Approaches to Ancient Judaism
Volume IV

Program in Judaic Studies
Brown University
BROWN JUDAIC STUDIES

Edited by

Jacob Neusner,
Wendell S. Dietrich, Ernest S. Frerichs,
Alan Zuckerman

Editorial Board

David Blumenthal, Emory University (Approaches to Medieval Judaism)
William Scott Green, University of Rochester (Approaches to Ancient Judaism)
Martin Hengel, University of Tübingen (Hellenistic Judaism)
David Hirsch, Brown University (Modern Jewish Literature)
Baruch A. Levine, New York University (Ancient Israel)
Alan Mintz, University of Maryland (Hebrew Literature)
Valentin Nikiprowetzky, University of Paris (Ancient Judaism)
Marc L. Raphael, Ohio State University (Approaches to Judaism in Modern Times)
Peter Schäfer, University of Cologne (Ancient Judaism)
Jonathan Z. Smith, University of Chicago (Studia Philonica)
Uriel Tal, Tel Aviv University (Modern Judaism)
David Vital, Tel Aviv University (Modern Judaism)
Geza Vermes, University of Oxford (Ancient Judaism)

Corresponding Editors

David Altshuler, George Washington University
Alan J. Avery-Peck, Tulane University
Baruch M. Bokser, Dropsie University
Joel Gereboff, Arizona State University
David Goldenberg, Dropsie University
Robert Goldenberg, State University of New York, Stony Brook
David Goodblatt, Haifa University
Peter Haas, Vanderbilt University
Martin Jaffee, University of Virginia
Shamai Kanter, Temple Beth El, Rochester, New York
Jack L. Lightstone, Concordia University
Irving Mandelbaum, University of Texas, Austin
Ivan Marcus, Jewish Theological Seminary of America
Louis E. Newman, Carleton College
Gary G. Porton, University of Illinois
Richard S. Sarason, Hebrew Union College–Jewish Institute of Religion, Cincinnati
Lawrence Schiffman, New York University
Tzvee Zahavy, University of Minnesota

Editorial Committee

Roger Brooks
Paul Flesher
Howard Schwartz
Judith Romney Wegner

Number 27

APPROACHES TO ANCIENT JUDAISM
Volume IV

Studies in Liturgy, Exegesis, and Talmudic Narrative

edited by
William Scott Green

APPROACHES TO ANCIENT JUDAISM
Volume IV

*Studies in Liturgy, Exegesis,
and Talmudic Narrative*

edited by
William Scott Green

Scholars Press
Chico, California

APPROACHES TO ANCIENT JUDAISM
Volume IV

Studies in Liturgy, Exegesis, and Talmudic Narrative

edited by
William Scott Green

© 1983
Brown University

Library of Congress Cataloging in Publication Data
Main entry under title:

Approaches to ancient Judaism.

(Brown Judaic studies ; no. 1, 9, 11, 27)
Includes bibliographical references and index.
1. Judaism—History—Post-exilic period, 586 B.C.–210 A.D.—Addresses, essays, lectures. 2. Rabbinical literature—History and criticism—Addresses, essays, lectures. 3. Rabbinical literature—Study and teaching (Higher)—Addresses, essays, lectures.
I. Green, William Scott. II. Series: Brown Judaic studies; no. 1, etc.
BM173.A66 1983   296'.09   76-57656
ISBN 0-89130-673-0

Printed in the United States of America

For the Greens --
John, Marlene, David, Suzanne, and Peter

TABLE OF CONTENTS

	Page
Preface	ix
List of Abbreviations	xi
Transliterations	xv
INTRODUCTION	xvii

William Scott Green, The University of Rochester

I. THE LITURGY OF THE SYNAGOGUE: HISTORY, STRUCTURE, AND CONTENTS 1

   Jakob J. Petuchowski, Hebrew Union College - Jewish Institute of Religion

II. TRANSLATING LEVITICUS RABBAH: SOME NEW CONSIDERATIONS 65

   Jacob Neusner, Brown University

III. READING RABBINIC BIBLE EXEGESIS 81

   Lewis M. Barth, Hebrew Union College - Jewish Institute of Religion

IV. THE "MIDRASHIC" PROEM: TOWARDS THE DESCRIPTION OF RABBINIC EXEGESIS 95

   Martin S. Jaffee, University of Virginia

V. YERUSHALMI'S COMMENTARY TO MISHNAH TERUMOT: FROM THEOLOGY TO LEGAL CODE 113

   Alan J. Avery-Peck, Tulane University

VI. THE MISHNAH IN TALMUDIC EXEGESIS: OBSERVATIONS ON TRACTATE MAASEROT OF THE TALMUD YERUSHALMI 137

   Martin S. Jaffee, University of Virginia

VII. HISTORY AND IDEOLOGY IN TALMUDIC NARRATIVE 159

   Robert Goldenberg, State University of New York, Stony Brook

Index of Liturgical Terms, Rubrics, and Concepts 173
Index of Biblical Sources 175
Index of Rabbinic and Other Ancient Sources 177
General Index 183

PREFACE

My gratitude goes to the editors of *Brown Judaic Studies* for their continuing interest in, and material support for, *Approaches to Ancient Judaism*. In particular, Professor Jacob Neusner has persistently supplied the inspiration, encouragement, and commitment that have allowed this fledgling series to develop. As editor, and on behalf of the series' contributors, it is a pleasure to acknowledge his generosity and his help.

Martha Morrow, Institute for the Advanced Study of Religion, University of Chicago, and Claire Sundeen, University of Rochester, typed portions of the manuscript. I thank them both. The bulk of the typescript and parts of the indices were prepared by Mary Jane Haddad, Office of the Dean, William Smith College. Her skill, patience, sharp eye, and keen wit made the entire exercise an uncommon pleasure, and I owe her much.

As usual, I have tried to maintain uniformity in the transliteration of unvocalized Hebrew and Aramaic terms. The transliteration of vocalized Hebrew and Aramaic, the spelling of proper names, and other matters of style and notation largely reflect the preferences of the various authors.

This book is dedicated with deep affection to my cousins, John and Marlene Green, and to their family, as a gesture of appreciation for a wonderful, supportive, and authentic friendship that transcends the ordinary and inevitable obligations of kinship.

W. S. G.

Department of Religious and Classical Studies
The University of Rochester

ABBREVIATIONS

Ar.	ʿArakhin
A. Z.	Abodah Zara
b.; B.	Babylonian Talmud
B. B.	Baba' Batra'
B. M.	Baba' Meṣia'
Bek.	Bekhorot
Ber.	Berakhot
Beṣ.	Beṣah
Contributions	Jakob J. Petuchowski, ed., *Contributions to the Scientific Study of Jewish Liturgy.* New York, 1970
Dem.	Demai
Deut.	Deuteronomy
Eccl.	Ecclesiastes
Ed.	ʿEduyyot
EJ	*Encyclopaedia Judaica.* Jerusalem/New York. 1971/72, 16 Volumes
Elbogen	Ismar Elbogen, *Der jüdische Gottesdienst in seiner geschichtlichen Entwicklung.* Hildesheim, ⁴1962
Ex.	Exodus
Ez.	Ezekiel
Gen.	Genesis
GR	Genesis Rabba
Hertz	Joseph H. Hertz, ed., *The Authorized Daily Prayerbook.* Reviewed Edition. New York, 1948
HUCA	*Hebrew Union College Annual*
Heinemann	Joseph Heinemann, *Prayer in the Talmud-- Forms and Patterns.* Berlin/New York, 1977
Hor.	Horayot
Is.	Isaiah
J.	Palestinian Talmud
JE	*The Jewish Encyclopedia.* New York/London, 1901/04, 12 volumes
JJS	*Journal of Jewish Studies*
Jer.	Jeremiah
JQR	*Jewish Quarterly Review* (N.S.-New Series)
JT	Palestinian Talmud
Ker.	Keritot
Ket.	Ketubot

Ki.	Kings
Kil.	Kilalim
Lam. R.	Lamentations Rabba
Lev.	Leviticus
Literature	Joseph Heinemann with Jakob J. Petuchowski, *Literature of the Synagogue*. New York. 1975
LPJL	Jakob J. Petuchowski and Michael Brocke, eds., *The Lord's Prayer and Jewish Liturgy*. New York, 1978
LR	Leviticus Rabba
Ma.	Ma'aserot
Makh.	Makhshirin
Mal.	Malachi
Meg.	Megillah
M.	Mishnah
Me.	Me^{c}ilah
Men.	Menaḥot
Miq.	Miqva'ot
MGWJ	*Monatsschrift für Geschichte und Wissenschaft des Judentums*
M. S.	Ma^{c}aser Sheni
Num.	Numbers
Pe.	Pe'ah
Pes.	Pesaḥim
PRK (*PRK*)	Pesiqta de Rav Kahana
Prov.	Proverbs
Ps.	Psalms
Qoh.	Qohelet
Reform	Jakob J. Petuchowski, *Prayerbook Reform in Europe*. New York, 1968
Sam.	Samuel
San.	Sanhedrin
Shab.	Shabbat
Sot.	Sotah
Ter.	Terumot
T.	Tosefta
Ta.	Ta^{c}anit
Theology	Jakob J. Petuchowski, *Theology and Poetry*. London/Henley/Boston, 1978
T. Y.	Tebul Yom
Understanding	Jakob J. Petuchowski, *Understanding Jewish Prayer*. New York, 1972

y.; Y	Palestinian Talmud
Yeb.	Yebamot
Zeb.	Zebahim
Zech.	Zechariah

TRANSLITERATION OF HEBREW

א	=	ʾ	מ ם	=	m
ב	=	b	נ ן	=	n
ג	=	g	ס	=	s
ד	=	d	ע	=	ʿ
ה	=	h	פ ף	=	p
ו	=	w	צ ץ	=	ṣ
ז	=	z	ק	=	q
ח	=	ḥ	ר	=	r
ט	=	ṭ	שׁ	=	š
י	=	y	שׂ	=	ś
כ ך	=	k	ת	=	t
ל	=	l			

INTRODUCTION
William Scott Green
The University of Rochester

The essays gathered in this volume focus on three disparate literary remains of ancient Judaism: liturgy, scriptural and halakic exegesis, and talmudic narrative. Certain readers surely will find these unlikely candidates for joint appearance in a single anthology, but some important common traits may serve to justify their combination. However distinct from one another they may appear as types of writing, liturgical, exegetical, and narrative texts illustrate and represent fundamental activities through which Judaism was constituted as a religion, and through which it persisted, in the ancient world.

The making of prayers, the interpretation of texts, and the telling of stories all are primary ways in which ancient Jews objectified and consolidated both their distinctive pictures of reality and themselves as recognizable groups. The construction of liturgy formalized in language, and thereby codified, images, symbols, and concepts that religious specialists and laymen could use to understand what they regarded as their identity and destiny. The very act of textual interpretation differentiated primary from secondary documents and thus established a literary fundament, a material canon, that the literate could portray as a source of wisdom and authority greater than themselves. Finally, talmudic narrative erected idealized models of exemplary rabbinic behavior but recounted them as events in history to make them appear normal and, therefore, normative. The literary remains considered here thus palpably demonstrate how Judaism was made "real" to ancient Jews and how they acquired a sense of its, and hence of their own, autonomous existence.

But liturgical, exegetical, and talmudic narrative texts reveal more than the means of constituting a religion. They expose the dynamics of continuity and change in ancient Judaism and manifest the mechanisms of persistence through which it remained pertinent to the lives of Jews.

It is, of course, a commonplace, almost a triviality, to assert that Jews in antiquity adapted their religion to serve their current needs. But, while the claim of adaptation is routinely made in the scholarly literature, the exact procedures of modification and change are rarely demonstrated. In the study of ancient Judaism, as in the study of religion in general, scholars have devoted most of their attention to one of two broad topics, the elucidation of allegedly ubiquitous and indelible religious patterns, phenomena, and beliefs, or the description and explanation of dramatic and radical religious change. But for ancient Judaism, at least, these academic preoccupations stand at some variance with the historical course of the religion and the ongoing lives of the religious communities. On the one hand, part of the appeal of Judaism, or any other religion, surely derives from its visions of permanence and claims of certitude and truth. But it hardly follows as a theoretical axiom that all forms of Judaism necessarily exhibit the same structure, pattern of ritual, or theology, and that to identify these in ancient Judaism is to adequately describe or understand the religion itself. On the other hand, although much is made of the dramatic changes in Judaism during the first century, the more decisive trait is that from then on Judaism in the ancient world exhibited few signs of radical transformation. Judaism in antiquity was neither static nor fluid. Its path of development lay somewhere between the two artificial extremes that have so dominated scholarly interest and curiosity.

That neglected middle range is richly illustrated in the liturgical, exegetical, and narrative texts considered below. They suggest that the persistence of Judaism in antiquity is a story neither of theological constancy nor of turbulent revolution of meaning, but of little changes, shifts in emphasis, alterations in refraction made by Jews as they appropriated their cultural and religious heritage and applied it to their social and historical present. In the course of composing their prayers, expounding Scripture or explaining the Mishnah, or telling and retelling stories literate Jews in antiquity modified their textual legacy, pushed it into shape, in a myriad of small, often subtle, frequently ingenious, and sometimes nearly imperceptible ways. From this perspective, the texts before us emerge as laboratories of cultural experimentation, workshops of tradition, that reveal procedures of reading, thinking, imagining, and knowing through which some Jews in antiquity kept their religion vital and made it matter to themselves. The papers collected in this volume all take seriously the centrality of these processes of tradition, and of their critical description and analysis, in the study of ancient Judaism.

The volume opens with Jakob J. Petuchowski's comprehensive treatment of the history, structure, and contents of the synagogal liturgy. Petuchowski is the doyen of Jewish liturgical scholarship, and his essay, a masterpiece of concision, constitutes an authoritative and critical review of the state of liturgical research. In it he traces the origin and development of the various blessings, prayers, and liturgical rubrics, outlines the order of the various services, explains important concepts in Jewish worship, and evaluates influential scholarly theories. At the same time, he pays more than requisite attention to the phenomenon of diversity in the liturgy by discussing the differences among the various Rites, by underscoring the important dialectic of fixity and spontaneity in the history of Jewish worship, and by elucidating the processes of tradition that shaped the liturgy's incremental growth. It is fair to say that no form of Judaism as a religion can be understood without knowledge of how Jews prayed and what they prayed for. Ironically, liturgy is treated as a specialized and sometimes arcane sub-field in much scholarship on Judaism, and students often emerge from their studies knowing more about the Talmud, kabbalah, and Zionism than about Jewish worship. Petuchowski's essay should help correct such an imbalance, and it thus constitutes a timely and useful contribution.

The next three essays take up the subject of the rabbinic exegesis of Scripture. Jacob Neusner and Lewis Barth treat the related problems of translating and reading these texts. Neusner perceives translation as the first act of interpretation and quite properly argues that knowledge of the purpose of a whole exegetical work depends in large measure on the discovery and classification of its empirical literary traits. He calls for translations that represent "distinct units of thought, whole and comprehensive statements, to be set apart from other such units of thought." Only with such nuanced renderings, he suggests, can we grasp how a document works, comprehend its particular use of antecedent materials, and discern the purpose of the whole. Barth shares Neusner's concern for what he calls "adequate understanding" of rabbinic exegetical texts, and he argues that the reading of such works cannot ignore the primacy of philology. Reading, he argues, must begin with the determination of the possible meanings of words, to be followed by the connecting of those words into discrete units of thought, and those thoughts into the "larger

argument," whose understanding is the "primary goal of inquiry."
In the third paper of the set, Martin Jaffee offers an astute and
novel scrutiny of the midrashic proem, the *petiḥa*. In contrast to
prevailing theories, his analysis reveals the proem to be a
sophisticated literary form whose ingenious juxtaposition of
scriptural verses requires a rhetorically skilled and exegetically
informed audience. In Jaffee's view, the proem is both "an act of
exegesis and object of exegesis," a literary form that "extends
the domain of Torah beyond the confines of Scripture and into the
entire deposit of rabbinic tradition." All three papers offer
examples of the texts they discuss, and their analyses demonstrate
the vigor and novelty with which Scripture was read and thought
about in rabbinic Judaism.

From the exegesis of Scripture we turn next to the rabbinic
exegesis of the Mishnah, the foundation document of the rabbinic
canon. Alan Avery-Peck and Martin Jaffee show how two tractates of
the Palestinian Talmud, Terumot and Maaserot, read, appropriated,
and expounded the Mishnah. Their results suggest that, in different
ways, the authorities behind these two talmudic tractates
bypassed the Mishnah's own intellectual agendum and used it for
their own purposes. Avery-Peck suggest that y. Terumot ignored
M. Terumot's theology of sanctification, read the Mishnah as a
rule-book, and attempted to make its regulations contemporary and
applicable. Jaffee carefully demonstrates that the framers of y.
Maaserot read the Mishnah according to their own, non-Mishnaic,
interpretative framework and built literary structures that seem
designed to obscure the Mishnaic text entirely. Their fresh and
persuasive analyses graphically illustrate the processes of tradition in rabbinism.

Finally, Robert Goldenberg examines the talmudic accounts of
rabbinic opposition to the patriarchal leadership of Gamaliel II
and Simeon b. Gamaliel. He shows that talmudic narrators recast
and reshaped these accounts to reflect distinct and conflicting
ideological attitudes towards the Patriarchate. He illustrates
the traditionality of such accounts, and in so doing raises serious
questions about their historicity.

All these papers indicate the importance of careful text-
centered research in the study of ancient Judaism, and each, in
its own way, reveals something important about the ways ancient
Jews appropriated their cultural legacy and applied it to themselves.
Together, these essays may help to draw scholarly attention away
from the polarities of permanence and radical change and direct it
to the study of the middle range, the processes of tradition.

THE LITURGY OF THE SYNAGOGUE: HISTORY, STRUCTURE, AND CONTENTS
Jakob J. Petuchowski
Hebrew Union College-Jewish Institute of Religion

I. THE SYNAGOGUE

What is said in the following pages about synagogal worship applies for the most part also to the prayers of the Jewish individual--either where there is no synagogue or when the individual is unable to attend the local synagogue that does exist. Jewish worship is both the duty of, and an opportunity for the individual. It is tied to no particular place--not even to the synagogue. There are, admittedly, certain prayers and ritual acts that can only be performed in the midst of a congregation. Such are the prayers that elicit a congregational response, like the Call to Worship, "Praise the Lord who is to be praised!," to which the congregation responds: "Praised be the Lord who is to be praised for ever and ever!," or like the *Qaddish*, the Jewish doxology *par excellence*, in which the congregation responds: "May His great name be praised for ever and unto all eternity!" to the hallowing of God's name and the plea for the coming of His kingdom. Also, the formal way in which the Pentateuchal pericopes are read from a parchment scroll necessitates the presence of a congregation.

The presence of a congregation, but *not* of a building designated as a "synagogue." A congregation, as traditionally defined, is a gathering of ten or more Jewish males above the age of thirteen. It is the word for "congregation" in the Priestly Code of the Pentateuch, *'edah*, that the Septuagint usually translates as *synagogē*; and it is the fact of the gathering of a congregation, rather than the particular place in which the gathering takes place, that, from a liturgical point of view, has remained decisive in distinguishing synagogal from private prayer.

In the course of time, specific buildings were, of course, erected to serve the devotional and intellectual needs of Jewish communities. But those buildings were not necessarily always sponsored by the same people who were responsible for laying down the rules of liturgical procedures. Thus, there are synagogues from the early centuries of the Common Era, which have been excavated in the Mediterranean region, whose decorative motifs do not correspond to the requirements and prohibitions established by the rabbis who devised the liturgical rubrics. We also read of early rabbis who refrained from worshipping in synagogues and preferred to pray in the academies where they studied and lectured.[1] Withal, through the centuries the rabbis ultimately succeeded in shaping the synagogues according to their own pattern, and the synagogues became one of the major expressions of rabbinic Judaism. With the rise of Reform Judaism in the nineteenth century, there again appeared synagogues that to greater or lesser degrees departed from the provisions of rabbinic Judaism.

Yet the rabbi is not a priest, and his presence is not required for the conduct of synagogal worship. Anybody who has the requisite knowledge and ability may lead the prayers and read and expound the Scriptures. Synagogal worship, in contrast to the strictly hieratic worship in the ancient Jerusalem Temple, is the people's worship, an expression of *religio laici*. It is highly unlikely that Jesus of Nazareth was an ordained rabbi. But his technical status as a layman did not prevent him from reading the Scriptures and preaching in Palestinian synagogues.[2]

The origin of the synagogue is shrouded in mystery. The range of theories concerning it is immense--from Julian Morgenstern's assertion that the synagogue originated in pre-Exilic times as a substitute for the "high places" (*bamoth*) that were destroyed as part of the Deuteronomic Reformation,[3] through the most commonly accepted (but unproved) view that the synagogue originated in the Babylonian Exile,[4] and the evidence some scholars see in Psalm 74:8 that "there must have been" synagogues in the Maccabean period.[5] None of those theories has sufficient proof to assure its universal acceptance. The one certainty may be found in the evidence presented by the New Testament, Josephus, and early rabbinic literature that synagogues in both Palestine and the Diaspora were well-established institutions in the first century of the Common Era. Important in this connection is the report in the Mishnah that, toward the end of the period of the Second Temple, the priests of the Jerusalem Temple would interrupt the sacrificial cult of the early morning hours by adjourning to the Chamber of Hewn Stones for a prayer service that consisted of elements still (though, no doubt, in a somewhat different form) included in today's synagogue worship.[6]

II. STANDARDS AND VARIETY

While the synagogue, as a building, is only one of the places where Jewish prayers can be said, it is likewise true that Jewish prayers antedate the origin of the synagogue--whenever that might have been. Biblical figures like Hannah, Solomon, Jeremiah and, above all, the Psalmists are portrayed as praying; confessions of sin accompanied the bringing of sin-offerings;[7] and a declaration of *heilsgeschichtliche* import was intoned by the farmer who brought his first fruits to the sanctuary. The wording of that declaration has been transmitted.[8] The text of the confession of sins has not, and it is quite likely that it was flexible enough to suit the needs of the individual penitent. Early rabbinic literature, however, does record the text of the High Priest's confessions on the Day of Atonement.[9] Official Temple rituals called for greater standardization than did the outpourings of an individual's heart--a contrast that also was to provide the dialectics of later Jewish liturgical developments.

True prayer, as we are repeatedly told in rabbinic sources, is the prayer of *kawwanah*, i.e., inwardness, concentration, and spontaneity. But the needs of a worshipping community also call for a liturgical continuum, for elements that are permanent and identical whenever and wherever members of the community meet for worship. That is $qebha^c$, i.e., the fixed liturgical routine. The history of Jewish prayer is the history of ongoing dialectics between *kawwanah* and $qebha^c$.[10]

Prayer, then, preceded and accompanied the Temple cult. The synagogue, whatever its time and place of origin, had co-existed, at least for a while, with the Second Temple; and it took the place of the Second Temple when that Temple was destroyed. Some two decades after that destruction the first steps were taken--by Rabban Gamaliel II in Yavneh (ca. 90 C.E.)--to bring some uniformity and standardization into the prayer-life of the Jews. It was then, for example, that the Prayer of the Eighteen Benedictions (also known as $^c amidah$, i.e., the prayer to be said while one is standing), *the prayer par excellence* of Judaism, was decided upon.[11] But the decision was confined to the number of the benedictions to be recited, to the ideas to be expressed, and, but only to some extent, to the sequence of the benedictions. There was at that time no thought of fixing the *wording* of that prayer. On the contrary, still in later centuries some rabbis deemed it important that the worshipper would incorporate some new formulations each time the Prayer of the Eighteen Benedictions was recited.[12] That is how the respective claims of *kawwanah* and $qebha^c$ were met and harmonized at this early stage of Jewish liturgical development.

Moreover, the ancient rabbis frowned upon the writing down of prayers,[13] and this, of necessity, made for the preservation of greater flexibility and variety. Altogether, the absence of written prayerbooks until the ninth century of the Common Era, and the costliness of producing prayerbooks until the invention of movable type and the availability of printed prayerbooks, are factors that must never be underestimated in any attempt to understand the development and the variegated nature of Jewish liturgy. They account, in part, for the institution of the *sheliaḥ ṣibbur* (i.e., "messenger of the congregation"), a layman (in the technical sense) who "led the congregation in prayer," and who, in much later centuries, was succeeded by the (professional) cantor as the leader of synagogue prayers. People, ignorant of the prayers or unable to formulate their own, would listen to the recitation by the *sheliaḥ ṣibbur*, and voice their assent to what they heard him recite by responding with '*amen*.

The absence of prayerbooks also accounts for the distinction made in the Mishnah by Rabbi Aqiba (2nd century C.E.) between the Jew, praying in private, who has a fluent mastery of the text of the Prayer of the Eighteen Benedictions and the Jew who lacks such fluency. The former is required to recite the full Eighteen Benedictions, while the latter fulfills his obligation by reciting an abbreviated version that consists of only seven benedictions.[14] Finally, the absence of prayerbooks during such a long period accounts for the fact that, when crystallization of the liturgy ultimately did take place, and when printed prayerbooks at long last became available, there was more than one crystallization and more than one "authorized" prayerbook. Local traditions (*minhagim*) played a major role in the crystallization process.

Within Orthodox Judaism today, and disregarding the Liberal and Reform prayerbooks that began to be published in the nineteenth century, and continue to be published in ever varying editions to this day, the following different liturgical Rites are still in actual use: the *Ashkenazi* (i.e., German-Polish) Rite, with its more localized subdivisions into the Rites of Poland, of Southwest Germany, of Bohemia, Moravia and Hungary, and of Russia; the Spanish and Portuguese (*Sepharadi*) Rite proper, and its local variations in North Africa, Aleppo and Baghdad; the Yemenite (*Teman*) Rite; the Italian (*Roma* or *Italiani*) Rite; the Balkanese (*Romani*) Rite; and the Ḥasidic Rite, called *Nosaḥ Sepharad* on account of some elements of the Spanish and Portuguese Rite that have been superimposed upon a basically *Ashkenazi* liturgy. In pre-modern times, French-Jewish communities like those of Carpentras and Avignon had their own distinctive Rites, which, curiously enough, retained elements of the ancient Palestinian Rite, unknown to other communities.

The Palestinian Rite (*Nosaḥ 'Ereṣ Yisrael*) itself fell into oblivion in the early Middle Ages, and only began to be reconstructed by modern scholarship on the basis of fragments that were discovered in the famous Cairo *Genizah* (i.e., storage chamber of a synagogue, in which old and dilapidated books and documents are kept) at the end of the last century--a reconstruction process that is, as yet, by no means completed.

Still, with all the differences that obtain between one Rite and another, the basic structure of the liturgy is the same throughout, and the identical rubrics can be found in all of the prayerbooks. There are differences in wording, but not in the underlying theology; differences in the order in which certain prayers and psalms are recited; and differences of a major kind in the medieval poetical embellishments (*piyyuṭim*) that are either included or excluded. But all of the various Rites currently in use include the rubrics laid down in the Mishnah and in the Talmud as well as the statutory prayers of which textual fragments (but not complete texts) are contained in talmudic literature. All of the liturgical Rites currently in use, albeit to greater or lesser degrees, are indebted to the ancient Babylonian Rite, of which the very first written prayerbook, that of Rav 'Amram Gaon in the ninth century C.E., was the first literary repercussion. 'Amram Gaon, head of a talmudical academy in Babylonia, was asked by a Jewish community in Spain to tell them how a Jewish service is to be conducted properly, and his responsum constitutes the first Jewish prayerbook. (Even so, there is no certainty that the actual prayer texts that have come down to us in 'Amram's name really go back to him in all cases, since scribes and copyists throughout the centuries have been in the habit of substituting prayer texts of their own times and places for manuscript readings that were unfamiliar to them.)[15]

'Amram's prayerbook was followed, in the tenth century C.E., by that of Rav Sa'adya Gaon.[16] Like 'Amram before him, Sa'adya was the head of a talmudical academy in Babylonia. But, prior to assuming that office, he had lived in Egypt, where he became familiar with the Palestinian Rite, which was then used there; and traces of the Palestinian Rite can be found in Sa'adya's liturgy.

The liturgical rulings of the eleventh-century Rabbi Solomon ben Isaac of Troyes (and Worms) are found in the *Siddur Rashi*, a compendium of rules and interpretations, which, however, does not contain the text of the prayers themselves.[17] But a student of Rabbi Solomon's, Simḥah ben Samuel of Vitry, in *Maḥzor Vitry*, reproduced the texts as well as the regulations.[18] In the twelfth century, Moses Maimonides appended his "Order of Prayers" to that section of his legal compendium, *Mishneh Torah*, in which the "Laws of Prayer" are codified;[19] and Maimonides' version of the liturgy exerted a great influence on the prayerbook of the Yemenite Jews.

Although all current Jewish liturgical Rites, to greater or lesser degrees, are indebted to the ancient Babylonian Rite, it

must be understood that the Babylonian Rite itself arose upon
Palestinian foundations. The Jewish liturgy *per se* originated in
Palestine, and the Babylonian rabbis accepted the definitions and
liturgical requirements that were laid down in the Palestinian
Mishnah. Also, throughout the talmudic period there was a constant
coming and going of scholars between Palestine and Babylonia. We
have mentioned that the Palestinian Rite is reflected in many of the
fragments from the Cairo *Genizah*, and that Rite also influenced the
ancient Egyptian Rite. Other reflections of that Rite are, in the
first place, the post-talmudic tractate, *Sopherim*,[20] and, to a somewhat lesser extent, the twelfth century *Seder Ḥibbur Berakhoth*,
composed in Italy.[21] This *Seder Ḥibbur Berakhoth*, in turn, was of
some influence upon the crystallization of the Italian Rite. If
one bears in mind that the Roman Jewish community was founded by
Palestinian Jews, and that the movement of the Jews in Western
Europe was from Italy to the North, up the Rhineland and beyond,
one will understand that the *Ashkenazi* Rite crystallized under
greater Palestinian influence than did the *Sepharadi* Rite, which
took shape in Muslim Spain while the Jews there were under the religious jurisdiction of the Babylonian rabbinic authorities in England.

III. THE EIGHTEEN BENEDICTIONS

When we turn to the first attempts at standardization of the
Jewish worship service, at the end of the first century C.E. in
Yavneh, under the auspices of Rabban Gamaliel II, we are confronted
by the question of what was actually standardized. As we have
already mentioned, the major achievement in the liturgical field
was that *the* prayer *par excellence*, the Prayer of the Eighteen
Benedictions, had its number of benedictions, eighteen, fixed at
that time. Rabban Gamaliel II was also instrumental in determining
the form of the domestic Passover Eve observance, the *seder*. The
practice of reciting the "Hear, O Israel" twice daily (of which
more below) had already been current in Temple times.

When we come to the formulation of the Eighteen Benedictions,
the relevant passage in the Talmud uses the verb *hisdir*, i.e., "to
arrange, to set in order." "Simeon Hap'qoli *hisdir* the Eighteen
Benedictions according to order, in the presence of Rabban Gamaliel
in Yavneh."[22] The verb, *hisdir*, does not imply any literary
creatio ex nihilo, but rather the arrangement of already extant
materials. Where did that material originate? The Talmud itself
contains different traditions about that. One, of a more legendary
character, would ascribe the composition of the Eighteen Benedictions and their threefold daily recitation to the biblical

Patriarchs, Abraham, Isaac and Jacob.[23] Another, more prosaic tradition mentions the Men of the Synagoga Magna (sometimes rendered as "The Men of the Great Assembly") as the source of the Eighteen Benedictions.[24] The Synagoga Magna, according to tradition, was that body of men, supposedly also including some of the Latter Prophets, which, from the time of Ezra and Nehemiah until the beginning of the rabbinic period in the second century C.E., exercised the religious leadership of the Jews and served as the prototype of the later *sanhedrin*. There is some doubt about the historical existence of a body designated as the Synagoga Magna; and there is no proof whatsoever that the Eighteen Benedictions, used from the time of Gamaliel II on, go back to the Synagoga Magna, even if such a body did exist.

Yet there are indications that some of the components of the Eighteen Benedictions actually antedate the end of the first century C.E. The Hebrew text of Ecclesiasticus, a work of the second century B.C.E., contains a number of phrases that also occur in the concluding eulogies of some of the Eighteen Benedictions.[25] Also, two of the Eighteen Benedictions are mentioned among the prayers that were recited by the Jerusalem Temple priests when they interrupted the daily sacrificial cult of the morning by participating in a service of Scripture readings and benedictions.[26] Those are but a few examples. It is not at all impossible that other material likewise antedated the time of Gamaliel II.

What that material looked like, is a question modern scholars are liable to answer on the basis of the particular method they adopt for the study of Jewish liturgy. There is, on the one hand, the so-called "classical philological method," which proceeds from the assumption that, where we have a longer and a shorter version of the same prayer, the shorter version must of necessity represent the earlier text. This method also permits itself, on the basis of admittedly later texts, to "reconstruct" the putative *Urtext*. A representative of that method is the American Jewish scholar, Louis Finkelstein, who not only dates the origin of the Eighteen Benedictions before the Maccabean period, but who also offers us his reconstructed version of the Maccabean--and even of the pre-Maccabean --texts of the Eighteen Benedictions.[27]

Rejecting that "philological method" were the two pioneers of the application of the *formgeschichtliche* method to the study of Jewish liturgy, the late Arthur Spanier[28] and the late Joseph Heinemann.[29] Representatives of the *formgeschichtliche* method are far more cautious in "dating" liturgical materials, and they reject the attempts at reconstructing the putative *Urtext* of any prayer.

They are aware that even the authorities at Yavneh did not fix the wording of the Eighteen Benedictions, and that for long centuries different versions of the same prayer, as parts of an oral liturgical tradition, could well have been used in different localities.

It is perhaps not a case of "either/or" when it comes to the study of Jewish liturgy. The "philological method" has its justifiable applicability once the scholar concentrates on written texts. But for the period of purely oral traditions--and that is what we are dealing with when we speak about the origin of the Eighteen Benedictions--the cautions and the strictures of the *formgeschichtliche* method are clearly in order.

If, then, we adopt the *formgeschichtliche* method to obtain a picture of what actually transpired at Yavneh toward the end of the first century C.E., we would come to the conclusion that, long before the time of Gamaliel II, various Jewish communities had been in the habit of praying, and of couching their prayers in the form of "benedictions" (*berakhoth*), a form we shall consider presently. A series of such *berakhoth* would constitute a *seder berakhoth*, an "order of benedictions." There was, however, no uniformity in those orders, nor was the number of *berakhoth* universally fixed for such a *seder*. The prayers in the form of benedictions arose within worshipping communities, and were neither composed nor imposed upon the communities by a central religious authority. It was in order to bring uniformity to Jewish liturgical practice that the authorities of Yavneh decided upon the number eighteen as the standard complement of the daily *seder berakhoth*. Why the number eighteen was chosen, is not altogether clear. It may have been arbitrary; and the explanations offered by later generations are clearly homiletical[30] and cannot be taken at face value.

That a choice of eighteen benedictions was made out of a larger available number is made obvious by the Tosefta's ruling that the benediction about the heretics is to be included in the benediction about those who separated themselves from the ways of the community, the benediction about the proselytes in the benediction about the elders, and the benediction about the Davidic dynasty in the benediction about the rebuilding of Jerusalem.[31]

The Palestinian versions of the Eighteen Benedictions, which have come to light in the Cairo *Genizah*, do, in fact, follow the ruling of the Tosefta, while the Babylonian version of this prayer, now in common use in the various Rites, has separate benedictions about the rebuilding of Jerusalem. The result is that, although the prayer is still called "Eighteen Benedictions," in actual fact it consists of nineteen.

It should be understood that, contrary to a widely held misapprehension, shared also by Maimonides,[32] the benediction about--really, the malediction against--the heretics (quite possibly the Judaeo-Christians) was *not* a nineteenth benediction that was added to the Eighteen Benedictions, but merely the adaptation of an already existing benediction to take account of a particular heresy that was deemed a threat at that time. The Palestinian versions of the Eighteen Benedictions, which have been found in the Cairo *Genizah*, do specifically mention various sects of Judaeo-Christians and yet contain no more than the stipulated eighteen benedictions.[33]

It follows, then, as we have already noted, that what was done under the auspices of Gamaliel II was the fixing of the number eighteen for the daily *seder berakhoth*, the choice of the particular themes to be expressed in it, and, to some extent, the sequence in which the individual *berakhoth* were to be recited. The wording was not fixed. Nor did the particular choice made in Yavneh rule out the possibility that benedictions not included under the auspices of Gamaliel II might survive in oral tradition and reappear elsewhere--as the example of the separate benediction for the Davidic dynasty, as used in the Babylonian and later Jewish liturgical Rites, quite clearly demonstrates.

IV. THE *BERAKHAH*

In discussing the Prayer of the Eighteen Benedictions, we have already had occasion to make frequent references to the form of prayer which is called *berakhah*, "benediction." It will now be our task to speak about the pattern and the function of the *berakhah* (pl., *berakhoth*).

The noun is derived from the verbal root *brk*, which the Septuagint usually renders as *eulogein*, and with which the New Testament use of *eucharistein* is synonymous. It means to bless, to praise, and also to give thanks. There is a Hebrew noun, *berekh*, which means knee; and it is not impossible that the two words are related --so that the root meaning of *brk* might well be: "to fall on one's knees in adoration of God," and then "to praise or exalt God." In II Chronicles 20:26, the place name, *'Emeq Berakhah*, is explained by the statement: "for there, they blessed the Lord." In Nehemiah 9:5, where *berakhah* is mentioned in connection with *tehillah* ("praise"), the word seems to be already used in a technical sense-- although the rabbinic discussions about the mandatory components of a technical *berakhah* continue into the third century C.E.[34]

The rabbinic form of the *berakhah* begins with the words, *barukh 'attah 'adonai* ("Praised are You, O Lord"). While the word *barukh* ("praised, blessed") is applied to God in the third person some twenty-five times in the Hebrew Bible, there are only two biblical passages in which God is addressed in the second person with *barukh*: I Chronicles 29:10, the opening words of a lengthy prayer of praise, and Psalm 119:12, which almost has the form of a rabbinic *berakhah*. It seems indeed to have been used as such in some circles. It obviously was contained as a *berakhah* in the Talmud text that Rabbi Solomon ben Isaac (Rashi) had in front of him in the eleventh century, for Rashi saw fit to correct that text, noting that Psalm 119:12 was not a *berakhah*, praising God for what He had done, but a *petitionary prayer*, which has to be understood as follows: "O Lord, You who are praised, teach me Your statutes."[35]

In his comment, Rashi showed remarkable sensitivity to what a rabbinic *berakhah* is all about. A petitionary prayer can indeed take the form of a *berakhah*. It is the genius of Jewish prayer that even a petitionary prayer can be recited as a praise of God, and all the petitionary prayers that form the bulk of the Eighteen Benedictions do, in fact, appear in this form. But for this to happen, the concluding sentence must be pure praise, without any admixture of petition. The *berakhah* praises God for what He has done, or for what He is doing. It presupposes an *answered* petition. That is why Psalm 119:12 is *not* a *berakhah* in the technical rabbinic sense--despite its three opening words. That is also why the rabbis devoted so much thought and discussion to the formulation of the proper *berakhah*.

It is in the nature of a rabbinic *berakhah* that, while it begins with an address to God in the second person, it continues in the third person. For example, the *berakhah* before eating bread reads: "Praised are You, O Lord our God, Ruler of the Universe, who brings forth bread from the earth." Before drinking wine, the *berakhah* is: "Praised are You, O Lord our God, Ruler of the Universe, who creates the fruit of the vine." There is no enjoyment, physical or spiritual, for which a *berakhah* has not been devised. A liturgical act, too, is always preceded, and often also followed, by one or more *berakhoth*. In fact, Rabbi Meir (2nd century C.E.) is credited with the statement that a man is obligated to recite one hundred *berakhoth* every day.[36] This may sound hyperbolic, but it really is not beyond the realm of the possible for the average pious Jew. He recites the "Hear, O Israel" with its framework of three or four *berakhoth* (of which more below) twice a day; he prays the Prayer of the Eighteen (really nineteen) Benedictions three times a day; he recites *berakhoth* when he dons the garment with the ritual fringes,[37] when he puts on phylacteries, when he washes his hands before he eats, and four *berakhoth* of Grace after each meal, when he drinks a glass of water, after he leaves the lavatory, before and after he recites Psalms as part of his daily devotions, when he hears good news, and when he hears bad news, when he sees lightning, when he hears thunder, etc., etc.

There are two forms of the *berakhah*: the long form and the short form. This designation has less to do with the actual length of the *berakhah* than with its structure. A *berakhah* that begins as well as ends with the words, "Praised are You, O Lord," is considered a "long form." A *berakhah* that uses the words, "Praised are You, O Lord," only once is considered a "short form." The *berakhoth* for bread and wine, mentioned above, are examples of the "short form." An example of the "long form" would be the first of the Eighteen Benedictions:

> Praised are You, O Lord,
> our God and God of our fathers,
> God of Abraham, God of Isaac, and God of Jacob,
> the great, mighty and awe-inspiring God,
> God Supreme,
> who bestows loving-kindnesses
> and possesses all things,
> who remembers the loving-kindnesses of the fathers,
> and who will bring a redeemer to their children's children,
> for the sake of His name,
> in love.
> King, Helper, Savior and Shield!
> Praised are You, O Lord, Shield of Abraham.

The second "Praised are You, O Lord" in one and the same *berakhah*, or, in the case of the "short form," the *berakhah* at the end of a prayer that does not begin with "Praised are You, O Lord" is called the *ḥathimah* or "concluding eulogy." A *ḥathimah* cannot introduce any ideas not previously expressed in the prayer; and, in the case where several themes are expressed in a prayer, the *ḥathimah* must revert to the main theme of the prayer that it concludes.

Although discussions about the proper structure of the *berakhah* continued until the third century C.E., the *berakhah* formula began to assert itself, over against other forms of praise, already at an earlier time. We have drawn attention to some of the phrases in the Hebrew text of the second-century B.C.E. work, Ecclesiasticus,[38] that also occur in the Eighteen Benedictions. In Ecclesiasticus, however, the phrase, *barukh 'attah* ("Praised are You") is not used. Instead, the recurring phrase there is *hodu le...* ("Make grateful acknowledgment to ..."). This is also the verb almost uniformly used in the Thanksgiving Hymns (*Hodayoth*) found among the Dead Sea Scrolls, hence the Hebrew name given to that particular scroll. The Hodayoth Scroll is to be dated at the latest to the first century B.C.E.

Interestingly enough, in one of the hymns of that scroll, the standard opening word, *bdekha* ("I make grateful acknowledgment to You"), has been crossed out by a scribe, and the words *barukh'attah* ("Praised are you") have been inserted above the crossed-out *'odekha* --thus testifying to the growing use of the *berakhah* formula.[39] A report in the Mishnah, telling us about the Temple service performed by the High Priest on the Day of Atonement in the Second Temple, states that the High Priest recited eight *berakhoth*: "concerning the Torah, concerning the cult, concerning thanksgiving, concerning the forgiveness of sin, concerning the sanctuary, concerning Israel, concerning the priesthood, and concerning "the rest of the prayers."[40] We are, unfortunately, not given the actual texts of those *berakhoth*--any more than we are given the texts of the *berakhoth* that were recited by the priests as part of the prayers and Scriptural lections with which they interrupted the daily morning sacrifice.

The growing acceptance of the *berakhah* formula does not mean that other forms of prayer were either given up or even discouraged. No liturgical or aesthetic restrictions were placed on the private, spontaneous prayer of the individual. Some of those private, non-*berakhah*-type prayers indeed ultimately found their way into the official prayerbooks. But, in general, a clear distinction was made between voluntary and statutory prayers. Voluntary prayers were unrestricted in form. Statutory prayers, with all the freedom that originally obtained concerning their actual wording, had to be couched in the *berakhah* form.[41]

V. THE EIGHTEEN BENEDICTIONS--CONTINUED

Chief among the statutory prayers is the Prayer of the Eighteen Benedictions. It was understood to correspond to, and--later, after the destruction of the Second Temple--to replace the statutory sacrifices ordained in the twenty-eighth and twenty-ninth chapters of the Book of Numbers.[42] Since there were two daily sacrifices, at dawn and in the late afternoon, there were two statutory recitations of the Eighteen Benedictions every day, morning and afternoon. (On Sabbath and festivals, a prayer of only Seven Benedictions took the place of the Eighteen, but the same times of prayer were observed.) It has also become customary to pray the Eighteen Benedictions a third time every day, in the evening. But, because there was no statutory Temple sacrifice to serve as a prototype, the obligatory nature of the evening Eighteen Benedictions, already affirmed by Rabban Gamaliel II, but denied by Rabbi Joshua, in Yavneh,[43] has never been fully established. Maimonides, in the twelfth century, held that, although there was no obligation to recite the Eighteen Benedictions in the evening, Jews have nevertheless become accustomed to this prayer in all their habitations, and "have accepted it upon themselves as though it were an obligatory prayer."[44] The uncertain legal status of this evening prayer, however, is still reflected in traditionalist synagogues, where, in the evening, the Eighteen Benedictions are prayed silently only, while, at all other times, the Eighteen Benedictions are first prayed silently and then repeated aloud by the prayer leader.

On Sabbaths, New Moons, the three Pilgrim Festivals, New Year, and the Day of Atonement, for which additional sacrifices (*musaphim*) are prescribed in Numbers 28 and 29, an additional recitation of the Prayer (here, because of the occasion, of Seven, not of Eighteen Benedictions), called *Musaph*, takes place. (The *Musaph* Prayer on New Year consists of nine benedictions.) Originally the *Musaph* Prayer, unlike other recitations of the Eighteen or the Seven Benedictions, seems to have been regarded as a congregational obligation only, rather than an obligation for the individual to fulfill with or without the presence of a congregation.[45] But it has been a part of the Jewish prayerbook ever since 'Amram's edition in the ninth century, and it undoubtedly was recited by individuals already in the talmudic period.[46]

The Day of Atonement is liturgically distinguished by having, in addition to the *Musaph* Service, also a Concluding Service (*Ne^{c}ilah*) during which the Prayer of the Seven Benedictions is said--although, in the early rabbinic period, other fast days, too, had a *Ne^{c}ilah* Service.[47]

The text of the Eighteen Benedictions as used in the *Ashkenazi* Rite, and going back to a Babylonian prototype, is readily available.[48] But the text of the Eighteen Benedictions that was found in the Cairo *Genizah*, and which represents an earlier Palestinian version, should here be made available:

(1) Praised are You, O Lord our God and God of our fathers,
God of Abraham, God of Isaac, and God of Jacob,
the great, mighty and awe-inspiring God,
God Supreme, Possessor of heaven and earth,
our Shield and Shield of our fathers,
our trust in every generation.
Praised are You, O Lord, Shield of Abraham.

(2) You are mighty, bringing low the proud;
powerful, judging the arrogant;
ever-living, raising up the dead;
causing the wind to blow and the dew to descend;
sustaining the living, quickening the dead.
O cause our salvation to sprout as in the twinkling
of an eye.
Praised are You, O Lord, who quickens the dead.

(3) Holy are You,
    and awe-inspiring is Your name;
    and beside You there is no God.
    Praised are You, O Lord, the holy God.

(4) Our Father, favor us with knowledge from You,
    and with discernment and insight out of Your Torah.
    Praised are You, O Lord, gracious Giver of knowledge.

(5) Turn us back to You, O Lord, and we shall return;
    renew our days as of old.
    Praised are You, O Lord, who delights in repentance.

(6) Forgive us, our Father, for we have sinned against You.
    Blot out and remove our transgressions from before
        Your sight,
    for Your mercies are manifold.
    Praised are You, O Lord, who abundantly pardons.

(7) Look at our affliction, and champion our cause,
    and redeem us for the sake of Your name.
    Praised are You, O Lord, Redeemer of Israel.

(8) Heal us, O Lord, of the pain of our hearts.
    Remove from us grief and sighing,
    and bring healing for our wounds.
    Praised are You, O Lord, who heals the sick of His
        people Israel.

(9) Bless, O Lord our God, this year for us,
    and let it be good in all the varieties of its produce.
    Hasten the year of our redemptive End.
    Grant dew and rain upon the face of the earth,
    and satiate the world out of the treasuries of
        Your goodness;
    and grant a blessing to the work of our hands.
    Praised are You, O Lord, who blesses the years.

(10) Sound the great horn for our freedom,
     and lift up a banner to gather in our exiles.
     Praised are You, O Lord, who gathers in the
         outcasts of His people Israel.

(11) Restore our judges as at first,
     and our counsellors as at the beginning;
     and reign over us -- You alone.
     Praised are You, O Lord, who loves justice.

(12) For the apostates let there be no hope,
     and uproot the kingdom of arrogance, speedily
         and in our days.
     May the Nazarenes and the sectarians perish as
         in a moment.
     Let them be blotted out of the book of life,
     and not be written together with the righteous.
     Praised are You, O Lord, who subdues the arrogant.

(13) May Your compassion be aroused towards the true
         proselytes;
     and grant us a good reward together with those who
         do Your will.
     Praised are You, O Lord, the trust of the righteous.

(14) Have compassion, O Lord, in Your abundant mercies,
     upon Israel, Your people, upon Jerusalem, Your city,
     upon Zion, Your glorious dwelling-place,
     upon Your Temple and upon Your abode,
     and upon the kingdom of the House of David,
         Your righteous anointed,
     Praised are You, O Lord, God of David,
         Builder of Jerusalem.

(15) Hear, O Lord our God, our prayerful voice,
and have mercy upon us,
for You are a gracious and merciful God.
Praised are You, O Lord, who hears prayer.

(16) Be pleased, O Lord our God, to dwell in Zion;
and may Your servants worship You in Jerusalem.
Praised are You, O Lord, whom we worship with reverence.

(17) We acknowledge to You
that You are the Lord our God and the God
of our fathers;
and we thank You
for all the goodness, the loving-kindness and the
mercies
which You have bestowed upon us,
and which You have wrought for our fathers before us.
And were we to say: "Our foot is slipping,"
Your loving-kindness, O Lord, would sustain us.
Praised are You, O Lord, to whom it is good to
give thanks.

(18) Grant Your peace
upon Israel, Your people,
upon Your city,
and upon Your inheritance.
And bless us -- all of us together.
Praised are You, O Lord, the Maker of peace.[49]

The first three and the last three benedictions, known as "Praise" and "Thanksgiving" respectively, remain the same (in the ideas they express, although there is a change in the wording of the last benediction for afternoon and evening use in the *Ashkenazi* Rite) on all occasions. They, as it were, represent the framework of the Eighteen Benedictions. The intermediate benedictions (twelve in the Palestinian, thirteen in all other Rites) are of a petitionary character, and are restricted to weekday use only. On Sabbath and festivals, they are replaced by a single benediction, the function of which is to express the "holiness of the day."

The suggestion that this is due to a conscious avoidance, on Sabbath and festivals, of the cares and concerns that find expression in the petitionary *berakhoth* may be no more than a homiletical conceit.[50] Those cares and concerns do find expression in other parts of the Sabbath and festival liturgy as well as in the Grace after Meals recited on those occasions. Moreover, the scheme of a Prayer of Seven Benedictions may, even for weekdays, be more ancient than the later scheme of the Prayer of Eighteen Benedictions. The Mishnah knows of a daily Prayer of Seven Benedictions, called, "The Essence of the Eighteen," which, according to Rabbi Joshua can be used by anyone to fulfill the obligation of prayer, and which, according to Rabbi Aqiba, is the prayer to be used by him who is not fluent in the recitation of the full Eighteen Benedictions;[51] and both the Palestinian and the Babylonian Talmud give us versions of the daily Prayer, for use by workmen and in cases of emergency, in which the twelve (or thirteen) intermediate petitionary *berakhoth* have been condensed into a single *berakhah*, while the first and last three *berakhoth* remain unabridged.[52] At any rate, it is not at all unlikely that public worship on Sabbaths and festivals antedated public worship on weekdays, and that an Order of Seven Benedictions for Sabbaths and festivals was in existence before the Order of Eighteen Benedictions for weekdays was devised at Yavneh.

The Seven Benedictions of the *Musaph* Service seem, at first, to have been identical with those of the morning Seven Benedictions --on the principle of "one recitation of the Seven Benedictions for each sacrifice mandated by Scripture." But already in the third century C.E. the view gained ground that the hope for the restoration of the sacrificial cult ought to find expression in the fourth benediction, and that the appropriate verses from Numbers 28 and 29, designating the additional sacrifices of the particular occasion, ought to be quoted. In the absence of printed, or even written, prayerbooks, this must have called for quite a feat of memory. Perhaps this is why the recitation of the Scripture verses was originally considered to be optional; but it was apparently only Maimonides who, in the Middle Ages, felt free to omit them.[53]

From the early nineteenth century on, the Seven Benedictions of the *Musaph* Service, because of their intimate connection with the sacrificial cult, presented a problem to the editors of Liberal and Reform Judaism prayerbooks. Progressive Judaism sees in the sacrificial cult an outgrown stage of Jewish worship, and does not look forward to its restoration. Some of those new prayerbooks retained the references to the sacrificial cult as a historical reminiscence. Others omitted those references. In America and England, the *Musaph* Service was dropped altogether in Liberal and Reform synagogues, while the prayerbook of American Conservative Judaism adopted the device of some of the earlier German Liberal prayerbooks, i.e., to let the prayer express a memory of the past, rather than a hope for the future.[54]

A unique form of the *Musaph* benedictions is that for the New Year festival. It consists of nine, and not of seven benedictions. There is reason to believe, however, that, originally, the *seder berakhoth* for all New Year services consisted of nine benedictions, and that the exclusive use of the Nine Benedictions in the *Musaph* Service represents a later stage in liturgical development--seeing that the earliest sources that mention the Nine Benedictions for the New Year do not specify the *Musaph* Service.[55]

The New Year *Musaph* Service, in its present form,[56] is the result of a complicated process of development. The Mishnah merely indicates that ten Scripture verses each, on the themes of God's Kingship, God's remembering, and the sound of the ram's horn, are to be included, with four chosen from the Pentateuch, and three from each Hagiographa and Prophets. The actual verses were not laid down, although the worshipper was warned not to choose verses that suggest divine punishment.[57] The use of Scripture verses dealing with God's remembering and the sound of the ram's horn were also included in the liturgy of public fast days in times of drought, and there they are provided with appropriate concluding eulogies (*ḥathimoth*). The verses dealing with God's Kingship were peculiar to the New Year liturgy at the time they were introduced there, and, consequently, without a previously known *ḥathimah*. They therefore had to be combined with one of the other standard Seven Benedictions in order to be suitably concluded with a *berakhah*; and the ancient rabbis argued whether the Kingship verses should be included in the benediction dealing with the "Holiness of God," or in the benediction dealing with the "Holiness of the Day." The practice that ultimately developed is based upon the latter view; but the special insert in the "Holiness of God" benediction, still used on New Year and the Day of Atonement,[58] is regarded by some scholars as a remnant of the opposite practice.

The selection of appropriate Scripture verses in due course became standardized, and various liturgical and poetic frameworks were created for those Scripture verses, among them one by the earliest synagogal poet known by name, Yosé ben Yosé (fourth or fifth century, C.E.).[59] But the text that ultimately gained universal acceptance in all rites goes back, at least in part, to the third-century Babylonian Amora, Abba Arikha (Rav). It combines the idea of God's remembering with the notion of divine judgment, and it stresses the themes of Revelation and Redemption in connection with the various mentions of the sound of the ram's horn. Once printed prayerbooks became available, many of the printers managed, in the Nine Benedictions meant for the prayer leader's recitation, to interweave the poetic compositions of Yosé ben Yosé and others with the liturgical framework ascribed to Rav in such a way that the unsuspecting worshipper no longer realizes that the poetic compositions were meant to be alternatives, not supplements to Rav's framework.[60] This, too, may serve as an illustration of the working out of a law of Jewish liturgical development, which can be stated as follows: If there is a choice between various formulae for one and the same occasion, the chances are that *all* the different versions will be adopted.[61]

VI. THE PROCLAMATION OF THE *SHEMA^c* AND ITS BENEDICTIONS

In the Evening Service (*Ma^{c}aribh*) and in the Morning Service (*Shaḥarith*)--but not in the Afternoon Service (*Minḥah*), the *Musaph* Service and the Atonement Concluding Service (*Ne^{c}ilah*)--the Prayer of the Eighteen (or Seven) Benedictions is preceded by a rubric called "The Proclamation of the *Shema^c* and its Benedictions." That rubric consists of a concatenation of three Pentateuchal passages (Deuteronomy 6:4-9, Deuteronomy 11:13-21, and Numbers 15:37-41) set within a framework of *berakhoth* that express, in this order, the ideas of Creation, Revelation and Redemption.[62] The rubric takes its name, *Shema^c* (="Hear," sc. "O Israel"), from the opeing word of Deuteronomy 6:4. If prayer is that which man addresses to God, then the *Shema^c* is not, strictly speaking, a prayer; for the *Shema^c* is the word addressed by God to man. That is why the ancient rabbis, always very careful in their choice of terminology, do not use the verb, *hithpallel* ("to pray"), in connection with the *Shema^c*, but the verb, *qara'* ("to read, to recite, to proclaim"). Since written prayerbooks were unknown in the rabbinic period, and since very few ordinary people were liable to have at hand a Pentateuch scroll from which they could read the three biblical passages twice a day,[63] it is best to understand the phrase, *qeri'ath Shema^c*, in the sense of "reciting" or "proclaiming" the *Shema^c*. For the *Shema^c* is the creedal affirmation of Judaism, the proclamation of ethical monotheism: "Hear, O Israel, the Lord our God, the Lord is uniquely One." This, in addition to its regular liturgical use, is also the last affirmation that the dying Jew seeks to make with his last breath.[64]

"Acceptance of the Yoke of the Kingdom of Heaven" was the name given by the rabbis to Deuteronomy 6:4-9; and they called Deuteronomy 11:13-21, "Acceptance of the Yoke of the Commandments."[65] Although the third paragraph, Numbers 15:37-41, is primarily concerned with the ritual fringes, it concludes with a reference to the Exodus from Egypt. Consequently, "The Exodus from Egypt" is the name the rabbis gave to the whole of the third paragraph.[66]

The recitation of the three paragraphs of the *Shema^c*, together with the Ten Commandments, was part of the daily prayer service conducted by the Jerusalem priests in the Second Temple.[67] That the practice of reciting the *Shema^c* twice daily, morning and night, goes back to Moses himself, as Josephus indicates,[68] seems unlikely. Kaufmann Kohler's theory that the practice originates among early Pietists, from whom he thinks the Essenes emerged in Palestine during the Persian period,[69] is suggestive but highly speculative. But the practice is definitely old. This conclusion is suggested not only by Josephus' hyperbolic claim and by the role of the *Shema^c* as part of the daily morning service in the Jerusalem Temple, but also by the way the Mishnah simply takes the practice for granted. The Mishnah reports differences of opinion about the exact times when the *Shema^c* is to be recited[70] and about the bodily posture to be adopted while reciting it,[71] but records no disagreement about the obligation *per se* of reciting the *Shema^c* twice daily. The matter-of-fact way in which the Mishnah presupposes this practice is noted by the Talmud, which then--retroactively, as it were--supplies the missing derivation from Scripture by referring to the injunction of Deuteronomy 6:7 to the Israelite to "speak of" God's words "when you lie down, and when you rise up."[72]

None of this need suggest that in pre-rabbinic times the *Shema^c* necessarily consisted of the three particular paragraphs that have comprised that rubric since the time of the Mishnah. We would be justified in reckoning with a gradual evolution and crystallization of the components of the *Shema^c*. We know, for example, that, in the Jerusalem Temple, Deuteronomy 6:4-9 was preceded by the Decalogue.[73] We also know that attempts were made to combine the Decalogue with the *Shema^c* outside the Temple as well, but that those attempts were discountenanced to prevent heretics from using the prominence given the Decalogue by such singling out to justify their claim that *only* the Decalogue "was given to Moses on Sinai."[74] Perhaps the heretics (*minim*) in question were a particular Judaeo-Christian sect. We know among the Ebionites there were those who did not ascribe the whole of the Pentateuch to divine revelation.[75] Yet the use of the Decalogue in conjunction with the *Shema^c* seems nevertheless to have broken out of the confines of the Temple precincts. A second century B.C.E. Hebrew fragment of Egyptian Provenance, the so-called "Nash Papyrus," contains the Decalogue, followed by the beginning of the *Shema^c*.[76]

On the other hand, the inclusion of Numbers 15:37-41 in the evening recitation of the *Shema^c* appears to have been problematic for a number of centuries--despite Josephus' assertion, made with particular reference to the remembrance of the Exodus from Egypt, that the twice daily recitation of the *Shema^c* goes back to Moses.[77] The Mishnah ascribes to Josephus' younger contemporary, Rabbi Eleazar ben Azariah, the inability to understand why Numbers 15:37-41 should be included in the evening *Shema^c*--until he was supplied with the requisite proof by Simeon ben Zoma.[78] Nevertheless, centuries later we are still told that, while the Numbers passage was indeed a part of the evening *Shema^c* in Babylonia, it was still absent from the evening liturgy of the Palestinian Jews.[79]

We have noted that the ancient rabbis used not the verb *hithpallel* (="to pray") in connection with the *Shema*^{c}, but the verb, *qara'* (="to recite," "to proclaim"). Indeed, the "Proclamation of the *Shema*^{c}" was originally recited by the Jew twice daily quite independently of any statutory prayer services, and more literally in fulfilment of Deuteronomy 6:7, "when you lie down and when you rise up." As a matter of fact, as far as the evening *Shema*^{c} is concerned, the Talmud tells us specifically why, on his way home from work, a man should stop by at the synagogue to recite the *Shema*^{c}. It was lest, going straight home to eat and nap a little before reciting the *Shema*^{c}, sleep overpower him, and he would sleep through the night without having said the *Shema*^{c} at all.[80] Moreover, the requirement that the *Shema*^{c} immediately precede the prayer of the Eighteen Benedictions in the morning and evening services does not seem to have gained universal acceptance until the third century C.E.[81]

In the light of what has been said above about the *berakhah*, it would follow that, as a liturgical rubric, the *Shema*^{c} must be embedded within a framework of *berakhoth*. This is indeed the case. The Mishnah lays down that the morning *Shema*^{c} be preceded by two benedictions and followed by one benediction,[82] and that the evening *Shema*^{c} be both preceded and followed by two benedictions.[83] In the recitation of the *Shema*^{c} by the priests in the Jerusalem Temple, the *Shema*^{c} was followed by a benediction, *'emeth weyaṣibh*, which--though doubtless in considerably elongated form--remains the benediction following the *Shema*^{c} in Jewish morning services today. The *Shema*^{c} in the Jerusalem Temple was also preceded by one benediction,[84] and not by two, as the Mishnah requires. Which one of the two current *berakhoth* before the *Shema*^{c} the priests recited, even the talmudic Amoraim no longer knew for sure.[85]

The first benediction before the morning *Shema*^{c} appears to have been much shorter at first than the version now in current practice.[86] In all likelihood it omitted the elaborate angelology and the *Trisagion*, which have since become standard in all Rites.[87] The purpose of that first benediction is to affirm God the Creator; and it begins as follows:

> Praised are You, Lord our God, Ruler of the universe,
> Fashioner of light and Creator of darkness,
> Maker of peace and Creator of all.
> In mercy You give light to the earth
> and to those who dwell upon it.
> In Your goodness You renew the work of creation
> every day, perpetually.

The opening words are, of course, derived from Isaiah 45:7--

with one important difference. Isaiah 45:7 speaks of God as the
"Maker of peace and the Creator of evil." The Jewish liturgy
changed the reference to God's creation of evil to one of God's
creation of all--a change not due, as the Talmud informs us, to
any disagreement with Deutero-Isaiah's theology (difficult as that
might be), but to a feeling for the fitness of things, which, in
prayer, preferred a euphemism to the express mention of evil.[88]

Kaufmann Kohler may or may not be correct in ascribing this
benediction to the early Pietists in the Persian period.[89] But
there can be no doubt that Deutero-Isaiah's affirmation itself was
meant as a rejection of the dualism that posited a god of light
(and goodness) and a god of darkness (and evil), the kind that
Deutero-Isaiah may have encountered in his Persian environment.[90]
Certainly, the ancient rabbis were impressed by the anti-dualistic
polemical edge of Deutero-Isaiah's utterance when, after it had
become the opening of the first benediction before the morning
Shema^c, they insisted that the morning benediction must include a
reference to darkness, and the evening benediction must include
a reference to light.[91]

In whatever guise it manifested itself, dualism was heresy
par excellence for the rabbis, whose faith was in the One and Only
God. The dualistic heresy (*shetey reshuyoth*) therefore, was perceived in Gnosticism as well as in Zoroastrianism. It may well be
as a barb against the former that some further phrases occur in
this benediction. God, it says, gives light to the world and its
inhabitants in *His mercy*. He daily renews the act of Creation in
His goodness. Yet we know that in the various Gnostic systems the
god of whom mercy and goodness can be predicated is the Unknown
God, the god who is all spiritual and who has no contact whatsoever with matter. On the other hand, in Gnosticism the *demiourgos*,
the world-creating god, is anything but a god of goodness and
mercy.[92] As against Gnosticism, then, the Jewish liturgy affirms
the goodness and the mercy of the One God--precisely in this God's
act of physical Creation!

The corresponding *berakhah* in the evening service praises
God,
> who by His word brings on the evening twilight,
> who in wisdom opens the heavenly gates, ...
> He is the Creator of day and night.
> He rolls the light away from before the darkness,
> and the darkness from before the light.
> ...
> Praised are You, O Lord,
> who brings on the evening twilight.[93]

The second *berakhah* before the *Shema^c* is thematically identical in both morning and evening services, though different texts are used on the two occasions.[94] Its theme is God's love for Israel, which He has manifested through His Revelation of the Torah. It concludes in the morning service with "Praised are You, O Lord, who has chosen His people Israel in love," and in the evening service with: "Praised are You, O Lord, Lover of His people Israel."

The main theme of the benediction immediately following the *Shema*ᶜ in both the morning and evening services--though, here again, the wording is different for the two occasions--is Redemption, with special emphasis placed upon the Exodus from Egypt.[95] The benediction appropriately concludes with "Praised are You, O Lord, who has redeemed Israel." (The ancient Palestinian Rite concluded with "Praised are You, O Lord, the King, Israel's Rock and his Redeemer.") In this sense, it links up with the last sentence of the third paragraph of the *Shema*ᶜ, a paragraph, as we have seen, that the ancient rabbis called in its entirety "The Exodus from Egypt."

When has just been said applies more directly to the benediction after the *Shema*ᶜ in the evening service. While the corresponding benediction in the morning service also expatiates on the Exodus theme, it begins with various hymnic affirmations that make reference to the truth of the other two paragraphs of the *Shema*ᶜ: the "Acceptance of the Yoke of the Kingdom of Heaven," and the "Acceptance of the Yoke of the Commandments." But even the evening benediction, albeit in a single sentence with which it begins, affirms the truth of the first two paragraphs of the *Shema*ᶜ as well:

> True and trustworthy and established
> is all this for us:
> that the Lord is our God,
> and that there is none beside Him,
> and that we are Israel, His people.

We see, then that the rubric called "The Proclamation of the *Shema*ᶜ and its Benedictions" is the expression that Jewish liturgy gives to the creedal element in Judaism. In addition to the belief in the One God and the duty to obey His commandments, it articulates the biblical-rabbinic *weltanschauung*, which is based upon the doctrines of Creation, Revelation, and Redemption. That this is done in the form of hymnic praise, rather than in prosaic and minutely defined "creeds," is typical for the role that dogma plays in the Jewish scheme of things.[96]

Yet another benediction follows the *Shema*ᶜ in the evening:
> Cause us, O Lord our God, to lie down in peace,

and let us rise again, O our King, to life.
Spread over us the tabernacle of Your peace, ...[97]

On weekdays, this prayer concludes with "Praised are You, O Lord, the eternal Guardian of His people Israel." On Sabbaths and festivals, it concludes with "Praised are You, O Lord, who spreads the tabernacle of peace over us, over all His people Israel, and over Jerusalem." The latter version seems to have been also the regular *weekday* conclusion in the ancient Palestinian Rite.[98]

This prayer is clearly a bedtime prayer, and must have been recited originally when the *Sitz im Leben* of the "Evening *Shema^c*" was literally "when you lie down." It is, in fact, still recited to this day by the pious Jew in that particular situation--in addition to, not as a substitute for, its recitation during the evening service.[99] But in the third century C.E., when emphasis began to be placed on reciting the Eighteen Benedictions immediately and without interruptions after the "Benediction of Redemption" that follows the *Shema^c*, and when the *Shema^c* became part of a quasi-statutory evening service,[100] a problem was seen in the fact that this prayer, called *hashkibhenu* from its opening word, interrupted the required sequence of "Benediction of Redemption" and Eighteen Benedictions. The difficulty was (superficially) resolved by calling the *hashkibhenu* prayer an "elongated form of the Benediction of Redemption."[101] This was not altogether unreasonable because the daily protection granted by God, for which this prayer pleads, may indeed be seen as an aspect of God's redemptive activity. But the real (and historical) origin of the problem--that *hashkibhenu* was a bedtime prayer, customary *before* the practice arose of praying the Eighteen Benedictions in the evening, at a time, moreover, when the *Shema^c* and the Eighteen Benedictions were two entirely unrelated liturgical rubrics--was perhaps already beyond the ken of the rabbinic discussants who agreed to call the *hashkibhenu* an "elongated form of the Benediction of Redemption."

Altogether, the (originally) optional character of the evening Eighteen Benedictions accounts for a certain variety that now obtains among the different Rites after the *hashkibhenu* has been said. When the optional character of the evening Eighteen Benedictions was still a matter of common knowledge, some people, instead of praying the Eighteen Benedictions in the evening, would recite a catena of Scripture verses that contained in their aggregate eighteen mentions of the name of God. Different Rites have preserved different selections of Scripture verses. In their present form, none of the different selections contains exactly eighteen mentions of the name of God, and the Sepharadi Rite does not have those Scripture verses at all. Nor do the other Rites on Sabbaths and festivals.[102]

Where the Scripture verses are recited, the feeling for the fitness of things liturgical, which abhors Scripture verses trailing off into a vacuum, quite naturally called for a concluding prayer with a *ḥathimah*. And, to introduce that *ḥathimah*, some, but not all Rites have a lofty messianic prayer:

> May our eyes see,
> our hearts rejoice,
> and our souls truly be glad in Your salvation,
> when Zion will be told:
> "Your God is enthroned!"
> ...
> Praised are You, O Lord, the King,
> who, in His glory,
> will perpetually and eternally rule over us
> and over all His works.[103]

Not all Rites that include Scripture verses after the *hashkibhenu* have this particular prayer to introduce the concluding eulogy. But, to the extent to which they do have Scripture verses, they also have a concluding eulogy. Thus the Italian Rite lacks this prayer, but it concludes the Scripture verses with the following *berakhah*: "Praised are You, O Lord, the King, the everliving God who endures for ever."[104] The Yemenite Rite, on the other hand, which also lacks this prayer, concludes its selection of Scripture verses with a *ḥathimah* very similar to that of the Ashkenazi Rite, which we have quoted above.[105]

Thus, instead of the two benedictions that, according to the Mishnah, should follow the "Evening *Shema^c*" many of the Rites, in fact, have three. Where the Scripture verses originally served as a substitute for the Eighteen Benedictions, this arrangement made sense--as did the variety among the Rites--since the rubric in question was not initially deemed to be mandatory. But the persistence of this arrangement even after the Eighteen Benedictions of the evening had become universal Jewish practice merely illustrates a law of Jewish liturgical development to which reference has already been made: If there is a choice between various liturgical options, the chances are that *all* of the options will be adopted.[106]

VII. THE EARLY STRUCTURE OF THE SYNAGOGUE SERVICE

If we have devoted apparently disproportionate space to the two rubrics, "The Proclamation of the *Shema^c* and its Benedictions" and "The Prayer of the Eighteen Benedictions," which, in terms of the number of prayerbook pages involved, have long been overshadowed by numerous other devotional texts, it is because, when the sources of classical Rabbinic Judaism speak about obligatory prayer, those were the two rubrics intended--at any rate, as far as communal worship was concerned. The *berakhoth* before partaking of various foods, and particularly the Grace after Meals, were also deemed to be obligatory,[107] but they were not a part of the synagogue service.

There are other rubrics, too, that in their geminal form, are already mentioned in the Talmud and that have since been incorporated into the synagogue worship service. But the Talmud understands them as liturgical duties of the individual, rather than as components of congregational worship. For example, there are a number of *berakhoth* that the Jew is meant to recite upon waking up in the morning, upon washing his hands, upon putting on his shoes, his belt etc., the so-called "Morning Benedictions" (*birkhoth hashaḥar*). These are now a part of public worship,[108] but the Talmud specifically assigns them to the individual within the particular setting of rising and getting dressed in the morning.[109] There are the "Verses of Song" (*pesuqey de-zimra'*), a group of Psalms and other Scriptural passages of praise, long since incorporated into public worship,[110] which, in the talmudic period, had by no means been clearly defined. At that time, they were an expression of individual piety rather than of congregational liturgy.[111] Also, the rubric variously called *taḥanunim* ("entreaties"), *debharim* ("words"), or *nephilath 'apayim* (falling with the face to the ground"), for which, in later centuries, elaborate texts were provided,[112] was, in its origin and intent, precisely that part of the service in which the individual was left free to use his own words and to express his own thoughts and concerns --in contrast to the more or less standardized prayers of the congregation.[113]

The earliest form of the synagogue service, as Elbogen has reconstructed it, consisted solely of the *Shema^c* and its Benedictions.[114] It did not contain any petitionary prayers at all. But the individual could add his private and personal prayers after the benediction following the *Shema^c*.

The second stage in the development of the synagogue service, around the year 100 C.E., was reached when a prayer leader led the congregation in the Eighteen Benedictions. The transition from the first to the second stage is still evident in the provision: "One does not say *debharim* ("words," i.e., personal prayers) after *'emeth weyaṣibh* (i.e., the benediction following the *Shema^c*), but one says *debharim* after the Prayer (sc. of the Eighteen Benedictions), and then they can be as long as the

confession of sins on the Day of Atonement."[115] That provision
clearly recalls the earlier procedure, when private prayers *were*
offered following the benediction after the *Shema^c*, and when that
benediction concluded the official public act of worship.

Throughout the centuries, those private prayers were not
regarded as part of the statutory worship until they were treated
as such by the sixteenth-century code of rabbinic law, the
Shulhan ^{c}Arukh.[116] Those prayers crystallized only gradually, and,
even in their crystallized form, they are by no means uniform in
various Rites.[117] From the talmudic period a number of the private
prayers of some of the rabbis have been preserved, prayers
that they would utter after the conclusion of the Eighteen
Benedictions.[118] Some of those prayers were already included in
the first Jewish prayerbook, the ninth-century *Seder Rabh 'Amram
Ga'on*.[119] Interestingly enough, it was the private prayer of a
Rabbi *not* included by 'Amram that ultimately was adopted by all
of the current Rites. We refer to the prayer of the fourth-century
Mar, son of Rabbina, which begins as follows:

> My God, keep my tongue from evil,
> and my lips from speaking guile.
> To those who curse me let my soul be silent;
> and may my soul be as dust to everyone.
> Open my heart to Your Torah,
> and may my soul pursue Your commandments.[120]

That public worship originally began with the *Shema^c* and its
Benedictions, and that anything preceding that rubric in the Jewish
prayerbook today is a later addition, may still be deduced very
easily from the fact that it is to the benedictions before the
Shema^c, and not to any rubric preceding them, that the "Call to
Worship" is attached. The prayer leader intones: "Praise the
Lord who is to be praised!," and the congregation responds:
Praised be the Lord who is to be praised for ever and ever!"[121]
The formulation of the "Call to Worship" in this form goes back
to Rabbi Ishmael of the second century C.E.[122] The response,
"Praised be the Lord, etc.," is also found in a source contemporaneous with the Mishnah.[123] But it is not clear from the context
there whether this was the response to the invitation to praise
the Lord at the beginning of public worship or the response to
the same invitation during other parts of the service in which
that invitation recurs--such as in connection with the reading
from the Pentateuchal scroll. At any rate, the "Call to Worship"
seems at first not to have been followed by a congregational
response, but immediately by the benedictions preceding the
Shema^c.[124]

The problem is complicated by the fact that there are *Genizah* manuscripts of the Palestinian Rite that do not have this "Call to Worship" at all--even though some others do, albeit in a slightly different form. Those that do not have the customary "Call to Worship," however, do have a *berakhah* preceding the benedictions before the *Shema^c*, a *berakhah* completely unknown to the Talmud and to all the current Rites. It reads:

> Praised are You, O Lord our God, Sovereign of the universe,
> who has sanctified us through His commandments,
> and has commanded us the commandment of the Proclamation
>   of the *Shema^c*,
> so that we may proclaim His Kingship with a perfect heart,
> declare His Unity with a single mind,
> and serve Him with a fervent heart.[125]

Whether the manuscripts that lack the customary "Call to Worship" were meant for individual, rather than communal prayer, or whether, as Mann surmises,[126] this non-talmudic *berakhah* may have taken the place of other forms of the "Call to Worship," it is impossible to determine with any certainty.

VIII. THE READING OF SCRIPTURE

From its very inception, whenever that might have been, the synagogue has combined its prayer services with the reading and expounding of Scripture--if, indeed, chronologically speaking, the latter was not originally the synagogue's primary function. At any rate, there are days when the *debharim*, the private prayers of the individual, are not and were not the end of public worship, but when, instead, a reading from the Scriptures follows. Pentateuchal pericopes are read as part of the Morning Service of every Sabbath, festival, fast-day, New Moon, Monday, and Thursday, as well as on Purim and Hanukkah. Pentateuchal pericopes are also read as part of the Afternoon Service of Sabbaths and fast-days. The morning reading of the Pentateuch on Sabbaths, festivals and fast-days is also followed by a pericope from the Prophets (*Haphtarah*), which, in the Jewish division of the Scriptures, include also the historical Books of Joshua, Judges, Samuel and Kings. A *Haphtarah* also follows the Pentateuchal pericope on the afternoon of fast-days. In addition to the Pentateuchal and Prophetic lections, the Five Scrolls, contained in the Hagiographa of the Hebrew Bible, are also read in the synagogue: Song of Songs on Passover, Ruth on Pentecost, Lamentations on the Ninth of Abh, Ecclesiastes on Tabernacles, and Esther on Purim.

An old tradition records: "Moses ordained for Israel that they should read in the Torah on Sabbaths, festivals, New Moons, and on the intermediate days of the festivals. ... Ezra ordained for Israel that they should read in the Torah on Monday and Thursday and on Sabbath afternoon."[127] Even if the institution of regular Scripture readings on specified occasions should be of a somewhat more recent origin than that assumed by the Palestinian Talmud in the above quotation, there can be no doubt that the institution was already so old by the time of the Talmud that its historical origin had been forgotten. It may well be that the original fixed pericopes were those for the festivals and for the four special Sabbaths preceding the Festival of Passover. In connection with those latter, the Mishnah, which already presupposes a consecutive lection of the Pentateuch, tells us that the consecutive cycle is to be interrupted by the special pericopes—and *not*, as was to become the later and present practice, that the special pericopes were to be read *in addition* to what would have been the regular Sabbath lection.[128]

The present Jewish custom (with the exception of Liberal, Reform and some Conservative synagogues) is to read through the entire Pentateuch within the span of one year. It goes back to the Amoraic practice in Babylonia, as recorded in the Babylonian Talmud. Since the Babylonian Talmud became authoritative for all Rabbinic Jews, the authority of that Talmud also established the almost universal validity of the Babylonian custom of reading the Pentateuch in an annual cycle of pericopes. *Almost* universal, but not absolutely universal. For the Palestinian Jews a different practice is recorded, and, to the extent to which—right into the eleventh century—some diaspora communities still stood under the influence of the Palestinian religious authorities, the Palestinian practice in the matter of Pentateuchal readings was also followed in some diaspora communities—to be revived, with some modifications, by a number of non-Orthodox Jewish congregations since the nineteenth century.

Unfortunately, the early sources are neither quite clear nor unequivocal about the precise nature of the Palestinian cycle of Pentateuchal readings. It would appear, however, that, in Palestine, it took something like three to three and a half years to complete the reading of the Pentateuch. Consequently, the Palestinian pericopes must have been much shorter than the Babylonian ones.[129] The problem has intrigued scholars ever since Adolph Büchler, in 1893-4, argued for the existence of a definite Palestinian triennial cycle of Pentateuchal pericopes and Prophetic readings.[130] Büchler had access to a manuscript, found in the Cairo *Genizah*, that listed Pentateuchal periocopes in a triennial cycle. By adducing various rabbinic statements that linked certain historical events recorded in the Pentateuch with certain seasons of the year, and by assuming that the pericopes narrating those events must have been read at those seasons, Büchler proceeded to identify the triennial cycle of the manuscript with "the" triennial cycle that in his view had already been adopted in the Palestine of the early rabbinic period.

Many scholars have since built upon Büchler's foundations--even though, in detail, some of their conclusions (e.g., about the time of the year in which the presumed triennial cycle was started) differed considerably from his. In the meantime, some fragments have been published of early (sixth-century?) Palestinian synagogal poetry, from which it could be seen (a) that the early poets composed poems based on the Pentateuchal pericopes for every Sabbath of the year, and (b) that the pericopes were those of a triennial cycle.

But it does not follow that *a* triennial cycle, in use during the sixth or the eighth centuries, was necessarily identical with *the* Palestinian Pentateuchal readings of the first and second centuries. It was left to Joseph Heinemann to explode the notion of a definite early Palestinian triennial cycle altogether--by redirecting attention to what the Mishnah itself had to say on the subject of Scripture readings.[131] The Mishnah, for example, lays down the rule that none of the seven people who read from the Pentateuchal scroll on a Sabbath must read fewer than three verses.[132] While this gives us a minimum of twenty-one verses to be read on a Sabbath morning, no maximum is laid down; and this would, of course, lead to a situation where different congregations, on one and the same Sabbath, could read different verses of the Pentateuch. Similarly, the Tosephta informs us: "Where they finished reading on Sabbath morning, they begin reading on Sabbath afternoon; where they finished reading on Sabbath afternoon, they begin reading on Monday; where they finished reading on Monday, they begin reading on Thursday; and where they finished reading on Thursday, they begin reading on the following Sabbath. But Rabbi Judah says: Where they finished reading on Sabbath morning, they begin reading on the following Sabbath."[133] With such variations in practice presupposed in the tannaitic sources, it is impossible to speak about a definite Palestinian triennial cycle of Pentateuchal pericopes at that early time, whatever the situation might have been in later centuries. In any case, as we have said, in the course of time the Babylonian annual cycle displaced the earlier Palestinian custom or customs.

The Prophetic lections have remained far less universally standardized than the readings from the Pentateuch. Here, there are considerable differences between the *Ashkenazi* and the

Sepharadi Rites,[134] and between both of them and the Italian Rite.[135] The *Haphtarah*, whose time of institution is quite uncertain, is often thematically, but occasionally only verbally, connected with the Pentateuchal pericope. There are also Prophetic lections that bear no relation to the Pentateuchal pericope, but are instead connected with events in the liturgical year. For example, when the Sabbath coincides with the New Moon, or when the Sabbath coincides with a New Moon Eve, or on the three Sabbaths preceding and the seven Sabbaths following the Fast of the Ninth of Abh, or on the "Great Sabbath," i.e., the Sabbath immediately preceding Passover, the Prophetic readings are determined by the particular season in the liturgical year, and not by any theme or phrase occurring in the Pentateuchal pericope.

There are ceremonies connected with removing the Pentateuchal scroll from the Ark in which it is kept, and with returning it there after the reading, that consist mainly of the recitation or chanting of Scripture verses and prayers. A very elaborate ritual for this occasion, reflecting Palestinian practice, is recorded in the post-talmudic tractate, *Sopherim*.[136] In this form, however, that ritual has not been taken over by any of the current Rites, which, moreover, differ considerably among themselves particularly in this matter.[137] Since the statutory part of this whole rubric was the actual reading from the scroll, and not the ceremony connected with its removal from, and return to the Ark, that ceremony may well have been left to local custom and predilections. Indeed, one might suggest that the development of that ceremony (or those ceremonies) could have been causally connected with the development of synagogue architecture and synagogue furnishings. For, at first, the Pentateuchal scroll was kept in a *portable* wooden box, called *tebhah*.[138] It was probably brought into the House of Assembly only when the scroll was needed. Otherwise, it was kept behind a curtain in an adjoining room. But later, synagogues began to be constructed with a niche in the wall for a stationary Ark, in such a way that the worshipper's attention would be directed to it.[139] It stands to reason that the removal of the scroll from a portable wooden box called for less ceremony than did its solemn removal from a prominent archtitectural feature, a fixed Ark.

The reading from the scroll was done by members of the congregation--three on Monday, Thursday and Sabbath afternoon; four on New Moon and the intermediate days of the festivals; five on festivals proper; six on the Day of Atonement; and a minimum of seven on the Sabbath. The first reader recited a *berakhah* before his reading, and the last reader recited a *berakhah* after his reading, both *berakhoth* praising God for the gift of the Torah. The readers in between only read their verses, but did not recite any *berakhah*.[140] This custom changed in the course of time. With the general spread of the Babylonian practice of reading through the Pentateuch within a single year, the pericopes became very much longer than they had been in the ancient practice of Palestine, where a pericope of only twenty-one verses, divided among seven different readers, was considered sufficient for a Sabbath. Consequently, the number of verses to be read by the seven individuals also increased to such an extent that the ordinary Jew could no longer be expected to acquit himself of such an assignment --also on account of the correct cantillation of each word according to its musical notation, which had to be learned by heart beforehand. For the Pentateuchal scroll contains the consonantal Hebrew text only, with no indication of either vowels or musical notations. Thus it came about that the actual reading was left to an expert reader. People were still "called" to the Torah, but they merely stood next to the reader; and, also contrary to earlier custom, each one of those "called" recited the *berakhoth* before and after the passage read to him. This has remained the custom to this day.[141]

A framework of *berakhoth* also surrounded the reading of the Prophetic lection (*Haphtarah*), which, in all Rites, more or less follows the text given in *Sopherim*.[142] The *berakhah* before the reading of the *Haphtarah* thanks God for the Prophets. The *berakhoth* after the *Haphtarah*, four in number, have as their themes God's faithful fulfillment of His promises, the rebuilding of Jerusalem, the messianic kingdom, and the "holiness of the day." Since only the first *berakhah* after the reading of the *Haphtarah* directly deals with the Prophetic lection, Heinemann sees in this complex of benedictions a very early *seder berakhoth* ("Order of Benedictions"), which might well have been in use before the standardized Prayer of the Eighteen Benedictions for weekdays and the standardized Prayer of the Seven Benedictions for Sabbaths were introduced at the turn from the first to the second centuries.[143] When, in a subsequent development, the Seven Benedictions of the *Musaph* Service were added to the Scripture reading on Sabbath morning, the old *seder berakhoth*, which followed the *Haphtarah*, nevertheless maintained itself in its original position.

An official of the early synagogue was the *methurgeman* (="translator"), who rendered a free Aramaic translation of the

Hebrew pericopes read.[144] Aramaic was the language of the common people, and it was the very purpose of the readings from the Pentateuch and the Prophets to make the people know and understand the contents of the Scriptures. Elbogen is inclined to believe that the employment of a *methurgeman* is as old as the institution of the Scripture reading itself.[145]

It is difficult to determine precisely when the practice of translating the Scriptural pericopes into Aramaic fell into oblivion. But that is what happened some time in the post-rabbinic period--until, in a somewhat different form, the practice was revived in the nineteenth century by Reform Judaism. The latter did not, of course, introduce an Aramaic translation, but a translation into the vernacular of the countries in which Jews lived. Perhaps the fixation on Aramaic (though we do hear of isolated cases where Greek, Arabic, and Persian translations were used in earlier centuries) led to the disappearance of the *methurgeman* in the first place. For, while various dialects of Aramaic may have been the language of the ordinary Jews in Palestine and Babylonia, a time was to come when Aramaic would prove to be even less intelligible to the ordinary Jew than Hebrew. And for those who understood Aramaic, written Aramaic translations or paraphrases, the *Targumim*, became readily available.

The interpretation and the expounding of Scripture was also connected with the reading of Scripture.[146] This is the origin of the synagogal sermon. Leopold Zunz has shown that much of the rabbinic *midrashic* literature goes back to the sermons delivered in Palestinian synagogues in the first few centuries of the Common Era.[147] But the sermon has had no uninterrupted history in the synagogue. It could be that the interdiction of *deuterosis* (=the rabbinic interpretation of Scripture) by the Emperor Justinian in the year 553 C.E. had something to do with this.[148] And so did the rapid spread of didactic synagogal poetry, which utilized rabbinic lore related to the various Scriptural pericopes, and may itself have been a device to circumvent Justinian's law. But there was never a period in synagogal history when preaching ceased altogether, although it may have flourished in different localities at different times.[149] Thus, while, in eighteenth-century Germany, preaching may have been reduced to two occasions in the year--to the Sabbath before Passover, when the rabbi expounded the laws and dietary regulations of Passover, and to the Sabbath before the Day of Atonement, when the rabbi sounded the call of repentance--the Jewish village preachers of Eastern Europe, the *maggidim*, who were seldom enough ordained rabbis in any technical sense, entertained and edified their congregations with sermons every Sabbath afternoon, in that very period of history. Also at that time, regular sermons were not uncommon in Italy. But, by the beginning of the nineteenth century, regular sermons in Germany had fallen into desuetude for too long to be welcomed by the traditionalists when the early Reformers reintroduced regular preaching. It was, in part, to prove the legitimacy of the sermon in the synagogue that Zunz wrote his *Gottesdienstliche Vorträge* in 1832. Since that time, however, the sermon has found its way into all--even the Orthodox--synagogues of the Western world.

Also connected with the reading of Scripture are a number of prayers, which are partly of messianic import, but in their greater number deal with congregational concerns and public welfare. It is in connection with the reading of Scripture that prayers are offered for the physical and spiritual welfare of the congregation, that special blessings are invoked upon the scholars, the lay leaders and the charitable, that the dead are commemorated and the martyrs recalled, and that the forthcoming New Moon is announced.[150] What those prayers have stylistically in common is (a) that they avoid calling God, "Lord," but use a circumlocution instead (such as "The Holy One, praised be He," "Father of mercies," "He who wrought miracles for our fathers," etc.), and (b) that they do not address God in the second person, but speak of Him in the third person. Heinemann has shown that prayers of this pattern originated in the rabbinic House of Study (*beth hammidrash*) --as contrasted with prayers of Temple origin, prayers of private, non-statutory devotion, and prayers adopting the law-court pattern.[151] It is typical for prayers of *beth hammidrash* origin that they tend to cluster around the reading and expounding of Scripture and rabbinic texts.

IX. THE *QADDISH*

Perhaps the most famous of the "prayers of House of Study origin," and certainly the one that is most frequently repeated, in whole or in part, during synagogue services, is the synagogue's doxology *par excellence*, the *Qaddish* prayer. (*Qaddish* is Aramaic for "holy.") It is composed in a Judaeo-Aramaic dialect with Hebrew components, and it reads as follows:

> Exalted and hallowed be His great Name
> in the world which He created
> according to His will.
> May He establish His Kingdom
> in your lifetime and in your days,
> and in the lifetime of the whole household of Israel,
> speedily and at a near time.

And say: Amen.

May His great Name be praised for ever
and unto all eternity.

Blessed and praised,
glorified and exalted,
extolled and honored,
magnified and lauded
be the Name of the Holy One, praised be He,--
although He is above all blessings and hymns,
praises and consolations
which may be uttered in the world.
And say: Amen.

May the prayers and supplications
of the whole household of Israel
be acceptable before their Father in heaven.

May there be abundant peace from heaven,
and life,
for us and for all Israel.
And say: Amen.

May He who makes peace in His high heavens
make peace for us and for all Israel.
And say: Amen.

The focus of this whole prayer, and probably its earliest component, is the congregational response: "May His great Name be praised for ever and unto all eternity." It is a variation on such biblical verses as Psalm 113:2, and Daniel 2:20. At that, the original function of the *Qaddish* was not so much liturgical as it was homiletical, i.e., the congregation responded with this doxology to the messianic peroration at the conclusion of the preacher's homiletical discourse. Thus the prayer, or, at any rate, its major response, is referred to as "'May His great Name be praised' of the homiletical discourse."[152] While the *Qaddish*, as we now have it, is in a form of Aramaic, there may also have been Hebrew versions of it, as is indicated by the form in which the major response is quoted in b. *Berakhoth* 3a. Another quotation of this response in Hebrew is given by the second-century C.E. Rabbi Yose, from whom we also learn that the response itself was recited responsively by prayer leader and congregation.[153]

The first reference to the *liturgical* use of the *Qaddish* comes to us from the post-talmudic tractate *Sopherim*, which reflects the liturgical usage of the Palestinian synagogues. There we read that the *Qaddish* is to be recited as a doxology at the conclusion of the reading from the Pentateuchal scroll.[154] The same source also tells us that, after the termination of the *Musaph* Service on the Sabbath, the prayer leader would comfort the mourners at the gates of the synagogue, and then recite the *Qaddish*.[155] This is the first reference we have to a connection between the *Qaddish* and the mourners--a connection that was to become much more firmly established several centuries later.

Apart from its use as a mourners' prayer, to which we shall revert, the main function of the *Qaddish* is to serve as a concluding prayer for a whole service, in which case the version of the *Qaddish* we have reproduced above is used, or to divide one rubric of the service from another, in which case the paragraphs "May the prayers and supplications," "May there be abundant peace," and "May He who makes peace" are omitted.

A special form of this prayer, called *Qaddish de-Rabbanan*, is recited when ten or more adult males have studied rabbinic literature in the synagogue, or have read those passages from that literature which have been included in the prayerbook. This form of the *Qaddish* uses the following paragraph in place of "May the prayers and supplications":

> For Israel and for our rabbis,
> for their disciples.
> and for the disciples of their disciples,
> and for all who engage in the study of the Torah,
> here and everywhere,
> for them and for you
> may there be abundant peace,
> grace and loving-kindness,
> mercy and long life,
> ample sustenance and salvation
> from their Father who is in heaven.
> And say: Amen.

Yet another form of the *Qaddish*, the so-called "*Qaddish* of Renewal," begins as follows:

> Exalted and hallowed be His great Name
> in the world which He will renew,
> resurrecting the dead,
> and raising them up to eternal life.
> He will rebuild the city of Jerusalem,
> and establish His temple in its midst.
> He will uproot idolatry from the earth,
> and restore the worship of God to its place.
> The Holy One, praised be He, will reign
> in His sovereignty and in His glory.
> May this be in your lifetime and in your days,
> and in the lifetime of the whole household of Israel,
> speedily and at a near time.
> And say: Amen.

This *Qaddish* then continues like the other versions, but omits the paragraph, "May the prayers, etc." It is the only *Qaddish* that mentions the dead and the Resurrection; and it is appropriately enough recited as part of the burial service at the cemetery. But it is not, strictly speaking, a "prayer for the dead." It merely spells out in greater detail the eschatological picture implicit in the phrase, "May He establish His Kingdom," which is contained in all the other versions of the *Qaddish*.[156] So little is this form of the *Qaddish* inherently related to death that the only other occasion when it is recited is the joyous and festive gathering, celebrating the completion of the study of a whole tractate of the Talmud.

No mention at all of the dead is contained in the version of the *Qaddish* that has become known as the "Mourner's *Qaddish*." It consists of the regular form of the *Qaddish*, but omits the paragraph, "May the prayers and supplications." It is recited by the mourners at the conclusion of every service as well as after the recitation of certain Psalms within the service. The custom of having the mourners recite the *Qaddish* for eleven months after the death of a near relative, and then on every anniversary of the death, has been traced back to medieval Germany. The eleventh-century *Maḥzor Vitry*, not to speak of earlier sources, does not yet know that custom. Isaac Or Zaru'a (twelfth/thirteenth centuries) reports that, in Bohemia and in the Rhineland, it was the custom for mourners to recite the *Qaddish* at the end of every service, but that the custom was not yet observed in France.[157] Today the custom is known in all Jewish communities.

The association of the *Qaddish* with the mourners would seem to be related to the sentiment expressed in Job 1:21: "The Lord has given, and the Lord has taken away; blessed be the Name of the Lord." But, under the influence of a medieval legend,[158] and possibly also of the Catholic Mass for the Dead, the *Qaddish* has more and more assumed the character of a "prayer for the dead," by which the survivors sought to affect the fate of their departed in the Hereafter. It was, peculiarly enough, left to the nascent Reform movement in the nineteenth century to give in to the popular (and somewhat superstitious) notion of the *Qaddish* as a "prayer for the dead" by inserting in it a new Aramaic paragraph, which, in fact, turned the *Qaddish* into just such a prayer:

> For Israel and for the righteous,
> and for all
> who have departed from this world
> in accord with the will of God,
> may there be great peace,
> a good portion in the life of the World to Come,
> and grace and mercy
> from the Lord of Heaven and earth.
> And say: Amen.[159]

In Germany, not all Liberal congregations used this version of the *Qaddish*; and those that did also retained other forms of the *Qaddish* to serve the liturgical function of a doxology. In the Reform and Liberal synagogues of England, the new version never found acceptance. But in American Reform Judaism, this new form of the "Mourner's *Qaddish*" was to remain the one and only form of the *Qaddish* in worship service for well over a century--

until it was finally omitted from the 1975 revised edition of the American Reform prayerbook, which also restored the *Qaddish* as a doxology to some of the rubrics where it is found in the traditional Jewish liturgy.[160]

X. THE *QEDUSHAH*

The *Qaddish* is by no means the only doxology in the Jewish worship service. Apart from the concluding doxologies of the various Books of Psalms, which are used in the daily morning service as a component of the "Verses of Song,"[161] there is one prayer in particular, known as the *Qedushah* (="Sanctification"). It occurs in various parts of the service and includes as congregational responses Isaiah 6:3, Ezekiel 3:12, and, with one exception, one or more verses from other parts of Scripture, linked together by introductions which are recited by the prayer leader.

The one exception is the *Qedushah* inserted in the first benediction before the *Shema^c* in the morning service, which has as responses Isa. 6:3 and Ez. 3:12 only. That benediction praises God as the Creator of the heavenly luminaries. In mystic circles, those luminaries were identified with intelligent beings and, hence, with the angelic hosts.[162] A favorite text describing those hosts was, of course, the vision in chapter 6 of the Book of Isaiah with its angelic *trisagion*.

The idea of the liturgical *Qedushah* is that Israel, on earth, joins the angelic hosts, on high, in singing the *trisagion*. This idea is explicitly stated in the introductions to the *Qedushah* that is included in the prayer leader's repetition of the Prayer of the Eighteen (or Seven or Nine) Benedictions, as well as in the "Prefaces" to the *Sanctus* in the Christian liturgy. (See the comparative table at the end of this chapter.)

The simplest form of the *Qedushah* is recited in the third of the Eighteen Benedictions on weekday mornings and afternoons, and in the third of the Seven Benedictions in the Afternoon Service of Sabbaths and festivals. A brief introduction leads into Isaiah 6:3. A very brief connecting link introduces Ezekiel 3:12; and a mere reference to its source in the Hagiographa introduces Psalm 146:10. This is followed by a liturgical "bridge" to the concluding eulogy (*hathimah*).[163]

A somewhat more elaborate form of the *Qedushah* is found in the third of the Seven Benedictions of the Morning Service for Sabbaths and festivals. The introduction to Isa. 6:3 remains the same, and so do the congregational responses. But the connecting links have been lengthened. A more graphic description than on weekdays introduces Ex. 3:12; and the messianic theme, implicit in

Psalm 146:10, is explicitly anticipated in the introduction which leads to this response.[164]

The most elaborate form of the *Qedushah* is in the *Musaph* Service for Sabbath and festivals and in the Morning, *Musaph*, Afternoon and *Ne^{c}ilah* Services of the Day of Atonement. Not only is the introduction to Isa. 6:3 longer and more festive, and suggestive of the "numinous" as described by Rudolf Otto in *Das Heilige*,[165] but the congregational responses, too, have been increased. Between Ez. 3:12 and Ps. 146:10, we here find Deuteronomy 6:4 and the end of Numbers 15:41, together with appropriate introductions. Those are, of course, the first and last verses of the *Shema^c*.[166]

What we have been describing refers primarily to the *Qedushah* of the ^{c}*Amidah* in the *Ashkenazi* Rite, and, but only to some extent, in the *Sepharadi* Rite. Maimonides knew of only one form of the *Qedushah* for all occasions.[167] The Yemenite Jews have followed Maimonides in this until recent times, when an exception was made in the *Musaph* Service, where the version of the Spanish and Portuguese Rite has been adopted.[168]

Another form of the *Qedushah*, known as *Qedushah De-Sidra'*, consists of Psalm 22:4 as an introduction. This is followed by Isa. 6:3, both in Hebrew and in its Aramaic paraphrase from the Targum. The latter speaks of God as being holy in the highest heavens, holy on earth, and holy in all eternity, and thus seems intentionally to foreclose any Christian trinitarian exegesis of this verse. Without any connecting link, Ez. 3:12 and Exodus 15:18 follow, again both in Hebrew and in the Aramaic paraphrase. This *Qedushah De-Sidra'* is embedded in a concatenation of Scripture verses and of prayers that, are clearly of, *beth hammidrash* origin.[169] It is obvious that in its origin the *Qedushah De-Sidra'* was connected with the sermons and the expositions of Scripture, which at one time followed the prayer service. It is now found at the conclusion of the daily Morning Service, the beginning of the Sabbath Afternoon Service, and in the service that marks the termination of the Sabbath.[170]

While it is relatively easy to describe the various forms of the *Qedushah* as they now occur in the diverse liturgical Rites, it is far more complicated to determine the origin of the *Qedushah*, the priority of one form over another, and the reason that the beginning and the end of the *Shema^c* are included in the *Qedushah* of the *Musaph* Service.

The only mention of the *Qedushah* in the tannaitic, i.e., the earliest, stratum of rabbinic literature merely tells us that

"Rabbi Judah used to respond 'holy, holy, holy' together with the one who recited the benediction."[171] Saul Lieberman takes it for granted that this refers to the *Qedushah* in the first benediction before the *Shema^c*.[172] From this one might infer that in the development of the liturgy the *Qedushah* of the first benediction before the *Shema^c* preceded the *Qedushah* of the Eighteen Benedictions. But that inference and Lieberman's identification of the *Qedushah* are by no means self-evident.[173] Nevertheless, Moshe Weinfeld has recently drawn attention to "traces" of the *Qedushah* of the first benediction before the *Shema^c*, which he has found in the scrolls of Qumran and Ecclesiasticus.[174] But neither Ecclesiasticus nor the Qumran scrolls represent the authorized rabbinic liturgy; and it is questionable whether, if Weinfeld is correct in his identification, inferences may be drawn from this material that validly apply to the *Qedushah* of the rabbinic period.

It is, however, suggestive that, as most scholars concede, the *Qedushah* in all of its forms arose in the circle of mystics who called themselves *Yoredey merkabhah*, i.e., "those who decend into the divine throne-chariot"--a group largely responsible for the post-talmudic *Hekhaloth* literature but whose origins go back to the tannaitic period.[175] Also, although the *Qedushah* might well be of Palestinian origin, it is nevertheless true "that while in Palestine the *Qedushah* was accepted only in the morning *^{c}Amidah* of Sabbaths and festivals (and that of the *Yoṣer* benediction, i.e., the first benediction before the *Shema^c*, too, was recited only on Sabbaths and festivals), in Babylonia it spread to all *^{c}Amidoth* (except the evening one) and both forms of *Qedushah* came to be recited also on weekdays. In this, as in all other matters, present-day custom follows the Babylonian pattern."[176]

Jacob Mann, following up reports contained in Geonic literature, ascribes the insertion of the first and last words of the *Shema^c* into the *Qedushah* of the *Musaph* Service to times of religious persecution, both in Byzantium and in Persia, when the recitation of the *Shema^c* was prohibited by the government and, as a subterfuge, the Jews postponed the *Shema^c* from its regular place in the liturgy until the *Qedushah* of the *Musaph* Service--by which time the government spies would have left the synagogues. While the complete *Shema^c* was removed from the *Qedushah* after the persecutions had come to an end, the first and last words were retained as a memorial to those difficult days. Mann even tries to determine the specific persecutions in Byzantium and Persia that led to this subterfuge.[177] But, despite the vast learning Mann displays in his argumentation, one might still wish to conclude with Elbogen

that "those theories are by no means certain," and to accept his
warning that "the frequent attempt to relate prayers, etc. to
persecutions" might be nothing more than "an emergency use of
legends."[178] We shall probably never know for sure just how the
Shema^c got into the *Qedushah* of the *Musaph* Service.

We are on more solid ground if, with Kaufmann Kohler,[179] we
see in the liturgy contained in Book VII of the Apostolic Constitutions the slightly Christianized version of Hellenistic Jewish
prayers, and if we see in the quotations of Isa. 6:3 and Ez. 3:12,
together with their introductions and conclusions, in chapter 35
of Book VII of the Apostolic Constitutions, a reflection of the
synagogal *Qedushah*--to be precise, the *Qedushah* in the Seven
Benedictions of the Sabbath Morning Service.[180]

Moreover, since the present form of the Apostolic Constitutions derives from the fourth century C.E.,[181] and since the sole
reference to the *Qedushah* in the Tosephta is ambiguous,[182] and
since in the two places where the Talmud mentions the *Qedushah*[183]
no full text is given, it would seem that, chronologically speaking,
this Christian work contains the first literary repercussion of a
Qedushah text that in many ways resembles the kind of introduction,
responses, and connecting links that are familiar from the later
and more crystallized Jewish liturgical Rites, beginning with the
first Jewish prayerbook, the ninth-century C.E. *Seder Rabh 'Amram
Gaon*.[184]

Without going into the merits of Kaufmann Kohler's claim that
the text in the Apostolic Constitutions is an "Essene" text,[185]
other than to note that Moshe Weinfeld's more recent findings[186]
might be construed as some sort of support for Kohler's hypothesis,
the Apostolic Constitutions do, at any rate, give us a *terminus
ad quem* for the introduction of a full *Qedushah* text that
resembles those which are still in use. It is quite unlikely, if
not downright impossible, that in that period the Synagogue would
have borrowed any liturgical texts from the Church. It stands to
reason, therefore, that, in the case of the *Qedushah*, as in the
case of several of the other prayers in the Apostolic Constitutions,
the Church is indebted to the Synagogue.

XI. THE DIALETICS OF *KAWWANAH* AND *QEBHA^c*

In chapter II, above, when dealing with "Standards and Variety," and elsewhere in the development of our topic, we have
already had occasion to note the dialectics between *kawwanah*, the
requirement that prayer be spontaneous, the free outpouring of
the human heart before God, and *qebha^c*, the need of worshipping
faith-community for fixed liturgical elements. We saw how that

conflict was resolved in the first century C.E., under the auspices of Rabban Gamaliel II. The number of benedictions that made up the statutory daily prayer was fixed, and the themes that have to be expressed in prayer were laid down, but the actual wording of the prayers was left to the inspiration of the individual worshipper or, at any rate, the individual prayer leader. We also have had the opportunity to observe in action a law of Jewish (and perhaps not only Jewish) liturgical development: that the *kawwanah* of one generation tends to become the $qebha^c$ of a succeeding generation.

Now that we have traced the evolution, development and crystallization of a number of key components of the Jewish worship service, including the $Shema^c$ and its Benedictions, the prayer of the Eighteen Benedictions, the *Qaddish* and the *Qedushah*, it is appropriate for us to take another look at the ongoing dialectics.

One of the more striking things to note is that, not only in the Amoraic period, but still well into the Geonic period, the Palestinian Rite preserves a much greater flexibility and variety than does the Babylonian Rite and its offshoots. It can perhaps be said that no two manuscripts of the Palestinian Rite ever present us with totally identical versions of the same prayer-- and that is said not only with respect to more or less minor variations in wording, but also, and primarily, with respect to entire structural formulations of the prayers.[187]

Just how far-reaching the liturgical creativity of the Palestinians could be might be illustrated by two versions of the second benediction before the $Shema^c$ in the Morning Service, published by Mann from *Genizah* finds. That benediction, which deals with God's love for Israel as manifested through the giving of the Torah, is quite a lengthy one in the versions of the liturgy that ultimately derive from the Babylonian crystallization.[188] Even the variations between the *Ashkenazi* and the *Sepharadi* versions are of a relatively minor character; and although their very opening words differ,[189] both the *Ashkenazi* and the *Sepharadi* version of those opening words go back to Amoraic authorities.[190]

Yet the two Palestinian versions, published by Mann, differ not only from the *Ashkenazi* and the *Sepharadi* version, but also from each other. One of them consists of no more than a verse from the Psalms (87:2), followed by a concluding eulogy. It reads as follows:

> The Lord loves the gates of Zion
> more than all the dwellings of Jacob
> Praised are You, O Lord, who loves His people Israel.[191]

How that verse from Psalm 87 expresses the ideas that this benediction is meant to express may not be immediately clear to the uninitiated reader. But it is perfectly clear to those who are familiar with the rabbinic exegesis of this verse, which puns on the word, Zion (Hebrew: *Ṣiyyon*), and understands it as *meṣuyyanim* (="distinguished"). The verse is made to say: "The Lord loves the gates that are distinguished by the Law more than all the other dwellings of Jacob."[192] Thus both God's love and the Torah are found in, or read into, this verse; and the benediction expresses all the ideas it is meant to.

The other Palestinian version of the same benediction, to which we would like to draw attention, is only slightly longer. It is cast in poetic form, alluding to Psalm 80:9, Psalm 78:16, and to Sinai/Horeb as the mountain of Revelation. It reads as follows:

> A vine from Egypt our God has brought up.
> He drove out nations and planted it.
> From Sinai He gave it water to drink,
> Yea, running waters from Horeb.
> Praised are You, O Lord, who loves Israel.[193]

The water is clearly understood in a metaphorical sense here, as, for example, in Isa. 55:1.

Those two illustrations must suffice to convey to the reader the liturgical flexibility and creativity of the Palestinian Jews still at a time when the Babylonian Jewish authorities increasingly tended to be rigid about the very wording of the benedictions. As we have repeatedly seen, e.g., in connection with the annual cycle of Pentateuchal readings, the Babylonian authorities ultimately succeeded in making their customs and practices the universal Jewish norm and in suppressing the traditions of Jewish Palestine. It did not always go without a struggle--a struggle, moreover, that may have had as much to do with the battle for the hegemony over Jewish life as with theological and liturgical considerations.[194]

The Babylonian Amoraim began the standardization process of the liturgy, in which they gave the *qebhaʿ* aspect a much more decisive role than the Palestinian Tannaim or even the Palestinian Amoraim had ever done; and the Babylonian Geonim successfully completed the process. In accounting for this phenomenon, Joseph Heinemann notes that (a) the Hebrew language remained a living language for the Palestinian Jews longer than it did for the Babylonian Jews; that (b) because of their love for the Hebrew language, which was no longer a living language for most Babylonian Jews, the Babylonian Jews did not avail themselves of the

Mishnah's ruling that the *Shema^c*, the Eighteen Benedictions, the Grace after Meals and other liturgical components "may be recited in any language,"[195] and that (c) as a consequence of the combination of (a) and (b), it would have been difficult for Babylonian and other Diaspora Jews to continue the free improvisation of prayer formulations in Hebrew. "For this reason, liturgical innovation gradually gave way in Babylonia to standard formulations which could easily be memorized and, eventually, written down."[196]

Yet, even after the Bablonian Geonim had done their work of standardization, Jewish liturgy remained receptive to fresh outpourings of *kawwanah*. Biblical psalmists and Pharisaic teachers, rabbinic preachers and meditative mystics, folk piety and educated selectivity had left their traces on the prayers and meditations that the Geonim were to standardize. But Palestinian, Spanish, Italian, French and German synagogal poets, Spanish-Jewish philosophers and mystics as well as German-Jewish Pietists, and again Spanish-Jewish mystics, this time in sixteenth-century Palestine, that is, after the printed prayerbooks had become available, were yet to make their contributions--not only to their local rites, but also beyond. Thus, the recitation of Psalms 95 through 99, Psalm 29, and the hymn *Lekhah Dodi*, which now precede the regular service on Sabbath Eve and constitute the rubric "Welcoming the Sabbath" even in the standardized prayerbook of the *Ashkenazi* rite,[197] are a contribution of the sixteenth-century mystics, gathered in Safed, Palestine, just as, centuries before, the passionate song of Zion of the Spanish-Jewish poet, Judah Halevi (11th/12 centuries), found its place among the laments and dirges recited by the German and Polish Jews on the day commemorating the destruction of Jerusalem.[198] And the Polish-Jewish Hasidim of the eighteenth century not only created their own liturgical Rite by superimposing elements of the Spanish and Portuguese rite upon a basically *Ashkenazi* liturgy, but some of their innovations even found their way into editions of the Orthodox *Ashkenazi* liturgy, which are not intended for Hasidim at all.[199]

The inclusion of new liturgical materials into the worship service after printed prayerbooks had become generally available is particularly remarkable. After all, the printers of prayerbooks had as much--if not more--to do with stunting *kawwanah* and promoting *qebha^c* as did the Babylonian Geonim and the later Jewish legal authorities. But even before the invention of printing it had never been easy to introduce innovations into the Jewish service. Additions to the liturgy, no less than omissions from it, indicate that a new generation's spiritual needs are no longer

completely met by what has become "traditional." There will always
be "traditionalists" who consider the past to be the final arbiter
of what is good, proper, and acceptable in liturgical usage,
people, that is to say, who stand at the extreme opposite of those
early rabbis who insisted, even with respect to the Prayer of the
Eighteen Benedictions, that one must say something new in it every
day.[200]

At the same time, once something new had succeeded in entering the liturgy, it could almost never be dislodged again. To
this day, Orthodox Jews offer a prayer every Sabbath for the
welfare of the rectorate of the Babylonian Talmud academies and
for the exilarchate, i.e., the secular and political leadership
of Babylonian Jewry,[201] although these institutions ceased to
exist almost a thousand years ago.

A good illustration of how difficult it is both to make
liturgical innovations and, once they have been made, to abolish
them again is provided by the *Kol Nidrey*. This is the declaration,
recited at the beginning of the Atonement Eve Service, in which
the Jew seeks annulment from God for any vows in the religious,
but not the civil, sphere that he is unable to keep.[202] Although
it is a legal formula, and not a prayer at all, and although the
great majority of modern Jews are quite unable to translate the
Aramaic text, its recitation on that particular occasion is nevertheless regarded by considerable numbers as one of the most solemn
and edifying highlights of the religious year. What has helped
the *Kol Nidrey* attain this great popularity is, above all, the
beautiful and haunting melody to which it is sung by the *Ashkenazi*
(but not by the *Sepharadi*) Jews.[203]

We first hear about *Kol Nidrey* in the eighth and ninth
centuries C.E., when various Babylonian Geonim mention it in their
writings. While a few of them favor this innovation, many others
come out in strong opposition. Some have heard about it and seem
to have no strong feelings about it, but merely indicate that in
their academies this sort of thing was not done. Still others go
so far as to call this innovation: "baseless," "erroneous," and
"foolish."[204]

But *Kol Nidrey* found its way into the liturgy of Atonement
Eve after all. And when, in the nineteenth century, the rabbis
of Reform Judaism abolished it, and substituted for it more
prayerful and edifying texts, they met with the kind of opposition
to be expected from those who sought to defend what had, after all,
been a $qebha^c$ component of the liturgy for about a thousand years.
It should be added that, after more than a hundred years of Reform

experimentations with substitutes for the traditional *Kol Nidrey* text, the latest edition of the American Reform Jewish prayerbook has gone back to the very formula that ninth-century Babylonian Geonim and nineteenth-century German Reform rabbis so vehemently opposed![205]

Another illustration of the same phenomenon is provided by the evolution and the fate of synagogal poetry, the so-called *piyyuṭim*.[206]

Piyyuṭim appear as inserts in the benedictions before and after the *Shema^c* and in the Prayer of the Eighteen (or seven or Nine) Benedictions. They have also been composed as litanies for the circumnambulation of the synagogue's reading desk with the festival bouquet (*lulabh*) on the Feast of Tabernacles, as elegies and dirges, bemoaning the destruction of the Temple and Jewish suffering in general, for the Fast of the Ninth of Abh, as penitential prayers for the Ten Days of Repentance and for fast-days, as poetic treatments of the narrative about the high priestly service in the Jerusalem Temple on the Day of Atonement for inclusion in the Atonement *Musaph* Service, and as poetic enumerations of the Six Hundred and Thirteen Commandments for the *Musaph* Service on the Feast of Pentecost. Other *piyyutim* serve as opening and concluding hymns of daily, Sabbath and festival services. *Piyyutim* are not only devotional and meditative, but also informational and didactic, utilizing biblical and rabbinic law and lore for the various occasions for which they have been composed.

The earliest synagogal poets whose names are known to us are Yose ben Yose, Yannai and Eleazar Kallir. They lived in the Byzantine Empire, most probably in Palestine itself, and, in all likelihood, flourished around the fifth and sixth centuries C.E. This has led some scholars to link the rise of the *piyyutim* with Emperor Justinian's interdiction of *deuterosis* in the synagogues, in 553 C.E.,[207] particularly since a twelfth-century source, albeit without mentioning Justinian's name, reports that when "the enemies decreed that the Israelites must not occupy themselves with the Torah," the Sages ordained the recitation of *piyyutim* in which the laws of Sabbath and festivals are contained.[208] Thus the *piyyutim* would have been a subterfuge to get around the prohibition. However, another twelfth-century report, also linking the introduction of *piyyutim* with government interference with Jewish worship, specifically mentions the Persian (!) government.[209] We do know of persecutions of Jews in Persia between 450 and 589 C.E., and it may well be that Persian Jews too used *piyyutim* as subterfuge to circumvent government interference. But the undoubted Byzantine provenance of the earliest known poets makes the initial connection between Justinian's edict and the rise of the *piyyuṭim* more plausible.

However, this refers specifically to certain types of *piyyuṭim*, the didactic ones. The real origin of synagogal poetry must be sought in a much earlier period. There are a number of anonymous poetic compositions that may well be older than the first known synagogal poet, Yose ben Yose. We have said above that "*piyyuṭim* appear as inserts" in various rubrics of the worship service. That is indeed the case, for thus we find them in the manuscript and printed versions of the liturgy with which we are familiar. But not all poems were meant to be mere "inserts." Some of them were actually intended as alternatives to the various prayers into which later generations inserted them, and go back to the period before the Babylonian Geonim had succeeded in stamping out the earlier freedom of making up one's own wording of the statutory prayers.[210] Of such a kind was the Palestinian version of the second benediction before the *Shema^c*, which we have discussed above.[211] Besides, the urge to "sing unto the Lord a new song" did not subside with the canonization of the biblical Book of Psalms.

On European soil, we find the *piyyuṭim* first developing in Southern Italy in the second half of the ninth century C.E. From there, they spread, in the tenth century, to central and Northern Italy. Franco-German Jewry, at first under Italian-Jewish influence, produced its own great school of poets in the tenth and eleventh centuries. That school tended to imitate the style of Eleazar Kallir, with his manifold allusions to biblical and rabbinic literature and his grammatical peculiarities. The Spanish school of synagogal poets began to flourish in the tenth century. Their poems are quite different in style and content from the Franco-German variety, for the Spanish-Jewish poets largely couched their poetry in biblical rather than rabbinic vocabulary, adhered to classical Hebrew grammar, and frequently adopted sophisticated schemes of rhyme and meter, often borrowed from Arabic prototypes.

The introduction of *piyyuṭim* into the liturgy was not only vehemently opposed by the same Babylonian circles which objected to the innovation of the *Kol Nidrey*, it also continued to be opposed throughout the centuries by some of the greatest legal authorities of Judaism.[212] But the opposition was to be of no avail.

Not only did synagogal poetry, originally considered to be optional *kawwanah* and voluntary by both its promoters and its opponents, assume all the authority of $qebha^c$, but its very existence necessitated a new nomenclature for the prayerbooks used by Jews. The Jewish prayerbook is called *siddur* or *seder tephilloth* (i.e., "order of prayers"). A one-volume *siddur* can easily contain all the statutory prayers of the whole year--for weekdays and Sabbaths, for festivals and High Holy Days. The standard edition of the *siddur*, which was in common use by Orthodox Jews in Germany, first published by Wolf Heidenheim in Rodelheim, in 1806, was the *Siddur Sephath 'Emeth*. Its 154th edition was published in 1931. This prayerbook contained 312 pages. But it did not include the poetic embellishments for the festivals and the High Holy Days. For those, the Jew needed separate prayerbooks, which, in addition to the poetry, also contained the statutory prayers.

Those separate prayerbooks are called *maḥzor*, which means "cycle," and is short for "cycle of the whole year." The early synagogal poets used to write poetry for each Sabbath, based upon the specific pentateuchal pericope according to a triennial lectionary *cycle*. Most of that poetry has been lost, since, with the general acceptance of the annual lectionary cycle, its relevance to the liturgy was gone. But those poets also wrote poetry for the festival *cycle* of the Jewish year. If, therefore, one collected the synagogal poetry of the whole year, one had a *cycle* of poems, a *maḥzor*. And that is the name Jews still give to their festival prayerbooks, as distinct from the daily and Sabbath prayerbook, which is still known as *siddur*.

A *maḥzor* for the whole year, according to the *Ashkenazi* Rite, printed in Venice in 1756, and bound in one volume, contained no less than 1,696 pages! That was the Hebrew text only, without any vernacular translation. In more recent years, beginning with the nineteenth century, vernacular translations have become a necessity for most Jews in the West, and it is no longer possible to confine the entire "cycle" within the covers of a single book. Modern editions of the *maḥzor*, with a vernacular translation, tend to run into six to nine volumes. At that, they contain no more than a small selection of the synagogal poetry which has been written. Israel Davidson's monumental *Thesaurus of Medieval Hebrew Poetry*,[213] on the two thousand and sixty pages of its four volumes, merely lists the opening words of, and bibliographical information about, the synagogal poems that were known to Davidson himself. Many others have come to light since Davidson's death in 1939. Such a wealth of poetic effusion had clearly drowned out "the voices of the oldest, most trustworthy Rabbis concerning the *piyyuṭim*," to use the title of A. A. Wolff's 1857 tract against the *piyyuṭim*.

If the proliferation of synagogal poetry represented a victory of *kawwanah* over *qebha^c*, it also represented an exemplification of the law that one generation's *kawwanah* becomes another generation's *qebha^c*. After the thirteenth century, there were few notable additions to the corpus of synagogal poetry; and the first printed Jewish prayerbook (1485/86) to all intents and purposes marked the beginning of the end for all future additions to the liturgy. The success of the sixteenth-century Safed mystics in breaking through this barrier is, therefore, all the more remarkable.

But the almost universal acceptance of synagogal poetry also illustrates something else: just as one generation's *kawwanah* becomes another generation's *qebha^c*, so do the reforming innovators of one period turn into the pillars on which the unbending conservatism of a future period builds; while those who, at a later period, maintain the conservatism of an earlier age will invariably be branded as radical innovators.

It is therefore not surprising that when the Reformers of the nineteenth century resurrected the arguments of earlier rabbinic authorities agains synagogal poetry, in order to justify the abolition of most of the medieval compositions, they, the Reformers, met with the strong opposition of the champions of the *status quo*.[214] It is somewhat ironic that this nineteenth-century battle in reality represented the struggle of a new generation's *kawwanah* with the *kawwanah* of earlier generations. For, in addition to the other reasons that motivated the Reformers, there was also the desire to reduce the sheer bulk of traditional material so that room might be found for the inclusion of liturgical texts expressing the concerns and aspirations, the *kawwanah*, of a new age.

It was indeed the striving for the expression of that new *kawwanah* that initially gave rise to the Reform movement in Judaism, in the early nineteenth century. For, whatever else Reform Judaism may have become in the course of its development, and however far-reaching its departures from past Jewish theology may ultimately have turned out to be, in its *origin* Reform Judaism manifested itself primarily as a movement of *liturgical* reform. Even its later theological transformations found their foremost expression in different editions of the Jewish prayerbook--of which there have been very many.[215]

By the beginning of the nineteenth century, the traditional Jewish worship service, particularly on Sabbaths and festivals, was a very long one, the product of centuries and millennia of liturgical development--of a development, moreover, that was one of constant additions, without ever allowing any significant omissions. That service was conducted entirely in Hebrew, with a few prayers in Aramaic. Neither language was understood by increasing numbers of Jews in the West. The sermon had long since fallen into oblivion. While the service was conducted by a cantor, there was no choral or even harmonious congregational singing, and instrumental accompaniment of the service was deemed by most rabbis of the time to be an infringement of Jewish religious law.[216] The effect of this kind of worship service upon many of the worshippers was one of complete boredom, and that boredom led all too often to a disregard of the decorum appropriate to a worship service. Many of the Jews who, in the period of Emancipation, had already enjoyed a Western education simply stayed away from the synagogue.

It was in order to make Jewish worship meaningful again, and meaningful enough to attract the young generation, that, in the second decade of the nineteenth century, the first Reformers introduced a number of liturgical changes. The worship service was to be shortened--mainly by omitting the frequent repetitions of the same prayer that occur in the traditional liturgy, as well as the greater part of the medieval synagogal poems. Some, though not all prayers were to be recited in the vernacular, and new prayers in the vernacular were to be introduced. Regular sermons of a moral and edifying nature were to be preached. Choir and organ music were to accompany the service. Of such a nature were the strivings of the early Reformers; and they even attempted to show that the changes they had introduced could be justified on the basis of the Talmud as well as of the medieval codes of Jewish religious law.[217]

Further changes, however, were introduced in a subsequent stage of Reform Jewish development, when the wording of some of the traditional prayers that had been retained was altered as well, to reflect the special emphases and nuances of Reform Jewish belief. This involved a stress on universalism and a de-emphasis of particularism, as well as Reform Judaism's modified view of messianic fulfilment--which no longer included the rebuilding of the Jerusalem Temple, the restoration of the sacrificial cult, and the return of all Jews to Palestine. The American Reform prayerbooks were to become even more radical--by omitting all references to angelology (already considerably reduced in the

European Reform rituals), by allowing for an even more extended use of the vernacular, and by consistently substituting references to the immortality of the soul for any traditional liturgical mention of the physical resurrection of the dead.[218] Within Reform Judaism itself, the ongoing dialetics between *kawwanah* and *qebha^c* have not infrequently led to liturgical results that can often be recognized only with difficulty as still belonging to the millennial Jewish liturgical tradition, which has here been described.

Be that as it may, the fact remains that the dialectics of *kawwanah* and *qebha^c*, so clearly taken for granted in the classical period of rabbinic Judaism and still in evidence even after the liturgy had become crystallized, had been brought to a halt for a number of centuries before the beginning of the modern period in history. *Qebha^c* seemed to have emerged as the ultimate victor. It was Reform Judaism that set the dialectics in motion again; and its beneficiaries, in this respect and to varying degrees, include all forms of Judaism practised in the Western world today.

COMPARATIVE TABLE
INTRODUCTION TO THE *QEDUSHAH*

I. In the Prayer of the Eighteen (or Seven) Benedictions in the Morning and Afternoon Services of Weekdays, Sabbaths and Festivals.

 (a) *Ashkenazi* Rite

We will sanctify Your Name on earth even as they sanctify it in the celestial heights, as it is written by Your Prophet: "And they called one unto another and said:"
Isaiah 6:3.

 (b) *Sepharadi* Rite

We will sanctify You and revere You in the pleasant manner of the holy Seraphim, who proclaim to You that threefold sanctification; and thus it is written by Your Prophet: "And they called one to another and said:"
Isaiah 6:3.

 (c) *Yemenite* Rite

We will sanctify You and revere You, and proclaim to You the threefold sanctification, according to the word which was spoken by Your Prophet: "And they called one to another and said:"
Isaiah 6:3.

II. In the *Musaph* of Sabbaths and Festivals.

 (a) *Ashkenazi* Rite

We will revere You and sanctify You in the mysterious speech of the holy Seraphim who sanctify Your Name in holiness, as it is written by Your Prophet: "And they called one to another and said:"
Isaiah 6:3.

 (b) *Sepharadi* Rite

The angelic hosts on high and Your people Israel gathered below will give You a crown, O Lord, our God. Together they proclaim to You the threefold sanctification, according to the word spoken by Your Prophet: "And they called one to another and said:"
Isaiah 6:3.

 (c) *Yemenite* Rite

Now identical with the *Sepharadi* Rite; but originally, following Maimonides. Using the same text as in the *Qedushah* for weekdays.

III. *Qedushah* in the First Benediciton before the "Hear, O Israel" of the Daily, Sabbath and Festival Morning Service.
The same in all the various Rites.

Be praised, You..., who have created the holy beings..., and all of whose ministers stand on the heights of the universe, loudly proclaiming together, in reverence, the words of the living God and eternal King. ... All of them open their mouth in holiness and purity, in song and praise, and they bless, praise, glorify, revere, sanctify and ascribe sovereignty to the Name of God, the great, mighty and awe-inspiring King. Holy is He! And all of them take upon themselves the yoke of the Kingdom of Heaven, one from another, and they grant permission, one to another, to proclaim the holiness of their Creator. In equanimity, in pure speech and in melody, they, all of them as one, intone the sanctification and recite in reverence:
      Isaiah 6:3.

The Ophanim and the holy Hayoth raise themselves up with a loud noise opposite the Seraphim. Opposite them, they offer praise and say:
      Ezekiel 3:12.

IV. *Qedushah* in the *Apostolic constitutions* (Book VII, ch. 35). Translation by Kaufmann Kohler, who omits what he considers to have been Christian interpolations, in *HUCA*, Vol. I (1924), pp. 415f.

And the shining host of angels and the intellectual spirits say one to another: "There is but One holy." And the holy Seraphim together with the six-winged Cherubim, who sing to Thee their triumphal song, cry out with never-ceasing voices;
      Isaiah 6:3.

And the other multitudes of the orders, the angels, the archangels, the thrones, the dominions, the principalities, the authorities, the powers cry aloud and say:
      Ezekiel 3:12.

But Israel, Thy Congregation on earth, emulating the heavenly powers, sings with a full heart and a willing soul night and day:
      Psalm 68:18 (LXX)

V. The *Sanctus* of the Roman Catholic Mass.
   (a) Regular Preface
   ... Per quem majestatem tuam laudant Angeli, adorant Dominationes, tremunt Potestas, Caeli caelorumque Virtutes ac beata Seraphim socia exsultatione concelebrant. Cum quibus et nostras voces ut admitti jubeas, deprecamur, supplici confessione dicentes:

   Isaiah 6:3, etc.

   (b) Preface on the Feast of the Most Holy Trinity
   ... Quam laudant Angeli, atque Archangeli, Cherubim quoque ac Seaphim: qui non cessant clamare quotidie, una voce dicentes:

   Isaiah 6:3, etc.

VI. *Qedushah de-Sidra'*
   "You are the Holy One, enthroned above the praises of Israel." (Psalm 22:4.)

   Isaiah 6:3.

   (*In Aramaic*): And they receive permission one from another and say: "Holy -- in the highest heavens, the abode of His Presence; holy -- upon earth, the work of His might; holy -- for ever and unto all eternity is the Lord of hosts; the whole earth is full of the radiance of His glory."

   Ezekiel 3:12.

   (*In Aramaic*): Then a wind lifted me up, and I heard behind me a sound of the mighty storm of those who were praising and abode of His Presence!"

   Exodus 15:18

   (*In Aramaic*): The Lord! His Kingdom endures for ever and unto all eternity.

NOTES

Synagogue Liturgy

[1] All translations from Hebrew and Aramaic texts are the author's own, even when page references are given to published prayerbooks with translations.

Grateful acknowledgment is made to the W. Kohlhammer Verlag of Stuttgart, Federal Republic of Germany, for the permission granted to publish this English version of my chapter, "Die Geschichte des synagogalen Gottesdienstes," scheduled to appear in the "Judentum" volume of their series, *Die Religionen der Menschheit*.

[2] Cf., e.g., Luke 4:16-27.

[3] Julian Morgenstern, "The Origin of the Synagogue," in *Studi Orientalistici in onore di Giorgio Della Vida*. Rome, 1956, Vol. II, pp. 192-201.

[4] See, e.g., Heinrich Graetz, *Geschichte der Juden*. Vol. II, Part 2. Leipzig, [3]1902, p. 18; and cf. Wilhelm Bacher, art. "Synagogue." in *JE*, Vol. XI, p. 619.

[5] See, e.g., George A. Buttrick et al., eds., *The Interpreter's Bible*. Vol. IV. New York/Nashville, 1955, pp. 392-394, where, however, this interpretation is rejected. For a brief survey of recent theories about the origin of the synagogue, see Joseph Gutmann, ed., *Ancient Synagogues--The State of Research* (Brown Judaic Studies 22). Chico, CA, 1981.

[6] Tamid 4:3 (end)-5:1.

[7] Lev. 5:5.

[8] Deut. 26:1-10.

[9] M. Yoma 3:8; 4:2; cf. b. Yoma 36b.

[10] See *Understanding*, pp. 3-16.

[11] Ber. 28b.

[12] Ber. 29b.

[13] Shab. 115b: "Those who write down prayers are like those who burn the Torah."

[14] M. Ber. 4:3.

[15] The latest scientific edition of this prayerbook is E. D. Goldschmidt, ed., *Seder Rabh 'Amram Gaon*. Jerusalem, 1971.

[16] See *Siddur Rabh Saadja Gaon*, ed. I. Davidson, S. Assaf and B. I. Joel. Jerusalem, 1941.

[17] See *Siddur Rashi*, ed. S. Buber and J. Freimann. Berlin, 1910.

[18] See *Maḥzor Vitry*, ed. S. Hurwitz. Nurnberg, 1923.

[19] See the scientific edition of this text in E. D. Goldschmidt, *On Jewish Liturgy*. (Hebrew.) Jerusalem, 1978, pp. 187-216.

[20] Cf. Michael Higger, ed., *Masekheth Sopherim*. Jerusalem, 5730², pp. 78-81.

[21] Cf. Abraham I. Schechter, *Studies in Jewish Liturgy*. Philadelphia, 1930, for the publication of parts of this text.

[22] Ber. 28b.

[23] Ber. 26b.

[24] Ber. 33a.

[25] Cf. M. H. Segal, ed., *Sepher Ben-Sira Hashalem*. Jerusalem, 1958², p. 355.

[26] Cf. M. Tamid 5:1.

[27] Louis Finkelstein, "The Development of the Amidah," in *JQR*., N.S., Vol. 16 (1925/26), pp. 1-43, 127-170. (Reprinted in *Contributions*, pp. 91-177.)

[28] Cf. e.g., his "Zur Formengeschichte des altjüdischen Gebetes," in *MGWJ*, Vol. 78 (1934), pp. 438-447; and his "Dubletten in Gebetstexten," in *MGWJ*, Vol. 83 (1939), pp. 142-149.

[29] Cf. *Heinemann*, pp. 1-12 and *passim*. For an over-all survey of various methodologies in the study of Jewish liturgy, see Richard S. Sarason, "On the Use of Method in the Modern Study of Jewish Liturgy," in William Scott Green, ed., *Approaches to Ancient Judaism*. Missoula, Montana, 1978, pp. 97-172. (Reprinted in Jacob Neusner, ed., *The Study of Ancient Judaism*, Vol. I. New York, 1981, pp. 107-179.)

[30] Cf. B. Ber. 28b, 29a.

[31] T. Ber. 3:25, ed. Lieberman, p. 18.

[32] Cf. Moses Maimonides, *Mishneh Torah, Hilkhoth Tephillah* 2:1.

[33] Cf. Jakob J. Petuchowski, "Der Ketzersegen," in Michael Brocke, Jakob J. Petuchowski and Walter Strolz, eds., *Das Vaterunser --Gemeinsames im Beten von Juden und Christen*. Freiburg, 1974, pp. 90-101. But see also Johann Maier, *Jesus von Nazareth in der talmudischen Überlieferung*. Darmstadt, 1978, p. 44, and Reuven Kimelman, "*Birkat Ha-Minim* and Lack of Evidence for an Anti-Christian Jewish Prayer in Late Antiquity," in E. P. Sanders *et al.*, eds., *Jewish and Christian Self-Definition*. Vol. II. Philadelphia, 1981, pp. 226-244.

[34] Cf. Joseph Heinemann, "The Formula *melekh ha ^{c}olam*," in JJS, Vol. XI (1960), pp. 177-179.

[35] See Rashi *ad* b. Berakhoth 11b, s.v. *barukh 'attah 'adonai*.

[36] Men. 43b.

[37] Numbers 15:37ff.

[38] See Note #25, above.

[39] See *Hodayoth* I QH V, 20, in Eduard Lohse, ed., *Die Texte aus Qumran*. Darmstadt, 1964, p. 130. English translation in Geza Vermes, *The Dead See Scrolls in English*. Harmondsworth, 1972, p. 166.

[40] M. Yoma 7:1; M. Sotah 7:7-8.

[41] Cf. *Heinemann*, pp. 77-103, for all the relevant sources.

[42] Ber. 26b.

[43] Ber. 27b-28a.

[44] Moses Maimonides, *Mishneh Torah, Hilkhoth Tephillah* 1:6.

[45] Cf. M. Ber. 4:7.

[46] Cf. b. Ber. 30b.

[47] Cf. M. Ta. 4:1; y. Ta. IV, 1 (p. 67a.); b. Ta. 26b.

[48] See the text in *Hertz*, pp. 131-157.

[49] Hebrew text published by Solomon Schechter in *JQR*, Vol. X (1898), pp. 654-659. (Reprinted in *Contributions*, pp. 373-378.) English translation in *LPJL*, pp. 27-30.

[50] Cf. Elie Munk, *The World of Prayer*. Vol. II. New York, 1963, p. 10.

[51] See Note #14, above.

[52] Y. Ber. IV, 3 (p. 8a); b. Ber. 29a.

[53] Cf. *Elbogen*, pp. 116f. and Notes, for the sources.

[54] Cf. *Reform*, pp. 240-264.

[55] For the sources and their development, see Jakob J. Petuchowski, "The 'Malkhuyoth,' 'Zikhronoth' and 'Shofaroth' Verses," in *Pointer* (London, England), Vol. VIII, No. 1 (Autumn 1972), pp. 4-6.

[56] English translation in *Hertz*, pp. 845-853, 867-887, 855-859.

[57] M.R.H. 4:6.

[58] English translation in *Hertz*, pp. 847-851.

[59] Cf. Aharon Mirsky, ed., *Piyyuté Yosé ben Yosé*. (Hebrew.) Jerusalem, 1977, pp. 87-95.

[60] Cf. Joseph Heinemann, in Hayyim Hamiel, ed., *Yamim Nora-im*. Vol. II. (=*Ma'yanoth*, Vol. 9). Jerusalem, 1968, pp. 555ff.

[61] For an early instance of the application of this law, see the discussion in b. Ber. 11b.

[62] English translation in *Hertz*, pp. 109-129; and in *LPJL*, pp. 21-26.

[63] For the rather unlikely eventuality that someone might be reading the *Shemaʿ* passage in a Pentateuchal scroll just at the time when the liturgical recitation of the *Shemaʿ* is called for, see M. Ber. 2:1.

[64] See S. Baer, ed., *Totse-oth Ḥayyim*. Rodelheim, ^{3}1894, p. 81.

[65] M. Ber. 2:2.

[66] M. Ber. 1:5.

[67] M. Tamid 5:1.

[68] *Antiquities*, IV, viii, 13.

[69] Cf. Kaufmann Kohler, *The Origins of the Synagogue and the Church*. New York, 1929, pp. 53-60; and *Studies, Addresses and Personal Papers*. New York, 1931, pp. 113-121.

[70] M. Ber. 1:1-2.

[71] M. Ber. 1:3.

[72] b. Ber. 2a.

[73] M. Tamid 5:1.

[74] b. Ber. 12a; Y. Ber. I, 8 (p. 3c).

[75] Cf. Hans Joachim Schoeps, *Theologie und Geschichte des Judenchristentums*. Tubingen, 1949, pp. 147ff. But see Johann Maier, *Jüdische Auseinandersetzung mit dem Christentum in der Antike*. Darmstadt, 1982, pp. 150-152.

[76] Cf. F. C. Burkitt, "The Hebrew Papyrus of the Ten Commandments," in *JQR*, Vol. XV (1903), pp. 392-408; and see Moshe Greenberg, art. "Nash Papyrus," in *EJ*, Vol. 12, col. 833.

[77] See Note #68, above.

[78] M. Ber. 1:5.

[79] b. Ber. 14b.

[80] b. Ber. 4b.

[81] Ibid.

[82] M. Ber. 1:4.

[83] Ibid.

[84] M. Tamid 5:1.

[85] b. Ber. 11a, b.

[86] English translation in *Hertz*, pp. 109-115.

[87] Sa'adya Gaon still knew of a brief version, which he included in the morning prayer to be said by the individual who prays without a congregation. See *Siddur Rabh Saadja Gaon*, ed. Davidson, Assaf and Joel. Jerusalem, 1941, p. 13.

[88] b. Ber. 11b.

[89] See Note #69, above.

[90] Cf. Martin Buber, *The Prophetic Faith*. New York, 1960, pp. 212f. But see, for a different interpretation of this passage, Yehezqel Kaufmann, *Toldedoth Ha'emunah Hayiśre'elith*. Vol. VIII. Jerusalem, 1956, pp. 86f.

[91] b. Ber. 11b.

[92] Cf. Kurt Rudolph, *Die Gnosis*. Gottingen, 1977, pp. 67-74 and *passim*. Cf. Robert M. Grant, *Gnosticism*. New York, n.d. (1961?), pp. 170-175.

[93] English translation in *Hertz*, p. 305.

[94] See *Hertz*, pp. 115-117, and 307.

[95] See *Hertz*, pp. 127-129, and 311-313.

[96] Cf. *Theology*, pp. 20-30.

[97] English translation in *Hertz*, p. 313.

[98] Cf. Y. Ber. IV, 5 (p. 8c). An alternative Palestinian concluding eulogy (*ḥathimah*) was: "Praised are You, O Lord, who spreads the tabernacle of peace over us and over all His people Israel, who comforts Zion and rebuilds Jerusalem." Cf. Jacob Mann, Genizah Fragments of the Palestinian Order of Service," in *HUCA*, Vol. II (1925), p. 304. (Reprinted in *Contributions*, p. 414.)

[99] See *Hertz*, p. 1001.

[100] See Note #80, above.

[101] b. Ber. 4b.

[102] Cf. *Elbogen*, pp. 101-105.

[103] English translation in *Hertz*, pp. 315-317.

[104] Cf. D. Camerini, ed., *Formulario di Orazioni secondo il Rito Italiano*. Torino, 1912, p. 141.

[105] Cf. *Tiklal Shibhath Tsiyyon*, ed. Joseph Kapiḥ. Vol. I. Jerusalem, 5712, p. 83.

[106] See Note #61, above.

[107] Cf. M. Ber., chapters 6 and 7.

[108] See *Hertz*, pp. 9-31.

[109] b. Ber. 60b.

[110] See *Hertz*, pp. 51-107.

[111] b. Shab. 118b.

[112] See *Hertz*, pp. 169-187.

[113] T. Ber. 3:6, ed. Lieberman, p. 13; b. B.M. 59b; and cf. *Elbogen*, pp. 73ff.

[114] Ismar Elbogen, *Studien zur Geschichte des jüdischen Gottesdienstes*. Berlin, 1907, pp. 38-44.

[115] T. Ber. 3:6, ed. Lieberman, p. 13.

[116] *Shulḥan ᶜArukh, Oraḥ Ḥayyim*, #131.

[117] Cf., e.g., *Hertz*, pp. 169-187, with Moses Gaster, ed., *The Book of Prayer...according to the Custom of the Spanish and Portuguese Jews*. Vol. I. London, 1949, pp. 39-46.

[118] Cf. b. Ber. 16b-17a. For English translations, see *LPJL*, pp. 40-43.

[119] Cf. *Seder Rabh 'Amram Gaon*, ed. E. D. Goldschmidt. Jerusalem, 1971, pp. 37f.

[120] English translation in *Hertz*, p. 157, and *LPJL*, p. 41.

[121] See *Hertz*, pp. 109 and 305.

[122] M. Ber. 7:3.

[123] *Siphre ad Deuteronomium, pisqa* #306, ed. Finkelstein, p. 342.

[124] Cf. *Elbogen*, p. 17; and Herman Kieval, art. "Barekhu," in *EJ*, Vol. 4, cols. 218-220.

[125] Mann, op. cit., p. 286. (Reprinted in *Contributions*, p. 396.)

[126] Mann, op. cit., pp. 285-288. (Reprinted in *Contributions*, pp. 395-398.)

[127] Y. Meg. IV, 1 (p. 75a).

[128] M. Meg. 3:4-6.

[129] Cf. Joseph Heinemann, "The Triennial Lectionary Cycle," Vol. XIX (1968), pp. 41-48.

[130] Adolph Buchler, "The Reading of the Law and Prophets in a Triennial Cycle," in *JQR*, Vol. V (1893), pp. 420-468; Vol. VI (1894), pp. 1-73. (Reprinted in *Contributions*, pp. 181-302.)

[131] Heinemann, see Note #129, above.

[132] M. Meg. 4:4.

[133] T. Meg. 3 (4):10, ed. Lieberman, p. 355.

[134] See the table in *JE*, Vol. VI, p. 137.

[135] Cf. Samuel David Luzzatto, *Mabho' Lemaḥzor Benéʹ Roma*, ed. E. D. Goldschmidt. Tel-Aviv, 1966, pp. 96-98, for the Prophetic readings in the Italian Rite.

[136] *Masekheth Sopherim* 14:8ff, ed. Muller, pp. XXIVf.

[137] Compare, e.g., the *Ashkenazi* liturgy for this procedure on weekdays, as given in *Hertz*, pp. 189-197, with the *Sepharadi* liturgy, as given in Gaster, op. cit., pp. 46-47, 50-51; and the corresponding Sabbath and festival procedure in *Hertz*, pp. 473-523, with Gaster, op. cit., pp. 110-116.

[138] Cf. *Elbogen*, pp. 469f.

[139] Cf. Franz Landsberger, "The Sacred Direction in Synagogue and Church," in *HUCA*, Vol. XXVIII (1957), pp. 181-203.

[140] M. Meg. 4:1-2.

[141] See *Hertz*, pp. 191-193.

[142] *Masekheth Sopherim* 13:10-14, ed. Muller, pp. XXIIf.

[143] *Heinemann*, pp. 227-229.

[144] M. Meg. 4:4; and cf. *Elbogen*, pp. 186f.

[145] *Elbogen*, p. 187.

[146] Cf. Luke 4:16-27.

[147] See Leopold Zunz, *Die gottesdienstlichen Vorträge der Juden*. Frankfurt a. M., ^{2}1892. For modern scholarly purposes, the Additional Notes by Chanock Albeck, in his Hebrew edition of this work (Jerusalem, 1954), should be taken into consideration.

[148] Cf. Heinrich Graetz, *Geschichte der Juden*. Vol. V. Leipzig, ^{4}1909, pp. 21ff.

[149] Cf. Israel Bettan, *Studies in Jewish Preaching*. Cincinnati, 1939.

[150] See *Hertz*, pp. 487-515.

[151] *Heinemann*, pp. 251-275.

[152] b. Sotah 49a.

[153] *Siphre ad Deuteronomium*, *pisqa* #306, ed. Finkelstein, p. 342.

[154] *Masekheth Sopherim* 21:6, ed. Muller, p. XLII.

[155] *Masekheth Sopherim* 19:12, ed. Muller, p. XXXVIII.

[156] Cf. Paul Volz, *Die Eschatologie der jüdischen Gemeinde im neutestamentlichen Zeitalter*. Tubingen, 1934.

[157] *Elbogen*, p. 95.

[158] Cf. *Seder Eliyyahu Zuta*, ed. Friedmann, p. 23, Note #52.

[159] Cf. *Reform*, pp. 323-329.

[160] For a detailed philogical study of the *Qaddish*, see David de Sola Pool, *The Kaddish*. New York, ^{2}1964.

[161] See *Hertz*, p. 97.

[162] See *Hertz*, pp. 111-113.

¹⁶³See *Hertz*, pp. 135-137; 277-279; 577-579.

¹⁶⁴See *Hertz*, pp. 453-455.

¹⁶⁵Cf. Bruno Italiener, "The Mussaf-Kedushah," in *HUCA*, Vol. XXVI (1955), pp. 413-424.

¹⁶⁶See *Hertz*, pp. 529-531.

¹⁶⁷Cf. E. D. Goldschmidt, *On Jewish Liturgy*. (Hebrew.) Jerusalem, 1978, p. 202.

¹⁶⁸Cf. the footnote in Kapih (Note #105, above), p. 186.

¹⁶⁹See Note #151, above.

¹⁷⁰See *Hertz*, pp. 203-205; 571-573; 731-735.

¹⁷¹T. Ber. 1:9, ed. Lieberman, p. 3.

¹⁷²Saul Lieberman, *Tosefta Ki-Fshutah, Zera^c im*, Part I. New York, 1955, p. 11.

¹⁷³Cf. *Elbogen*, pp. 61f.

¹⁷⁴See Moshe Weinfeld, "Traces of the *Qedushah de-Yotser* and the *Pesuqe de-Zimra* in the Qumran Scrolls and in Ben-Sira," (Hebrew), in *Tarbiz*, Vol. XLV (1975/76), pp. 15-26.

¹⁷⁵Cf. Heinemann, in *Literature*, p. 77.

¹⁷⁶Heinemann, in *Literature*, pp. 77f.

¹⁷⁷Cf. Jacob Mann, "Changes in the Divine Service of the Synagogue due to Religious Persecutions," in *HUCA*, Vol. IV (1927), pp. 241-310.

¹⁷⁸*Elbogen*, p. 587, Note to page 62.

¹⁷⁹Kaufmann Kohler, "The Origin and Composition of the Eighteen Benedictions," in *HUCA*, Vol. I (1924), pp. 387-425. (Reprinted in *Contributions*, pp. 52-90.)

¹⁸⁰Kohler, op. cit. in Note #179, above, pp. 415f. (=*Contributions*, pp. 80f.) See also David Flusser, "Sanktus und Gloria," in *Abraham unser Vater* (Festschrift für Otto Michel). Leiden/Koln, 1963, pp. 129-152; and Eric Werner, "The Doxology in Synagogue and Church, Part I," in *HUCA*, Vol. XIX (1945/46), pp. 275-328. (Reprinted in *Contributions*, pp. 318-370.)

¹⁸¹Cf. Berthold Altaner, *Patrologie*. Freiburg, ⁶1958, p. 50; and art. "Apostolic Constitutions," in F. L. Cross, *The Oxford Dictionary of the Christian Church*. London, 1957, pp. 73f.

¹⁸²See Note #171, above.

¹⁸³*Qedushah* in b. Ber. 21b; *Qedushah de-Sidra* in b. Sotah 49a.

¹⁸⁴See *Seder Rabh 'Amram Gaon*, ed. E. D. Goldschmidt. Jerusalem, 1971, p. 32.

¹⁸⁵See Note #179, above.

[186] See Note #174, above.

[187] Texts of the Palestinian Rite, in addition to those published by Schechter and Mann, and reprinted in *Contributions*, pp. 373-448, may be found in the following publications: Victor Aptowitzer, "Fragment d'un Rituel Pâque," in *REJ*, Vol. 63 (1912), pp. 124-128.

Simḥah Assaf, "Misseder hatephillah be-erets yisrael," in Yitsḥaq Baer et al., eds., *Sepher Dinaburg*. Jerusalem, 1949, pp. 116-131.

Israel Davidson, "Poetic Fragments from the Genizah--A Palestinian Liturgy for the New Year," in *JQR*, N.S., Vol. 8 (1917/18), pp. 425-454.

Israel Levi, "Fragments des Rituels de Prières Provenant de la Gueniza du Caire," in *REJ*, Vol. 53 (1907), pp. 231-241.

Joseph Marcus, "Gleanings from the Genizah," in *JQR*, N.S., Vol. 21 (1930/31), pp. 85-88.

Naphtali Wieder, "The Old Palestinian Ritual--New Sources," in *JJS*, Vol. IV (1953), pp. 30-37; 65-73.

[188] For the text, see *Hertz*, pp. 115-117; *LPJL*, pp. 21-22.

[189] Cf. Gaster, op. cit., pp. 27f.

[190] b. Ber. 11b.

[191] Jacob Mann, in *HUCA*, Vol. II (1925), p. 295 (=*Contributions*, p. 405).

[192] b. Ber. 8a.

[193] Mann, in *HUCA*, Vol. II (1925), p. 323 (=*Contributions*, p. 433). English translation in *Literature*, 217-218.

[194] See Lawrence A. Hoffman, *The Canonization of the Synagogue Service*. Notre Dame/London, 1979.

[195] M. Sotah 7:1. About this whole problem, see *Understanding*, pp. 43-55.

[196] *Heinemann*, pp. 284-287.

[197] See *Hertz*, pp. 347-363.

[198] Abraham Rosenfeld, ed., *The Authorised Kinot for the Ninth of Av*. London, 1965, pp. 152f.

[199] Cf. *Shilo Prayer Book*. New York, ^{6}1972, e.g., pp. 16-19, 34, 127f.

[200] See Note #12, above.

[201] See *Hertz*, pp. 501-503. Note, however, that this prayerbook has already "modernized" the prayer by adding the words, "and in all the lands of our dispersion," both in Aramaic and in English,--an addition *not* made in the majority of Orthodox prayerbooks.

[202] Cf. *Elbogen*, pp. 153f.; *Reform*, pp. 334ff.; Herman Kieval, art. "Kol Nidrei," in *EJ*, Vol. 10, cols. 1166-1167.

[203] Cf. A. Z. Idelsohn, *Jewish Music in its Historical Development*. New York, 1929, pp. 154f. and 160; and Eric Werner, *A Voice Still Heard*. University Park, PA/London, 1976, pp. 35-38.

[204] See the relevant Geonic responsa collected by B. M. Lewin, in his *Otsar Ha-Geonim*. Vol. XI. Jerusalem, 1942, pp. 21-24.

[205] Central Conference of American Rabbis, *Gates of Repentance*. New York, 1978, p. 252.

[206] Cf. *Elbogen*, pp. 280-353. The pioneering work in the scientific study of the *piyyuṭim* was done by Leopold Zunz. See his *Literaturgeschichte der synagogalen Poesie*. Berlin, 1865; and his *Die synagogale Poesie des Mittelalters*. Hildesheim, ^{3}1967. Still of some value is Michael Sachs, *Die religiöse Poesie der Juden in Spanien*. Berlin, ^{2}1901. The best modern introduction to this genre of literature is Ezra Fleischer, *Hebrew Liturgical Poetry in the Middle Ages*. (Hebrew.) Jerusalem, 1975. About the theological implications of some of the *piyyuṭim*, which are often quite radical and unconventional, see *Theology*. English translations in Arthur Davis and H. M. Adler, eds., *Service of the Synagogue*. ^{1}71949 (and many other editions), 6 vols.; in *Literature*, pp. 215-277; and in *Theology*, *passim*. But no translation can do full justice to both the poetic structure and to the nuances and allusions of the *piyyuṭim*.

[207] See Note #148, above.

[208] Judah ben Barzillai Al-Bargeloni, *Sepher Ha'ittim*, ed. Jacob Schorr. Gracow, 1902, p. 252.

[209] Cf. Martin Schreiner, "Samau'al b. Jahja al-Magrabi und seine Schrift 'Ifham al-Jahud'," in *MGWJ*, Vol. 42 (1898), p. 220.

[210] Cf. *Heinemann*, pp. 29f.

[211] See Note #193, above.

[212] See *Theology*, pp. 16f.; and A. A. Wolff, *Die Stimmen der ältesten glaubwürdigsten Rabbinen über die Pijutim*. Leipzig, 1857.

[213] New York, ^{2}1970.

[214] Cf. *Reform*, p. 406 (Indez, s.v. *Piyutim*).

[215] Cf. *Reform*, *passim*; W. Gunther Plaut, *The Rise of Reform Judaism*. New York, 1963, pp. 27-42; 152-184; Eric L. Friedland, *The Historical and Theological Development of the Non-Orthodox Prayerbooks in the United States*. Brandeis University, Ph.D. dissertation, 1967; Jakob J. Petuchowski, art. "Reform Judaism," in *EJ*, Vol. 14, cols. 23-28.

[216] Cf. Jakob J. Petuchowski, art. "Organ in the 19th and 20th Centuries," in *EJ*, Vol. 12, cols. 1454-1455.

[217] Cf. Alexander Guttmann, *The Struggle over Reform in Rabbinic Literature*. New York, 1977, pp. 177-208.

[218] Cf. Petuchowski's Supplement in the Hebrew edition of *Elbogen: Hatephillah Beyisrael*. Tel-Aviv, 1972, pp. 323-328.

TRANSLATING LEVITICUS RABBAH:
SOME NEW CONSIDERATIONS

Jacob Neusner
Brown University

With Leviticus Rabbah we enjoy the results of a truly great scholarly achievement, Mordecai Margulies, *Midrash Wayyikra Rabbah. A Critical Edition Based on Manuscripts and Genizah Fragments with Variants and Notes* (Jerusalem, 1953-1960, I-V). Margulies placed the study of Leviticus Rabbah on an entirely new foundation. How so? He supplied an authoritative account of the two basic issues of any ancient document: the text and the principal philological problems. At the same time he left open certain analytical questions. One of these may be called redactional. This is in two aspects.

First, we want to know how to distinguish the distinct components of the composition. The text clearly is composite. Then what are the individual units out of which the composition was constructed? A glance at the excellent translation by J. Israelstam and Judah J. Slotki, *Midrash Rabbah . . . Leviticus* (London, 1939) shows that differentiation among units of thought stands at a rather primitive stage. Israelstam and Slotki present us with long paragraphs, not indicating that these paragraphs are made up of numerous individual units of thought. They also do not systematically tell us which units of thought are shared among other documents, and which ones represent the contribution of the framers of the text at hand alone. It is not criticism of their excellent and pioneering work to recognize that, after nearly half a century, further translation--that is, a fresh and systematic commentary--may provide further insight into the original text. One point of emphasis of any new translation must be differentiation of the long columns of type into distinct units of thought, whole and comprehensive statements, to be set apart from other such units of thought.

Second, once we see the parts of which the whole has been assembled, we have to ask the redactional question. Why has the framer put together things in the way that he has, and not in some other way? What point did he wish to make by juxtaposing one item with some other? The alternatives prove important in assessing the large-scale meaning and significance of the document as a whole. If the framer of a given unit has so arranged things as to advance a polemic we discover time and again, then we may uncover a significant issue addressed by the document as a whole. If on the other hand the framer does little more than put together this, that, and the other thing, we have to entertain a quite different hypothesis about the context in which the work was done, the purpose motivating it, the intellectual framework encompassing it. This second redactional question, one of overall composition, becomes possible only when the first, the analytical one, has been answered. That is, before we can explain how and why things have been put together as they have, we must clearly distinguish the individual components of the aggregation in hand. None of this has ever demanded systematic inquiry.

A question lying at the other end of a systematic redactional analysis of the document, of course, promises still more critical insight. What in fact is "original" to the plan of the whole, and what has joined the document only later on? I place original in quotation marks, because I do not now know that there was any "original" text, that is to say, a well-planned foundation laid in the execution of a purposive and systematic exegesis of bits of Leviticus. Perhaps, as I indicated, all we have is an aggregation of things about Leviticus that, by one sort of accident or another, merely happened to pile up and reach closure. If, however, we are able to distinguish, in one unit after another, a given syntactic form, or a repeated mode of treating an exegetical problem, or even a single viewpoint, harped upon again and again, then we may affirm that the work proposed not only to collect things, but also to make points. But to test that hypothesis we must accomplish a fresh translation of the document, laying emphasis upon points of form-criticism and redaction-criticism, as I have explained. That is what I now undertake.

With the advantage of Margulies' text and philological commentary, not to mention his systematic citation of parallels, the new translation still cannot claim to represent a considerable advance over the existing one, except in the specified ways. By offering a small sample of it in this setting, I hope to gain the advantage of colleagues' suggestions about the theory of translation as such: how can I achieve my stated goals more effectively? And, further, are there ways in which I may still more critically define the inquiry at hand?

At the end lies the large and fundamental question of defining what, exactly, a midrash-compilation is. For close to a thousand years before the collection and closure of the materials we know as Leviticus Rabbah, exegetes read and explained Scripture. So the work of "midrash," meaning amplification of the basic canonical text, constitutes a convention of diverse forms of Judaism

even before the closure of the Hebrew Bible. What is new in
Leviticus Rabbah is not the reading and exposition of verses of
Scripture. What is an innovation is *assembling* these particular
expositions in just this way, at just this time, and for just the
purpose at hand. But until we know what way that was, what age
marked the completion of the work, and what purpose was supposed
to be served by the compiling of diverse exegeses ("midrashim") into
a single composition ("midrash"), we know nothing. That is, we
really cannot say *just what this book is*. We therefore do not now
know what it was meant to be, and, therefore, in its own context,
what (if anything) it meant as a whole. And that is the case, even
though, as is clear, we have a pretty clear notion of what each of
its words and phrases means, and even a first-class version of what
is original to the document and what was added only by copyists and
printers. In the sample translation that follows, as I said, I
mean to illustrate modes of translation leading to the answers to
the questions just now outlined.

LEVITICUS RABBAH
PARASHAH THREE

III.I

1. A. "When anyone brings a cereal offering [as an offering to
the Lord, his offering shall be of fine flour; he shall
pour oil upon it and put frankincense on it and bring it
to Aaron's sons the priests. And he shall take from it a
handful of fine flour...]" (Lev. 2:1-2).
   B. R. Isaac opened [discourse by citing the following verse]:
"'Better is a handful of quietness than both hands full of
labor, and it is the desire of the spirit' (Qoh. 4:6).
   C. "Better is the one who [learns by] repeating [and memo-
rizing] two divisions [of the Mishnah] and is at home in
them than the one who [learns by] repeating [a great many]
laws, but is not at home in them.
   D. "'...desire of the spirit'--he wants to be called a legal
authority [which is why he has tried to learn more than
he is able to accomplish].
   E. "[Along these same lines], better is the one who [learns
by] repeating [and memorizing] laws and is at home in them
than the one who [learns by] repeating [and memorizing]
both laws and exegetical principles but is not in home
at them.
   F. "'...desire of the spirit'--he wants to be called a master
of exegesis [of the law, through its overriding principles].

G. "Better is the one who [learns by] repeating [and memorizing] laws and exegetical principles and is at home in them than the one who [learns by] repeating [and memorizing] laws, exegetical principles, and Talmud, but is not at home at them.

H. "'...desire of the spirit'--he wants to be called a master of learning [and expert in the Talmud, so able to give practical decisions].

I. "Better is one who has [a total capital of only] ten gold coins, but who does business with them and earns his living with them, than one who goes and borrows [additional capital] on usurious rates.

J. "In a proverb it says, 'He [who borrows] loses both what is his own and what is not his own.'

K. "'...desire of the spirit'--for he wants to be known as a successful entrepreneur.

L. "'Better is the one who goes and works and gives charity from what he has earned than the one who goes and steals and seizes other people's property by violence and then gives to charity out of what in fact belongs to other people.

M. "In a proverb it says, 'She sells her body in exchange for apples, which she passes out among the sick.'

N. "'...desire of the spirit'--for he wants to be known as a charitable person.

O. "Better is the one who has a vegetable patch and who fertilizes it and hoes it and makes a living from it than one goes and undertakes to share-crop the plot of [a great many] others for half the harvest."

P. "In a proverb it says, 'If you rent one garden, you'll eat the birds too, and if you rent many gardens, the birds will eat you.'

Q. "'desire of the spirit'--he wants to be known as a big landowner.

2. A. Said R. Berekhiah [commenting on 'a handful of quietness' and reading the Hebrew, *kaf nahat* to mean footfall], "Better is one footstep that the Holy One, blessed be He, took in the land of Egypt.

B. "in line with the following verse of Scripture: 'And I shall pass through the land of Egypt' (Ex. 12:12),

C. than the two handfuls of furnace-ash [thrown] by Moses and Aaron.

D. "Why? Because with the former came redemption, and with the latter came no redemption."

3. A. Said R. Hiyya bar Abba, "'Better is a handful of quietness' (Qoh. 4:6)--this refers to the Sabbath-day.
B. "'Than both hands full of labor'--this refers to the six days of work.
C. "'...the desire of the spirit'--one wants to work on [the six days of labor].
D. "You should know that that is the case, for Israel, will be redeemed only on the Sabbath.
E. "That is in line with the following verse of Scripture: 'Through repentance (šwbh) and repose you will be saved' (Is. 30:15) [and that is on the Sabbath day] [meaning], in Sabbath repose you will be saved."

4. A. Said R. Jacob bar Qorshai, "'Better is a handful of quietness' (Qoh. 4:6)--this refers to the world to come.
B. "'Than both hands full of labor'--this refers to this world.
C. "'...desire of the spirit'--Bad people want to do whatever they want in this world and to have the penalty exacted from them in the world to come."
D. That [statement of Jacob bar Qorshai] is in line with the following passage, which we have learned in the Mishnah: "[Jacob] would say, 'Better is a single hour spent in repentance and good, deeds in this world than the whole of the world to come. Better, is one hour of serenity in the world to come than the whole of the life of this world' (Abot 4:17)."

5. A. R. Isaac interpreted the cited verse [Qoh. 4:6] to refer to the tribes of Reuben and Gad. When the tribes of Reuben and Gad came into the land and saw how rich was the potentials for sowing and planting here, they said, 'Better is a handful of quietness' in the [holy] Land 'than both hands full' in Transjordan.
B. "'...desire of the spirit'--It is what we want.
C. "That is in line with the following verse of Scripture: 'Let this land be given to your servants as a possession' (Num. 32:5).
D. "Then they went and said, 'Did we not choose [Transjordan] for ourselves?' [So we cannot retract?]"

6. A. Another possibility [for interpreting Qoh. 4:6]: "Better is a handful of quietness"--this refers to the handful of cereal offering brought as a freewill offering by a poor person, [the handful of cereal sufficing].

B. "...than both hands full of labor"--this refers to the finely ground incense of spices [Lev. 16:12] brought by the community as a whole.
C. [How so?] Said the Holy One, blessed be He, "I prefer the handful of cereal offering brought as a freewill offering by a poor person than the two handsfull of finely ground incense of spices brought by the community as a whole.
D. "for the latter bears with it expiation [for sin]."
E. And what is [the measure of the handful of cereal offering]? It is a tenth of an *ephah*.
F. "When anyone brings a cereal offering..." (Lev. 2:1).

We have a fully-worked out exercise, in which a verse of Leviticus is juxtaposed to a verse lacking all obvious relationship. But when we note that Qoh 4:6 refers to "handful," and the opening verses of Lev. 2:1 likewise make reference to "a handful," we are alert to the intent of the framer. Whether or not, therefore, he drew upon available exegetical materials pertinent to Qoh. 4:6, the plan is clear. How so? If we leap from 1.A-B to No. 6, we see the entire message. But, of course, the redactor has given us a much larger repertoire of materials, all of them pertinent only to Qoh. 4:6. Accordingly at some prior point in the aggregation of the composition, the entire message was contained at 1.A-B and 6. Provoked by reference to Qoh. 4:6, someone inserted masses of materials relevant to that passage. In any event we cannot doubt that the bulk of the interpolated materials had achieved completion prior to their encounter with the present passage.

Certainly No. 1 is a handsome and ample exposition, following self-evident formal lines carefully and meticulously, beginning to end. While No. 2 intersects with both Qoh 4:6, "hands full," Lev. 2:1 "handful," it seems to me a mere serendipity. Nos. 2, 3 4, and 5 prove disparate and miscellaneous, joined only by their tripartite exposition of the cited verse. So we see a two-stage process of formation--one devoted to selecting and briefly explaining a verse of Scripture from the prophets or writings relevant to the cited passage on Leviticus, the other a miscellany of exegeses of the same intruded verse. Clearly, it is the former of the two stages (whether earlier or later in actual composition) that bears the principal message of the systematic exegesis of Leviticus. Then the message is that a meagre offering, brought freely and not because of the need for repentance for sin, takes precedence over a lavish offering, provoked by the requirement to expiate sin.

Leviticus Rabbah/71

III.II

1. A. "You who fear the Lord, praise him! All you seed of Jacob, [glorify him and stand in awe of him, all you seed of Israel! For he has not despised or abhorred the affliction of the afflicted, and he has not hid his face from him but has heard, when he cried to him]" (Ps. 22:23-24).
   B. "You who fear the Lord, praise him!"
   C. R. Joshua b. Levi said, "This refers to those who fear Heaven."
   D. R. Ishmael b. R. Nehemiah said, "This refers to righteous converts."

2. A. R. Hezekiah, R. Abbahu in the name of R. Eleazar [= Y. Meg. 1:10]: "If the righteous converts enter [into the world to come], Antonius will enter at the head of all of them..."

3. A. What is the meaning of the verse, "All you seed of Jacob, glorify him"?
   B. This refers to the ten tribes.
   C. If so, then what is the referent of the clause, "Stand in awe of him, all you seed of Israel"?
   D. Said R. Benjamin b. R. Levi, "This refers to Benjamin, who comes last."

4. A. "For he has not despised or abhorred the affliction of the afflicted"--
   B. Under ordinary circumstances, when two people come to course, one poor and one rich, to whom does the judge turn? Is it not to the rich man? But here: "He has not hid his face from him but has heard when he cried to him!"

5. R. Haggai decreed a fast to bring down rain. He said, "It is not because I am worthy [of making such a decree and bringing down rain on account of my merit], but it is on account of that which is written: 'For he has not despised or abhorred the affliction of the afflicted.'"

6. A. Just as he has not despised his prayer, so he did not despise his offering.
   B. "And when one brings a cereal-offering" (Lev. 2:1).

Once more the main point comes at the end, No. 6. If all we had were Ps. 22:24 and then No. 6, we should come up with the entire point of the whole, so far as it refers to Leviticus at all. The point is that the offering of a poor man is accepted, as much as his prayer. Then the prayer is primary, not the cereal-offering. The rest is a composite on Ps. 22:23-24. 1.B-D take up the relationship of marginal pietists, God-fearers, then full converts; that leads at No. 2 to a brief allusion to a sizable passage, found at Y. Meg. 1:11 and other places, on Antonius. Nos. 3 and 4 pursue the phrase-by-phrase exegesis of the cited verse, and, as I said, No. 5 makes a contribution by telling a brief tale.

III:III

1. A. "Let the wicked abandon his way, and the man of evil his thoughts" (Is. 55:7).
   B. Said R. Biba b. R. Abina [=Y. Yoma 8:7], "How should a person recite the confession on the eve of the Day of Atonement?
   C. "A person has to say, 'I acknowledge everything that I did in the evil way in which I was standing, and the like of whatever I did I shall never do again. May it be your will, O Lord, my God, to forgive me for all my sins, and to bear with me for all my transgressions, and to atone for me for all my wicked deeds.
   D. "That is in line with the following verse of Scripture: 'Let the wicked abandon his way, and the man of evil his thoughts' (Is. 55:7).
   E. It is written, "Let [him] abandon..."
2. A. "[Let the wicked abandon his way, and the man of evil his thoughts], and let him return to the Lord, that he may have mercy on him, [and to our God, for he will abundantly pardon]" (Is. 55:7).
   B. R. Isaac and R. Yose b. R. Hanina:
   C. R. Isaac said, "It is like a man who fit together two boards and joined them to one another."
   D. R. Yose b. Hanina said, "It is like a man who fit together two legs of a bed and joined them together."
3. A. "And let him return to the Lord, that he may have mercy on him" (Is. 55:7).
   B. Rabbis and R. Simeon b. Yohai:
   C. Rabbis say, "All forms of atonemont-[offerings] did the Holy One, blessed be He, show to Abraham, our father, [at the covenant 'between the pieces,' Gen. 15] except for the form of atonement gained through offering a tenth of an *ephah* of fine flour [Lev. 2:1]."
   D. R. Simeon b. Yohai said, "Also the form of atonement-offering of the tenth of an *ephah* of fine flour did the Holy One, blessed be He, show to Abraham, our father.
   E. "The word, 'these' is used here [with reference to the meal offering, at Lev. 2:8: 'The meal-offering that is

made out of these'], and the same word occurs elsewhere [with reference to the account of the covenant 'between the pieces'; 'And he took him all these' (Gen. 15:10)].

F. "Just as the word, 'these,' used in the present context refers to the tenth of an *ephah* of fine flour, so the word, 'these' used with reference to [the modes of expiatory offering described at Gen. 15] likewise encompasses the tenth of an *ephah* of fine flour."

4. A. "...and to our God, for he will abundantly pardon."
   B. R. Judah b. R. Simon in the name of R. Zeirah: "The Holy One, blessed be He, further gave us a mode of attaining forgiveness out of what, in fact, belongs to him, namely, the tenth of an *ephah* of fine flour.
   C. "When any one brings a cereal offering as an offering to the Lord..." (Lev. 2:1).

This pastiche of materials relevant to Is. 55:7 aims, if not very directly, at Lev. 2:1. Once more we observe that only part of the construction serves the purposes of exegesis of Leviticus. We have a systematic construction addressed to Is. 55:7, with 1.B-D a completely autonomous unit, occurring at Y. Yoma 8:7, inserted whole. No. 2 (the meaning of which is not wholly clear) is joined to No. 1. Nos. 3 and 4 alone intersect with the present passage. If we did not have No. 3, No. 4 would be perfectly comprehensible on its own, that is, as a comment not pertinent to Gen. 15 but solely to Lev. 2:1. My guess is that Nos. 3 and 4 were joined to serve Gen. R., where the passage also occurs, but of course were repeated here because of their obvious relevance.

In the balance, it is difficult to demonstrate that at the foundation lay a citation of Is. 55:7 followed by the substance of No. 4. It seems plausible to see Nos. 3 and 4 as the base, so Gen. R. as the original location. If so, the polemic is clear. The cheapest form of expiation offering also is God's special gift, the act of grace above all others. Expensive beasts serve no better than a handful of flour.

III:IV

1. A. ["When any one brings a cereal offering" (Lev. 2:1).] Now what is written just prior to this statement?
   B. "And he shall take away its crop with the feathers [and cast it beside the altar on the east side, in the place for ashes, and he shall tear it by its wings, but shall not divide it asunder. And the priest shall burn it on the altar upon the wood that is on the altar; it is a burnt offering, an offering by fire, a pleasing odor to the Lord]" (Lev. 1:16-17).

74/Jacob Neusner

    C.   Said R. Tanhum b. R. Hanilai, "A bird such as this flies about and swoops all over the place and eats everywhere, so what it eats constitutes stolen property and comes by violence. Said the Holy One, blessed be He, 'Since this crop [of the bird] is filled with the result of thievery and violence, let it not be offered up on the altar.'

    D.   "That is why it is said, 'And he shall take away its crop with the feathers...'

    E.   "By contrast, a domestic animal is raised at the crib of its owner and so does not eat whatever it finds anywhere, things that are stolen or come by violence. Therefore one may offer up the entire beast.

    F.   "That is why it is said, 'And the priest shall offer the whole [of the burnt-offering of the flock or herd]' (Lev. 1:13)."

2.   A.   Since a person steals and gains through violence, come and see how much bother and effort [are necessary] before [food] comes out from it: from mouth to gullet, from gullet to stomach, from stomach to second stomach, from second stomach to maw, from maw to intestines, from the small winding intentine to the large winding intestine, from the large winding intestine to the mucal sieve, from mucal sieve to rectum, from rectum to anus, from anus outside [following Israelstam, p. 39].

    B.   So take note of how much bother and effort [are necessary] before its food exudes from it.

The passage serves Lev. 1:16, not Lev. 2:1. The opening phrase, I, is a feeble effort to provide some sort of linkage between the larger plan of the composition--exegesis of Lev. 2:1--and 1.B-F. The point of No. 2 is unclear; it is tacked on because of the issue of stealing and violence in connection with getting food. But the passage does not relate either to No. 1 or to the larger context.

III:V

1.   A.   "And he shall tear it by its wings but shall not divide it asunder, [and the priest shall burn it on the altar, upon the wood that is on the fire; it is a burnt offering, an offering by fire, a pleasing odor to the Lord]" (Lev. 1:17).

    B.   Said R. Yohanan, "If an ordinary fellow should smell the odor of the burning wings, it would turn his stomach, and yet you say, 'And the priest shall burn it on the altar' (Lev. 1:17).

    C. "Why go to all this trouble? It is so that the altar may be ornamented by the offering of [even] a poor man [who cannot afford a beast, Lev. 1:10, but can afford a bird, Lev. 1:14]."

2. A. King Agrippas wanted to offer a thousand bird-offerings on a single day. He sent a message to the priest, "Let no one beside me make an offering on this day."

    B. A poor man came, with two birds in his hand, and said to the priest, "Offer these for me."

    C. [The priest] said to him, "The king ordered me not to permit anyone but him to make an offering today."

    D. [The poor man] said to him, "My Lord, priest, I catch four birds every day, two which I offer, and two which I use for a living. If you do not offer these two up, you cut my living in half."

    E. The priest took them and offered them up.

    F. In a dream the message came to King Agrippas, "A poor man's offering came before yours."

    G. He sent a message to the priest, "Didn't I tell you not to let anyone but me make an offering that day?"

    H. He sent words to him, "My lord, king, a poor man came, with two birds in his hand and said to me, 'Offer these for me.' I said to him, 'The king ordered me not to permit anyone but him to make an offering today.' He said to me, 'I catch four birds every day, two which I offer, and two which I use for a living. If you do not offer these two up, you cut my living in half.' Now should I not have offered them up?!"

    I. He said to him, "You did things right."

3. A. $m^c \acute{s}h\ b$: People were leading an ox to be offered, but it would not be led. A poor man came with a bundle of endive in his hand, and held it out to the beast, which ate it. [The ox] sneezed and expelled a needle, and it then allowed itself to be led on to be offered. If the needle had not been expelled, it would have caused an internal perforation, resulting in a blemish invalidating the animal for sacrificial purposes (Israelstam, p. 40, n. 1).

    B. The owner of the ox saw a message in his dream: "The offering of a poor man came before yours."

4. A. $m^c \acute{s}h\ b$: A woman brought a handful of fine flour [for a cereal offering, in line with Lev. 2:1]. But the priest ridiculed her and said, "See what these women are bringing as their offerings! In such a paltry thing what is

>   there to eat? And what is there to offer up?"
> B.   The priest saw a message in his dream: "Do not ridicule
>   her on such an account, for it is as if she was offering
>   up her own soul."
> C.   Now is it not a matter of an argument *a fortiori*? If
>   concerning someone who doesn't offer up a living soul [of
>   a beast] Scripture uses the word, "Soul" ["When any soul
>   (RSV: one) brings a cereal offering"], if someone brings
>   a [contrite] soul, how much the more is it as if this one
>   has offered her own soul."

Nos. 1, 2, and 3 prove continuous and deal with Lev. 1:17.
No. 4 carries forward the polemic of the foregoing, in its stress
on the worth of the poor person's offering. But No. 4 can stand
independently as much as any of the first three items. It serves
Lev. 2:1 by underlining the deep meaning of Scripture's use of the
word, "soul," translated also as "any one." The meaning imputed to
4.C is familiar. God wants the sacrifice of a contrite heart. The
priest should understand that the woman's paltry sacrifice is all
she has, and perhaps more than she can afford. That message, of
course, is delivered by Nos. 1-3 as well.

The person who drew the materials together clearly can have
had Lev. 1:17 and 2:1 in mind. But then an exegetical composition
systematically and in order treating long sequences of scriptural
verses, such as Gen. R., will have been well served. A collection
such as this one, in which only a few verses are taken up, not systematically and not in their given order, will hardly have demanded
this kind of composition at all. So if the passage at hand was
written to serve the exegesis of Leviticus, then the literary requirements of the framer still did not envision the kind of document that Leviticus Rabbah turned out to be. For, the larger number
of passages do not go from one verse to the next, through a given
chapter, as does Gen. R.

III.VI
> 1. A. "[When any one brings a cereal offering as an offering to
>   the Lord, his offering shall be of fine flour; he shall
>   pour oil upon it and put frankincense on it,] and bring
>   it to Aaron's sons, the priests" (Lev. 2:1-2).
>   B. R. Hiyya taught [=Sifra Nedabah IX:10] "[That is the case]
>   even if they are many. Even if many priests have to be
>   involved with the paltry offering, e.g., in measuring the
>   flour, pouring on the oil, kneading it, putting on the
>   frankincense, taking the handful, and the like, each
>   priest must do his part, to show respect for the offering

Leviticus Rabbah/77

> even of a poor man (Margulies citing Rabad).]"

C. Said R. Yohanan [citing a proof-text for the foregoing proposition], "'In the multitude of people is the king's glory' (Prov. 14:28)."

2. A. "And he shall take from it a handful of fine flour and oil, with all of its frankincense, [and the priest shall burn this as its memorial portion upon the altar, an offering by fire, a pleasing odor to the Lord. And what is left of the cereal offering shall be for Aaron and his sons]" (Lev. 2:2-3).

B. "...of the fine flour"--and not the whole of the fine flour.

C. "...of the oil"--and not the whole of the oil.

D. Lo, [there was the case of] one brought his cereal offering from Gaul or Spain or those distant parts, and saw the priest taking [and offering only] a handful and eating the remainder. He said, "Woe is me for all the trouble I went to, [merely] so that this one should eat."

E. People made him feel better, telling him, "Now if this [priest], who has gone to the trouble of merely taking two steps, between the hall and the altar [Joel 2:17] gains the merit to allow him to eat [the meal-offering-remnant], you, who went to all this trouble, how much the more so [should you gain merit from this offering of yours]!"

F. Moreover, "And what is left of the cereal offering shall be for Aaron and his sons" (Lev. 2:3). [Margulies: "Not only does the officiating priest gain possession of the remainder, but he can pass on the right to his sons. The one who has brought the offering all the more so gains the right to pass on the merit of his deed to his children after him."]

3. A. [In Aramaic:] R. Hananiah bar R. Aha went to a certain place and found the following verse at the head of the order [of the reading of the Pentateuch in the synagogue on that Sabbath]: "And what is left of the cereal offering shall be for Aaron and his sons" (Lev. 2:3).

B. With what verse did he commence the discourse in that regard?

C. "From men beneath your hand, O Lord, from men whose portion in life is of the world, may their belly be filled with what you have stored up for them; may their children have more than enough; and may they leave something over to their babes" (Ps. 17:14).

>   D. [Understanding the Hebrew, *mmtym*, men, as *m(h) mtym*, who are (mighty) men, he proceeded:] "Who are mighty men? They are the ones who took their portion from beneath your hand, O Lord.
>   E. "And who might such a one be? It is the tribe of Levi.
>   F. "'From men whose position in life is of the world'--these are the ones who did not take a share in the land [but rather got their support from the leftovers of God's altar and agricultural dues].
>   G. "'Their portion in life'--this refers to the Holy Things of the sanctuary.
>   H. "'May their belly be filled with what you have stored up for them'--this refers to the Holy Things separated in the provinces [from the crops, that is, the priestly rations of various kinds supplied by the farmers].
>   I. "'May their children have more than enough'--'Every male among the children of Aaron may eat of it' (Lev. 6:11).
>   J. "'And may they leave something over to their babes'--'And what is left of the cereal offering shall be for Aaron and his sons' (Lev. 2:3).
> 4. A. Aaron imparted merit [to eat Holy Things] to his sons, whether valid or invalid [for service at the altar, for blemished priests also may eat priestly rations].
> 5. A. So Scripture states, "My covenant with him was a covenant of life and peace, and I gave them to him, that he might fear, and he feared me, he stood in awe of my name. True instruction was in his mouth, and no wrong was found on his lips. He walked with me in peace and uprightness, and he turned many from iniquity. For the lips of a priest should seek instruction from his mouth, for he is a messenger of the Lord of hosts"; (Mal. 2:5-7) [=Sifra Shemini Mekhilta de Miluim 37].
>   B. "My covenant with him was a covenant of life and peace," for he pursued the interests of peace in Israel.
>   C. "And I gave them to him, that he might fear, and he feared me" for he accepted upon himself the discipline of the teachings of the Torah in a spirit of fear, awe, trembling, and quaking.
> 6. A. What is the meaning of the following clause: "He stood in awe of my name?"
>   B. They say [=b. Hor. 12b, Ker. 5a]: When Moses poured out the anointing oil on Aaron's head, he trembled and fell backward, exclaiming "Woe is me! I might well have

committed sacrilege against the anointing oil [in using it in this way]!"

C. The Holy Spirit answered him, "'Behold, how good and pleasant it is when brothers dwell in unity! [It is like the precious oil upon the head, running down upon the beard, upon the beard of Aaron, running down on the collar of his robes!] It is like the dew of Hermon, which falls on the mountains of Zion! For there the Lord has commanded the blessing, life for evermore" (Ps. 133:1-3).

D. "Just as sacrilege does not apply to dew, so sacrilege does not apply to anointing oil."

7. A. "It is like precious oil upon the head, running down upon the beard, upon the beard of Aaron" (Ps. 133:2).

B. Now did Aaron have two beards, that the cited verse should make reference to the word, beard, two times, "the beard," "the beard of Aaron"?

C. But: When Moses saw the anointing oil running down the beard of Aaron, he rejoiced as if it ran down his own beard."

D. As it is written, "True instruction [torah] was in his mouth. [The oil that had flowed down on the mouth and beard of Aaron represented true Torah.]

8. A. [Continuing from Sifra, b. San. 6b:] ["True instruction (Torah was in his mouth)], and no wrong was found on his lips. He walked with me in peace and uprightness, [and he turned many from iniquity" (Mal. 2:6)].

B. "True instruction was in his mouth"--for he never called what was unclean clean, or what was clean, unclean.

C. "And no wrong was found on his lips"--for he never declared prohibited what was permitted, nor did he declare permitted what was forbidden.

D. He walked with me in peace and uprightness"--for he never entertained misgivings [Israelstam, p. 43] about the ways of Omnipresent, just as Abraham never entertained misgivings.

E. "And he turned many from iniquity"--for he turned sinners back to the study of the Torah.

F. And Scripture says, "Sincerely do they love you" (Song 1:4).

G. What is written at the end of the passage? "For the lips of a priest should seek instruction from his mouth, for he is a messenger of the Lord of hosts" (Mal. 2:7).

The unifying topic of the pastiche of materials at hand

concerns the priests' rights to what is left over of the cereal-offering, Lev. 2:3. But we begin, No. 1, with a continuation of the theme of the foregoing *parashah*, the importance of the offering even of a poor person. Then, the exegesis goes forward on the immediately following verse, as if the plan were to provide amplification for each verse in sequence. No. 2 spells the matter out, first explaining the meaning of the verse, B-C, then, D-E, making explicit the deeper issue at hand. Once more the rights and role of the priesthood present a question mark. The solution is to assign to the lay-Israelite still greater merit than accrues to the priest. So the polemic underlines the higher standing of ordinary folk, despite the liturgical primacy of the priesthood. If 2.E is integral, then Margulies' explanation of its relevance states this same matter still more forcefully. The priests enjoy the right to hand on their merit to their children; genealogy, after all, forms the basis for their primacy. But, he points out, lay people enjoy that very same right. If the passage is not integral, then 2.E would serve as the opening salvo of No. 3, that is, citing the verse to be discussed prior to the exposition.

No. 3 makes the point, by intersection of Lev. 2:3 and Ps. 17:14, that the Levites, inclusive of the priesthood, legitimately enjoy their share in the offerings because that takes the place of their right to hold a piece of land. Now the right to leave over part of their merit is seen in a different light. No. 4 is a brief addition, tacked on for obvious reasons.

Nos. 5-8 provide an entirely independent exegesis, centered, upon Mal. 2:5-7. In fact we have two sets, Nos. 5, 8, and Nos. 6-7. The former, lifted from Sifra, accomplishing a systematic exegesis of the cited verses, make entirely conventional points. The latter treats Mal. 2:5-7 as it intersects with Ps. 133. So the whole was put together to serve as an account of Mal. 2:5-7. Why was it inserted here? The overall theme, the priesthood and its value, accounts for its positioning.

So, in all, Nos. 5, 8, 6-7 were assembled on their own, then tacked on because of the general relevance to the theme of the larger construction. Nos. 2 and 3-4 clearly take up the explanation of the rule of Lev. 2:3 and justify the rights accorded to the priesthood by that rule. The principle construction of Nos. 2-4 is perfectly clear: the basis for bringing the whole together seems reasonable.

READING RABBINIC BIBLE EXEGESIS
Lewis M. Barth
Hebrew Union College - Jewish Institute of Religion

The techniques of scholarship, and those of teaching as well, must be appropriate to the subject matter of a discipline. In the case of a literature, they must be able to generate an adaquate understanding of the meaning of a particular text and its relationship to its literary and historical contexts. For midrash, this means its ties to other types of rabbinic literature, its connections with rabbinic Judaism, and its relations to the literatures and cultures of the late Hellenistic, Roman, and Christian worlds as well. "Adaquate understanding" is a comprehensive and therefore inexact phrase, and the question might be asked, adaquate for what and for whom? Much of my teaching and the work of my students is devoted simply to determining what a text says and how it says it. This activity is part of the larger issue of how one reads a text, a matter of considerable debate in our time. Clearly, some techniques of reading are common to literary documents in general, some to religious texts, others to imaginative fictional texts. In the case of midrash, the process of reading is complicated by our distance from text in time, cultural outlook, and language, but it is where one must begin. This paper offers one analytical reading of a midrashic text and reflections on the elements and presuppositions of that reading.

The text is *Pesikta de Rav Kahana*,[1] Chapter 13:1. The translation is presented in outline form.

> Rabbi Abba bar Kahana preached: *Raise a shrill cry, Bath-gallim; hear it, Laish, and answer her (or "O Poor) Anathoth* (Is. 10:30).
> 1. *Raise a shrill cry*--Cry aloud (Aramaic).
> 2a. *Bath-gallim*--Just as these waves *(gallim)* stand out in the sea, so your fathers stand out in the world.
>   b. Another interpretation: *Bath-gallim*--Daughter *(bath)* of wanderers *(golim)*; daughter of wanderers (Aramaic).
>   b1. Daughter of Abraham--What is written about him? *And the Lord said to Abram, "Leave your own country,* etc. (Gen. 12:1; the verse continues: *your kinsmen, and your father's house, and go to a country that I will show you.)"*

    b2. *Daughter of Isaac*--What is written about him?
        *...and Isaac went to Abimelech, the Philistine
        king at Gerar* (Gen. 26:1)
    b3. *Daughter of Jacob*--What is written about him?
        *...and that Jacob had obeyed his father and
        mother (and gone to Paddan-aram)*. (Gen. 28:7).
3. *Hear it*--Hear my commandments.
        Hear words of Torah.
        Hear words of prophecy.
    And if not,
4. *Laish*--Behold, a lion will attack you (Aramaic).
    This is Nebuchadnezzer the Wicked, for it is written
    about him: *A lion has come out of his lair* (Jer. 4:7).
5. *And answer her* (or *"O Poor"*)--
        Poor in Zaddikim.
        Poor in words of Torah.
        Poor in commandments and good deeds.
    And if not,
6. *Anathoth*--Behold, the man from Anathoth is going to
    come and prophesy against you words of rebuke.
Therefore, Scripture needs must say: *The words of Jeremiah,
the son of Hilkiahu* (Jer. 1:1).

Three simple questions may be asked of this text: 1) Where and when is it from?; 2) What is it?; and 3) What does it mean?

I

The first question is historical and literary in intent. The passage appears in the *Pesikta de Rav Kahana (PRK)*, probably a late fifth century Palestinian homiletic midrash-collection. *PRK* contains some twenty-eight original chapters, each of which comprises a complete "literary sermon" based on Torah or Haftarah readings for special Sabbaths or festivals. The Hebrew title of Chapter XIII, from which our text is taken, is *Dibrey Yirmiyahu*, the first two words of the book of Jeremiah. Jer. 1:1-2:3 is the first in a cycle of ten Haftarot known as "The Three of Retribution and Seven of Consolation", which are read on the Sabbaths proceeding and following the Ninth of Av, the day of mourning the destruction of the two Jerusalem Temples. *PRK* contains ten sermons that are based on the first or first few verses of each of these Haftarot, of which our text is the beginning. The passage is attributed to Rabbi Abba bar Kahana, a third generation Palestinian Amora, who was known as a prolific preacher and master of the aggadah. He flourished in the first half of the fourth century, that is to say, at least one hundred years prior to the compilation of *PRK*.

II

The second question, What is it?, requires an answer that describes the text's form. If the description were to be based on the translation, it would appear that this document is some sort of outline, a very short-hand exegesis/eisegesis or commentary on Is. 10:30 that concludes with the citation of Jer. 1:1. The verse from Isaiah is fragmented into six units of single words or phrases, each of which is followed by a comment; a brief transition formula leads from the last comment to Jer. 1:1.

The verb used to introduce our passage is *pataḥ*, a technical term I have translated as "preached". William Braude, throughout his monumental translation of *PRK*, renders it "began his discourse". What kind of a discourse is this? And if it "began", where does it continue and where does it end? We may assume that our text is some sort of homily, but then what is the sermon text: Is. 10:30 or Jer. 1:1? And yet another question, is it not so that rabbinic sermons usually end on a note of hope or consolation? This passage does not; what sort of a homily is it?

Our text is the first of six similar sections in Ch. XIII whose form is commonly designated *petiḥa* in Hebrew or *petiḥta* in Aramaic. These terms are often translated "proem", but they clearly describe a homiletical form quite different from the proem of Greek rhetoric or sermons of the Church Fathers. Over two thousand *petiḥtot* are found in rabbinic literature, some very brief, others quite lengthy. Those that appear in the "classical midrashim" (*Genesis Rabba, Leviticus Rabba,* and *PRK*) all have the same structure: the *petiḥa* begins with the exegesis/eisegesis of one or a few consecutive verses and ends with another seemingly unrelated verse. The concluding verse, however, is the goal of the *petiḥa*, for that verse begins either the Torah or Haftarah reading.

Scholars have debated the purpose of the *petiḥa* form. The late Joseph Heinemann argued that the extant *petiḥtot* are elaborations of actual sermons preached prior to and in order to introduce biblical lections. They are examples of the dominant form of the live Jewish sermon in Palestine in the third and fourth centuries, and gave way only later to more elaborate sermonic compositions preached on the Sabbath after the completion of the Torah readings during the morning service or in the afternoon. Richard Sarason has argued against Heinemann that the *petiḥtot* are literary constructions based on traditional exegesis that were created by an editor in his process of constructing an exegetical anthology.² Although Sarason stresses the literary origin of *petiḥtot*, he agrees with Heinemann that the *petiḥa* form "originated in the oral exegesis of Scripture."

For purposes of reading and interpreting such texts it is important to emphasize both the centuries-long process of oral transmission of exegetical traditions and the literary creativity that in the end constructed the "literary sermons". Heinemann proposed a three stage schema for the development of rabbinic sermons. First, the letter by letter, word by word, phrase by phrase, and verse by verse exegesis of Scripture was delivered by the Sages (*ḥakhamim*) before their students in the House of Study (*Bet Hamidrash*); second, the relatively brief comments of the Sages were expanded by the Preachers (*darshanim*) in oral sermons in synagogues before congregations composed primarily of lay people; finally, the selecting, compiling, and reshaping of earlier materials into larger compositions was accomplished by editors or compilers (*'orkhim* and *mesadrim*) for readers who could return again and again to ponder the meanings to be found in these complex texts. Such an extended process, whether the specific stages are correct or not, may be contrasted with the transcription and publication of the Church Father Origen's sermons, to take but one example. This third century Father had his live sermons taken by short-hand writers and transcribed in volumes bearing a title mentioning the passage commented upon. From such volumes the sermons were immediately recopied and disseminated. In the Jewish context, students in the academy may have taken down in writing comments of the Sages; it is not likely that this could occur in the synagogue setting of the oral sermon preached on a Sabbath or Festival.

Apart from the overall composition and shaping of traditional exegesis, the work of the editor/compiler is revealed in attributions of the *petiḥtot*, in additional extraneous interpretations that are introduced, and in the concluding formula, which links exegesis to lection verse. The problems of attribution are extremely complex. For example, one sage cannot be distinguised from another on the basis of individual style or content. One name could be substituted for another without any significant impact on the meaning of a passage. We do not know in most cases if the sage cited was in fact the author of the *petiḥa* attributed to him, or if his name was chosen simply to give the text authority. In many cases, authorship is attributed to a sage whose name clearly introduces only the last comment of the exegesis prior to the lection verse. To confound matters further, the majority of *petiḥtot* are anonymous. It has been suggested that more often than not these were invented by the editor; if so, this is another bit of evidence to support Sarason's hypothesis.

Another trace of the editor is the technical phrase *davar 'aḥer*, which introduces another alternate interpretation of the biblical verse or phrase. It can be used consciously to offer a single contrasting opinion, or it can be used mechanically to indicate the preservation of one or many alternate opinions, whether or not these are related to any central line of exegesis or thematic exposition. The concluding transition phrase found in a series of *petiḥtot* may be used in a similar manner, to offer a conceptual and significant linking, or a merely mechanical and external tie, between exegesis and lection verse.

I have discussed these matters at some length, and much more could be said, in order to suggest the complexity of problems found in interpreting texts such as the one before us. Oral exegesis, passed on for centuries, is likely to have become expanded and elaborated, and certainly to have absorbed independent exegetical units having no essential connection to one another. Numerous examples of this occur in midrashic literature, and for an additional reason too: the same tradition of exegesis may be transferred from one biblical verse to another because of some significant or artificial likeness between the verses. In the course of moving about, a tradition may become altered, take on new meanings, and even assume the wording of the new biblical context it comes to explain or of the different traditions in whose midst it has now settled. A *petiḥa*, then, may contain some extraneous comments that will appear alongside other, perhaps more original comments, exempla, parables, proverbs, and word-plays that serve to explain a verse in a more or less thematic way. The result is that this unique homiletic form, at the final stage of its development in the "literary sermon," forces the reader to analyze each unit of tradition in itself and then to attempt to determine its relation to the *petiḥa* verse as a whole, to the lection verse, to the surrounding traditions, and to the material drawn together in the larger sermonic chapter. In this regard, our modern notion, probably derived from Greco-Roman and Christian rhetoric, that a homily should display a unity of theme, does not exactly fit rabbinic homiletic texts. A midrashic homily does not communicate directly; interpretation of the interpretation is a necessity, a never-ending process and possibility built into the text itself.

III

The third question, What does it mean?, brings us to an interpretation of the interpretation found in our text. I suggest that this *petiḥa* provides a rabbinic argument to justify the life and mission of Jeremiah and the inclusion of his book in the canon of Scripture for a fourth or fifth century Palestinian theological-polemical context. The proem verse, Is. 10:30, is understood as Isaiah's warning of impending punishment to the Congregation of Israel, a people of once noble ancestry who had lost its religious virtues, social concern, and saintly individuals. The warning was rejected, the people urged to harken did not, and the defects of society and religious life were not overcome. Therefore, Scripture had to convey "the Words of Jeremiah", a phrase that signifies the terrible threats of punishment and their fulfillment found in the book of prophecies of this man of woe.

This message is presumably conveyed as an introduction to the reading of the Haftarah, Jer. 1:1-2:3, for the first Sabbath of retribution; it specifically serves to introduce the literary sermon found in *PRK*, Ch. XIII and the entire ten sermon cycle that deals with retribution and consolation. The specific form is that of the *petiḥa*, and the style of the exegesis exhibits numerous traces of oral homiletic rhetoric. Although the tone and intent of this passage are ominous, it nevertheless contains a significant metaphor, which is reversed at the conclusion of Ch. XIII to provide a closing note of consolation: the lion may have destroyed, but the Lion will rebuild forever an eternal Temple.

Such a prose statement of meaning needs to be justified, and what follows is an attempt to provide a detailed analysis of the text and to draw some broader implications from that analysis. The exegesis of Is. 10:30, attributed to Rabbi Abba bar Kahana, begins with a simple Aramaic translation of $ṣhly$ $qwlk$, "cry out" or "shout". The root $ṣhl$ can bear the nuance of crying out in terror or in joy and is used in both senses in the Hebrew Bible. So too can the Aramaic root used to translate it here, $lblb$, which, incidently, does not reflect the rendering of Is. 10:30 in the Targum. The tension between joy or terror is not incidental, for our editor delights in ambiguity, comparison and contrast. Later manuscripts add an interpolation at this point, perhaps to resolve this tension and surely to make clear that the Isaiah verse, which originally referred to a group of villages in the path of the Assyrian army marching toward Jerusalem, is applied to the people of Israel: "Isaiah said to Israel, 'Instead of occupying yourselves with songs and melodies to idolatry, raise your voices in joy with words of Torah'".

The audience is now reminded of its distinguished past: its ancestors stood out in the world. This exegesis has an involved development and a significant rhetorical function. The separation of the two elements in the place name *Bath-Gallim*, is quite ancient. The LXX translates, "O daughter Gallim." The rabbis extend the notion from "daughter" to "descendents" and then go on to compare *glym (gallim)*, with '*bwtykm*, "your ancestors". The wording and imagry of this metaphor are based on a tradition in *Genesis Rabbah (GR)* 44:7 (T.A., p. 429-30), which is an exegesis on Gen. 15:1, *Do not fear Abraham*. Although the comment in *GR* has nothing more to do with our text than the fact that Abraham, one of the *'avot*, is named, it does contain the following explanation of Is. 41:5 *"See, O Islands, and fear*--just as these islands stand out in the see, so Abraham and Shem stand out in the world". Now "islands", which stand out from the sea, is a much more vivid image than "waves". Nevertheless, Is. 10:30 reads "waves" and not "islands", and the comparison is adaquate enough for our editor to use the metaphor rhetorically to praise his audience by recalling their noble ancestry, in order to suggest later how far the people had fallen. To suit a verse then, the wording of a tradition is changed, or, stated differently, a new tradition of interpretation is born.

At this point the editor has chosen to insert an alternate interpretation of *Bath-gallim*. This is one of those additional comments that appear without connection to an overall thematic interpretation. It has a life of its own, so to speak, yet strikingly must be re-read in light of the context in which it appears. I have followed Braude's translation of *gwlym* here as "wanderers" because of the proof-texts that follow. However, I have rejected his full translation phrase, "forced to wander". First, there is no reason to assume negative compulsion in the prooftexts; each is an example of God's command and involves a blessing, not punishment. Second, all three prooftexts play on the verb *hlk*, "to go" and not on *glh*, "to go into Exile". *Galut*, "Exile", is a central biblical and rabbinic concept; it has the clear meaning of being sent away from the Land of Israel as punishment for previous sin. In our prooftexts, however, Abram is told to go to the Land; Isaac moves from one place to another within it; and only Jacob leaves, but with the mission to take a wife and return. Neither biblical nor rabbinic literature consider these cases to be examples of "Exile". They are instances of "wandering" from place to place, and it is

undeniable that the Patriarchs did move about. We cannot know
what historical need called such an interpretation into being; the
word *glym* is its pretext.

Nevertheless, we must double back and remind ourselves
that *golim* has a meaning much more common than "wanderers"; it is
"those who are sent into Exile". In the context of our *petiḥa* and
sermonic chapter, it would appear that we are to re-read the tradition that way, and perhaps even overlook the prooftexts, whatever
be their original intent. Exile is the constant threat and actual
punishment in the book of Jeremiah. It is also mentioned several
times in the remainder of this sermonic chapter. The introduction
of this theme fits the tripartite structure of our *petiḥa*, as if
it were the first of three threats that follow three direct appeals
to the audience, a kind of ominous reminder of past punishment
pointing to future concern. The other two threats, of Nebuchadnezzar and Jeremiah, are introduced with *w'm l'*, "and if not". Here,
davar 'aḥer, "another interpretation", states the alternative to
distinguished ancestors. The editor wants us to contrast these
two traditions and suggests the thought that "your ancestors, no
matter how distinguished, went into Exile, so might you."

A final point about these two comments on *Bath-gallim*: they
serve to evoke a subject that will come to be treated in highly
ironic ways throughout this chapter, the motif of ancestry. *Petiḥa*
3 has God upbraid Israel, in a play on Zech. 1:5, *My children, your
fathers who sinned before me, where are they?* (i.e. they are
punished, in Exile, or dead?). *Petiḥa* 4 opens with Prov. 17:2, *A
servant who deals wisely shall rule over a son that does shamefully*.
This is applied to Jeremiah. Although he descends from the pros-
titute Rahab, he will come to rebuke those of noble ancestry who
have acted corruptly. In the body of the sermon, Par. 8, Jeremiah,
along with other priest-prophets, Phineas, Uriah, and Ezekiel, was
derided by his contemporaries for having come from a family of
dubious geneology. God, therefore, had to re-write their biograph-
ies to give them distinguished pedigrees. Then they would possess
sufficient prestige for people to listen to their words and not
dispise their persons.

Next, the exegesis forces the audiences to attend to what it
must hear and what it lacks: commandments, words of Torah, words
of prophecy. Each of these is stated with utmost brevity, and no
proof texts are offered. These same objects of *hqšyby*, "harken",
are repeated with slight variations and in reverse order as the
comment of "O Poor". The form of the utterance is reminicent of
numerous similar sententious statements in rabbinic literature,

such as "The world stands on three things: Torah, Worship, and
Acts of Lovingkindness". Such statements attempt to encapsulate
essential elements in the rabbinic world view, without which the
continued existence of human society cannot be imagined. From a
rhetorical perspective, these concepts foreshadow defects in society that are emphasized in subsequent sermons in this ten chapter
cycle. These elements recur, particularly in *PRK*, Ch. XV, the
sermon entitled "Lamentations", to be read on the Sabbath just
prior to the Ninth of Av. Sections 8 and 9 of Ch. XV offer vivid
examples of the rejection of commandments of a social nature:
bribery, theft, and oppression. The theme of the neglect of the
study of Torah and its implications is treated in section 5 there.
And yet another paragraph (7) depicts the shameful murder of the
priest-prophets Uriah and Zechariah.

The interpretations of "harken" and "O Poor" are each followed
by threats of punishment: Nebuchadnezzar and Jeremiah. The first
threat is based on the traditional identification of Nebuchadnezzar
with the "lion". *Laish*, the town, is a homonym of $ly\check{s}$, "lion",
and a synonym of '*aryeh* in proof text Jer. 4:7, which is understood
to refer to Nebuchadnezzar, the "evil one" whom God will bring from
the north (Jer. 4:6). (This interpretation, incidentally, ignores
the actual contextual reference of the Isaiah verse to Sennacherib,
and in so doing stands in contrast to the parallel to our passage
in b. San. 94b).

"Lion", however, is a double edged symbol and has two referents in Ch. XIII: first, the threatening enemy, understood as God's
instrument of punishment, and second, the all powerful and saving
God, who appears as the "Lion" at the end of par. 15. This play
on words is remarkable because it formally ties the conclusion of
the chapter with its beginning. The linkage occurs in a context
that stresses the rabbinic requirement that a sermon must end on
a note of hope or consolation. Such a view is already evident in
the conclusion of several biblical books of the Prophets and recurs
up at the start of our sermon's conclusion in Par. 14. An argument
is related there between Rabbi Eliezer and Rabbi Yochanan, on the
theme: "all prophets opened with words of rebuke and closed with
words of comfort". Rabbi Eliezer states that the only exceptions
were Jeremiah and Isaiah. Rabbi Yohanan rejects the verses brought
for proof by his colleague and shows that even Jeremiah and Isaiah
ended their prophecy with comfort, although their books do not
explicitly confirm this. The editor of our sermonic chapter
develops the position attributed to Yohanan in order to end his
own sermon on Jeremiah with a note of hope. This is not a mere

formalistic gesture, but a surprising twist that finds in the
language of punishment the promise of future restoration. In his
peroration he utilizes as his point of departure the date of the
end of Jeremiah's prophecy "in the fifth month". "The lion
(Nebuchadnezzar) attacked, in the month of the Lion (Leo-Av), and
destroyed the Lion of God (Ariel-the Temple); in order that the
Lion (God) will come in the month of the Lion (Leo-Av) and rebuild
the Lion of God (Ariel-the Temple)". Suitable proof texts are
offered for each of these statements, and it is clear that the
reader is to understand the tradition that in the future God himself will rebuild the Temple to last forever, in the month of Av,
thereby turning "mourning into rejoicing".

This skillful conclusion of Ch. XIII is the most striking
rhetorical and artistic feature of a composition whose opening
petiḥa foreshadows so much of what follows. Nevertheless, it is
important to remember that the *petiḥa* itself does not conclude on
a note of hope, but rather that the exegesis of Is. 10:30 serves
to introduce the last threat of punishment represented by the man
from Anatoth, Jeremiah and his words. Implied in this formulation
and throughout this chapter is a conviction that the sermon editor
communicates implicitly and explicitly: the continuity of prophecy
and its fulfilment is to be found within Judaism. Our preacher
tells his readers that Isaiah's warnings to his own generation
were later fulfilled in the lifetime of Jeremiah; the latter's own
threats of punishment came to pass in the destruction of the Temple
in Jerusalem by the Babylonians. Another aspect of this theme is
revealed in *petiḥa* 3, where it is stated that although Moses and
other previous prophets have died, their prophecy has endured--
how much the more so will the prophecy of Jeremiah, who is alive,
be fulfilled. Yet another view is presented in *petiḥa* 6, in which
Deut. 18:18 is applied to Jeremiah. God says to Moses, *I will
raise up a prophet for them from among their own people like yourself;* Jeremiah is just like Moses, his career and teaching parallel
the great teacher in six particulars, the last of which is the
message of *twkḥh*, rebuke.

The theme of the continuity of prophecy and its fulfillment
within Judaism suggests by implication the context of theological
argumentation that provides the background against which we must
understand this text and to which this sermon and entire ten sermon
cycle is a response. This *petiḥa* and sermon, created for reading
in conjunction with the first of the three Sabbaths of Retribution,
deal with the two most painful events in the spiritual history of
biblical and first century Judaism: the destruction of the first

and second Temples. Christian theology, beginning with the New Testament and expanded in the writings of Justin Martyr and the Church Fathers of the third and fourth centuries, dwelt on these events. The continuing ruin of the Temple in Jerusalem was a tangible sign of God's punishment for the Jews' rejection of prophecy, the murder of prophets, and crucifixion of Jesus. On another level altogether, by the third century, the figure of Jeremiah had become a type of Christ. Such is Origen's exegesis, for example, in his first sermon on Jeremiah, to explain the text: *Before I formed you in your mother's womb I knew you, and before you were brought forth I sanctified you* (Jer. 1:5).

From the perspective of Palestinian rabbis, sin led to punishment and had to be acknowledged. However, they could grant neither any relationship between these events and Christianity nor the existence of similarities between Jeremiah and Jesus. Rebuke did not mean that the covenant was broken or that a new convenant existed, transferred to another people, the True Israel. Rabbinic method was to interpret the Hebrew Bible by applying its message of prophecy to the internal events and conditions of the Jewish people. Jeremiah was to be understood as a link in the chain of prophets, an associate of Isaiah, Ezekiel, Zechariah, and comparable in many respects to Moses. Even the form of the *petiḥa* itself eliminates the possibility of Christian biblical interpretation by excluding the application of the Hebrew Bible to anything but itself and the continuing life of the community depicted in it. This form, what might be called a closed circle of exegesis, serves as an unstated counter to the ubiquitous typological interpretations of the LXX by the Church Fathers and their efforts to view the entire "Old Testament" in light of the New.

IV

Having said all this, I must now return to reflect briefly on what has been said and its implications for our overall theme. To begin with something unstated, I have not defined the term "midrash". Rather I have chosen to analyze a text that self-evidently is an example of rabbinic homiletic midrashic exegesis. At this juncture in the history of scholarship, it would be pointless to attempt a restraining definition of the term or even to suggest that its early use should provide guidelines for a contemporary discussion. My comment is meant to be reasonably sarcastic, for I do not think that all biblical exegesis is midrash, but rather that midrash is one form of biblical exegesis. Equating the terms merely leads to blurring distinctions, and it is the business of scholarship and literary criticism to attempt to formulate meaningful distinctions even between related activities and literatures.

Second, such a text as our *petiḥa* does not stand alone. It is found in a midrashic collection whose provenance can be determined by philological methods and whose date can reasonably be inferred. The text also has a form, the developmental lines of which are fairly clear and about which a good deal is known. From a formal perspective, such texts are compilations within compilations. Tools of analysis must be applied to them that permit an both appreciation of their earlier oral rhetorical characteristics and an understanding of, perhaps an emphasis on, their final form and content as an expression of intent of the editor/compilor.

Finally, the purpose of reading such a text is to understand its intellectual and religious content, its literary and historical sources, its imagery, and its other literary qualities and devices that stimulate some individual or group to preserve it. Basic to such a reading is a philological evaluation: the determination of the possible range of meanings of words, the connections of words into discrete units of thought, and the placement of these units of thought into the formation of the larger "argument". The understanding and formulation of that argument, for me, is the primary goal of inquiry. It must be stated and defended as adequate to account for the significant features of the text, as a first step in the process of determining relationships to literary and historical contexts. The use of the insights of various disciplines, especially rhetoric and literary criticism, is extremely useful in achieving an understanding of a midrashic text. General statements on the nature of the rabbinic mind or rabbinic theology or the intellectual and cultural history of the rabbinic period all stand or fall on the reading of such texts.

NOTES

[1] The text is translated from *Peskita de Rav Kahana*, ed. Bernard Mandelbaum (New York, 1962). English translations of biblical passages follow *The New English Bible*.

[2] Richard S. Sarason,, "The Petihtot in Leviticus Rabba: 'Oral Homilies' or Redactional Constructions'," *JJS* XXXII/1-2 (1982), pp. 557-558.

THE "MIDRASHIC" PROEM:
TOWARDS THE DESCRIPTION OF RABBINIC EXEGESIS

Martin S. Jaffee
University of Virginia

The centrality of exegesis[1] as a mode of literary creativity in late-antique rabbinism points to an abiding trait of rabbinic religion and culture--the all-embracing character of Torah as a symbolic model of and for the cosmic and social orders.[2] The whole Torah of Moses, Written and Oral, contains within it the principles of order and meaning, which, in the hands of the qualified exegete, can be made to encompass all knowledge of the world and all experience of oneself in the world. This project of "exegetical totalization,"[3] by which the rabbinic Torah-canon is enabled to interpret and structure the worlds of concrete Jewish groups, accounts for the wide variety of exegetical methods represented in rabbinic literature. Torah, required for the shaping of life, must itself be shaped by the exegete so that it may address life. In time, the act of shaping--of exegesis--itself becomes a mode of life, a torah for interpreting Torah.

Rabbinic exegesis mediates knowledge of Scripture within the limits of specific exegetical methods that adhere to self-conscious conventions of form and style. These conventions are no less essential to the exegetical message than is the verbal sense of the exegesis itself. Indeed, the form in which Scripture is presented for exegesis, even more than the exegetical content, exhibits the operative meanings that inform the rabbinic way of life and world view.[4] It follows that an appreciation of rabbinic exegesis as cultured activity requires, on the one hand, description of the various exegetical forms typical of rabbinism and, on the other, analysis of the meanings such forms impose upon the materials that gain expression through them.[5]

This essay makes a preliminary contribution to such a task. I analyse a single clearly defined form of scriptural exegesis, the midrashic proem (*petiḥah* or *petiḥta*), which is normally employed in non-legal exegetical collections, such as Genesis Rabba (GR), Leviticus Rabba (LR), Lamentations Rabba (Lam.R.) and Pesikta d'Rab Kahana (PRK). The proem is intimately bound up with the emergence of rabbinism as a dominant expression of Palestinian Judaism, for the documents in which it most frequently appears (such as the above) emerge from the Palestinian rabbinic circles of the fourth through seventh centuries, the very centuries in which rabbinism became the major expression of Judaism in the Middle East and Mesopotamia. Study of an exegetical form ubiquitous in the literature of this period must offer insight into the character of rabbinism during the age in which its typical institutions and values reached classical form. The task is to permit the literary and intellectual traits of the proem--its technique--to elucidate its meaning as a cultural form, a product of human activity that acts back upon its creators and shapes the imagination of those who accept its conventions.

Before us, then, is what I take to be a typical example of the proem-form. I have translated it in such a way as to permit its characteristic literary traits to be clearly perceived. The comments following the translation reflect upon these traits and provide the foundations for a number of general conclusions about the cultural meaning of the proem as an exegetical form.

Before turning to our example, however, a few words are in order about the general traits of the proem-form. Since the pioneering work of Leopold Zunz early in the last century, a scholarly consensus has been reached about the fundamental elements of the form and their interrelationships.[6] The proem usually contains five identifiable literary units. These are:

   I. A superscription ("Rabbi X commenced" or "This is what Scripture says"),
  II. Scriptural citation + explanatory pericope,
 III. Sequence of independent pericopae related to the verse of II and/or a series of entirely unrelated verses,
  IV. Citation of the verse of II + explanatory pericope,
   V. Citation of a final scriptural verse unrelated to that cited at II.

The purpose of the proem, it is said, is to demonstrate that the verse cited at II contains the key to interpreting the verse at V. This is the burden of IV, which links the former to the latter. The demonstration, however, is indirect, for it proceeds through the intervening materials of III. These pericopae, often the lengthiest and most complex segment of a proem, are frequently unrelated to each other or to the crucial verses of II and V. Their context within the formal limits of the proem itself requires the reader to relate them to the other materials with which they appear. The superscription, I, plays no discernible exegetical role. In proems assigned to a specific authority, the superscription serves as an attributive, while in unattributed proems, the superscription seems merely to signal that a coherent exegetical unit is to follow.[7]

In rabbinic exegetical documents proems with identical concluding verses (V) typically are listed together, normally in groups of three or more. This list is followed by a series of pericopae that employ other exegetical forms, take up at length the exegesis of the verse cited at V, and usually follow the thematic lines adumbrated in the preceding sequence of proems. A set of proems and subsequent exegetical pericopae constitutes a "chapter" in rabbinic exegetical documents, for example, the *parashah* in LR or the *pisqa'* in PRK. In its present documentary context, then, the proem functions to introduce the exegesis of the verse it cites at V.[8]

Research since the work of P. Bloch in 1885 has shown, however, that the documentary context of the proem, particularly in earlier documents, is artificial.[9] The proem is an autonomous unit of literary expression. The content of proems may be altered or constructed to suit the needs of a single document, but the form itself imposes its own logic upon constituent materials and requires no explication beyond its own formal limits. The identification of the proem's autonomous literary character, an important result of the *wissenschaftliche* tradition of midrashic scholarship, is the foundation upon which the descriptive project of this study must be constructed. Through analysis of the traits of one proem in each of its extant versions, I hope to reach conclusions suggestive for the form as a whole.

The example before us appears in both LR and PRK. The two versions differ dramatically only at units IV and V, a result of the differing documentary contexts of each version. In LR, IV and V are relevant to the exegesis of Lev. 21:1ff., the verse upon which LR *parashah* 26 ("Emor") is centered. In PRK, to the contrary, IV and V serve Num. 19:1ff., the scriptural pericope to which PRK *pisqa'* 4 ("Parah Adumah") is devoted. That the materials of I-III serve the exegesis of separate scriptural verses requires explanation. For the time being, we simply note that the redactors of this proem into its different literary contexts felt free to alter its exegetical referent to suit their own purposes. As others have observed, this trait extends to the form as a whole, and is not unique to our example. We also shall see that the proem before us, like most in the earlier literature, is composed of materials originally formulated for use outside the formal limits of the proem. These materials, paralleled in the Palestinian Talmud and Genesis Rabbah, serve independent exegetical agenda in their primary literary contexts. That they have been sundered from their primary context and forced to make a point important to the proem's formulator indicates that these materials are believed to be multivalent in meaning. Their sense is defined not by their words alone, but by the context of other traditions and scriptural passages within which they are placed.

Let us now turn to LR 26:1-3/PRK 4:2:[10]

    I. R. Tanhum bar Hanilai commenced:

    IIa. *The promises ('mrwt) of the Lord are promises that are pure, silver refined in a furnace on the ground, purified seven times* (Ps. 12:6, RSV).

    IIb. (PRK adds: Said R. Tanhum bar Hanilai: "*The promises of the Lord are promises that are pure*--)
The promises of the Holy One Blessed Be He are promises, [but] the promises of [men of] flesh and blood are not promises."

In worldly practice a king of flesh and blood enters a province, and the men of the province flatter him with their acclaim. And [if] their acclaim meets with his favor, he promises them, "Tomorrow I will build public baths and lavatories for you, tomorrow I will install a sewage system for you." But [then] he falls asleep and fails to arise [ever again]. Where is he? Where are his promises? Truly, the Holy One Blessed Be He is not such a one. Rather, [as Jeremiah declares,] "*The Lord is the true God*" (Jer. 10:10, RSV).

(y.San.1:1,18a)   IIc. What is truth: Said R. Abyn: "For *He is the living God and the everlasting King*" (Jer. 10:10, RSV).

    IIIa. *[promises that] are pure* (*thrwt*, Ps. 12:6, RSV):

(GR 32:4)   IIIb. R. Judan in the name of R. Isaac (GR, PRK: R. Yohanan), R. Berekhiah in the name of R. Eleazar, R. Jacob of Kefar Hanin in the name of R. Joshua ben Levi (PRK: and all cite it in the name of R. Joshua ben Levi):
"We have found that Scripture (PRK: The Holy One) uses a circumlocution of two or three words in the Torah, in order to avoid any unseemly language (PRK: any mention of pollution). So is it written: *Take with you seven pairs of all clean animals, and a pair of the animals that are not clean, the male and his mate* (Gen. 7:2, RSV). And it is not written thus: "From the animal that is polluted"! Rather, [is it written:] *that are not clean, the male and his mate.*

(GR 32:4)   IIIc. Said R. Judan bar Menassah:
"Even when [the Holy One Blessed Be He] introduced [the Israelites] to the traits of polluted animals, he began his discourse [upon each animal] only with those traits of clean animals [which the polluted animal itself shares].
1. It is not written thus: "The camel [is unclean], for it does not part the hoof."

Rather, [the verse states:] [*The camel,*] *because it chews the cud* [as do permitted animals, *but does not part the hoof, is unclean to you*] (Lev. 11:4, RSV).
2. It is not written thus: "The rock-badger [is unclean], for it does not part the hoof." Rather, [the verse states:] [*The rock-badger,*] *because it chews the cud* [as do permitted animals, *but does not part the hoof, is unclean to you*] (Lev. 11:5, RSV).
3. It is not written thus: "The hare [is unclean], for it does not part the hoof.". Rather, [the verse states:] [*The hare,*] *because it chews the cud* [as do permitted animals, *but does not part the hoof, is unclean to you*] (Lev. 11:6, RSV).
4. It is not written thus: "The swine [is unclean], for it does not chew the cud." Rather, [the verse states:] [*The swine,*] *because it parts the hoof* [as do permitted animals, *but does not chew the cud, is unclean to you*] (Lev. 11:7, RSV).

IIId. R. Yose of Mimlah and R. Joshua of Sikhnin in the name of R. Levi:
"In the days of David, children who had not yet tasted sin [were so learned that they] knew how to interpret the Torah in forty-nine ways [so (cf. y.Pe.1:1, that a person or object could be] declared unclean, as well as in forty-nine ways [so that the same person or object could be] declared clean. And David would pray on their behalf and say, *Do thou, O Lord, protect them* (Ps. 12:7, RSV)— [that is,] preserve their [pure words of] Torah in their hearts. [And David would continue,] *Guard us ever from this generation* (Ibid.)— [that is,] from that generation which, as a whole, deserved destruction."

IIIe. And after all this praise they [i.e., the innocents] went out to war and fell? Only because there were slanderers among them (PRK adds: did they go out to war and fall).
This is as David says: *My soul is among lions: and I lie down among those who are aflame, the sons of men, whose teeth are spears and arrows, and their tongue a sharp sword* (Ps. 57:5, K).
1. *My soul is among lions*—these are Abner and Amasa, who were lions in Torah [but who failed David in his time of trouble].
(y.Pe.1:1,16a) 2. *I lie down among those who are aflame*—these are Doeg and Ahitophel, who were aflame after gossip.
3. *The sons of men, whose teeth are spears and arrows*—these are the men of Keilah [whom David suspected would betray him to Saul] (PRK adds: for it is written:) *Will the men of Keilah surrender me and my men [into the hand of Saul? And the Lord said "They will surrender you."]* (1 Sam. 23:12, RSV).
4. *And their tongue a sharp sword*—these are the Ziphites [who betrayed David to Saul] (PRK adds: for it is written:) *When the Ziphites came and told Saul, "David is hiding among us"* (Ps. 54:1).
At that very hour said David (PRK adds: before the Holy One Blessed Be He: "Lord of the Worlds!)

And what is your Holy Presence doing here on the earth [which is polluted by slander]? *Be thou exalted O God above the heavens*" (Ps. 57:6, K)-- [that is,] "Remove your Holy Presence from among them." [And with the Holy Presence gone from Israel, the innocent were killed in battle along with the slanderers].

But the generation of Ahab consisted entirely of idolators, yet since there were no slanderers among them, they went out to war and were victorious.

(y.Pe.1:1,16a) This [is proven by] what Obadiah said to Elijah: *Has it not been told my lord what I did when Jezebel killed the prophets of the Lord, how I hid a hundred men of the Lord's prophets by fifties in a cave, and fed them with bread and water* (1 Ki.18:13, RSV)?

If he brought bread, why [did he also bring] water? Only to teach that the water was more difficult to bring than the bread [and would therefore have attracted attention to the hiding place]. Yet Elijah declared on top of Mt. Carmel: *I, even I only, am left a prophet of the Lord* (1 Ki. 18:22, RSV). And the entire people heard, but did not reveal to the King [that one hundred other prophets had been spared by Obadiah]. [Clearly, then, there were no slanderers in the idolatrous generation of Ahab].

IIIf. Said R. Samuel bar Nahman:
1. "They inquired of the snake, 'Why are you found among fences?' He replies to them, 'For it is I who breached the fence of the world [by
(y.Pe.1:1,16a-b) enticing Adam and Eve to sin]'.
2. [They inquired further,] 'Why do you go about with your tongue extended upon the ground'? He replies to them, 'For it is the cause [of my punishment]'.
3. [They inquired further,] 'And what pleasure do you have? The lion attacks and eats, and the wolf mauls and eats, while you bite and cause death [and thus cannot eat what you kill]'. (PRK substitutes: 'Why is it that all other beasts and animals bite, but do not cause death, while you bite and cause death'?) He replies to them [with the following Scripture:] *'Does the serpent bite unless there be a whisper*? (Eccl. 10:11, B)-- How could I do anything if I were not commanded from above?
4. [Finally, they inquire,] 'And why is it that when you bite one limb all the limbs are affected'? He replies to them, "You inquire of me? Inquire of the gossiper, for he speaks here and kills [by his words] even in Rome, speaks in Rome and kills [by his words] unto the ends of the earth.'"

IIIg. And why is [gossip] known as "triplet"? Because it kills three:
the one who speaks it,
the one who heeds it,
and the one concerning whom it is spoken.

(y.Pe.1:1,16a)
                      And in the days of Saul it killed four:
                      Doeg, who spoke it,
                      Saul, who heeded it,
                      Ahimelekh, concerning whom it was spoken,
                      and Abner.

IIIh.   Abner--why was he killed?
(PRK: [Opinions are transmitted in the names of] R. Joshua ben Levi, R. Simeon ben Laqish and the Sages:)

1. R. Joshua ben Levi said: "[Abner was killed] because he made sport at the expence of the blood
(y.Pe.1:1,16a) of young men. So it is written: *And Abner said*
(y.Soṭ.1:8,17b) *to Joab, 'Let the young men arise and play before us'* . . . *[and each caught his opponent by the head, and thrust his sword in his opponent's side]*" (2 Sam. 2:14ff., RSV).

2. And R. Simeon ben Laqish said: "[Abner was killed] because he set his name before the name of David. So is it written: *And Abner sent messengers to David beneath him* (thtyw) *saying, 'Whose is the land?'* (2 Sam. 3:12). [That is,] he addressed [the message] 'From Abner to David' [and was punished for this act of disrespect]."

3. And the Sages say: "[Abner was killed] because he did not tarry to appease Saul in regard to David, so is it written (PRK: when David said to Saul:) *'See, my father, see the skirt of your robe in my hand; [for by the fact that I cut off the skirt of your robe and did not kill you, you may know . . . that there is no treason in my hands']* (1 Sam. 24:11, RSV). Abner said [to Saul], 'Pay no attention to this one's boasting, [for the cloak] was caught by the thorn [and David's loyalty thus remains in doubt]'. And when they reached the encampment, [David] said to [Abner], *'Will you not answer, Abner?'* (1 Sam. 26:14, RSV). [That is,] 'Regarding the cape, you claimed that it was torn off by a thorn. [Will you claim as well of] the spear and water jug [which I have taken from the defenseless Saul without harming him] that they were caught by a thorn?'"

4. And some say: "[Abner was killed] because it was within his power to protest [Saul's order to kill the priests of] Nob, the priestly city, but he did not protest" (cf. I Sam. 22:17ff.).

IV.   Said R. Tanhum bar Hanilai:
"Two scriptural lections [regarding the subject of] cleanness has Moses written for us in the Torah. And through whom were [these lections] given [to Israel]? Through the tribe of Levi, for of [that tribe] it is written: *Silver refined in a furnace on the ground* (Ps. 12:6). And [elsewhere] it is written: *[He will sit as a refiner and purifier of silver,] and he will purify the sons of Levi [and refine them like gold and silver]* (Mal. 3:3, RSV).

And which are these [scriptural lections]? These are [the lections regarding] the Red Heifer (Num. 19:1ff.) and the lection regarding [the priestly avoidance of] the dead (Lev. 21:1ff.).

V. And the Lord said to Moses, *"Speak to the priests, [the sons of Aaron, and say to them that none of them shall defile himself for the dead among his people]"* (Lev. 21:1, RSV).

(PRK IV.) R. Hanan bar Pazzi interpreted the verse [i.e., *purified seven times* (Ps. 12:6)] in light of the lection of the Red Heifer, for it contains seven [categories, each of which consists] of seven [independent references]:
Seven [references to] the heifer;
Seven [references to] the burning;
Seven [references to] sprinkling;
Seven [references to] washing garments;
Seven [references to] polluted individuals;
Seven [references to] clean individuals;
Seven [references to] priests.
If someone says to you that [seven references to the priests] are lacking [i.e., that priests are mentioned only five times], reply to him that Moses and Aaron are also included in the total.

(PRK V.) *Now the Lord said to Moses and Aaron, "This is the statute of the law [which the Lord has commanded]: Tell the people of Israel to bring you a red heifer* . . . (Num. 19:1ff., RSV).

The five structural units of LR/PRK conform to the pattern typical of the proem-form. In each version, units I-II+IV-V can be isolated as a complete and cogent exegetical argument that establishes a thematic and substantive relationship between the verse cited at II (Ps. 12:6) and its correspondent at V (Lev. 21:1 or Num. 19:1). Likewise, the body of the proem, III, is in function typical of the general pattern of extended proems. Despite the citation of Ps. 12:6 at IIa, the unit as a whole ignores the thematic context of Scripture, and instead lists a series of materials relevant solely to the single scriptural word, "pure." These materials themselves offer exegeses and comments to a variety of scriptural verses that have no obvious connection with either the verse of IIa or that of V. That there is little effort to spell out the relation of these pericopae to the materials of I-II+IV-V is, of course, the most widely recognized trait of the proem-form.

The impression, however, that III is an interpolation into a smooth argument of I-II+IV-V is incorrect. Closer analysis shows that III is carefully redacted to complement the thematic interests of II. Indeed, II-III themselves form an entirely coherent unit, requiring no reference to IV-V. The latter, which varies dramatically in each version of the proem, must be understood as an independent unit, a requirement of the proem-form itself, rather than as a constitutive element of an exegetical argument begun at II. The important observation is that II-III, which serves Lev. 21:1

(LR IV-V) or Num. 19:1 (PRK IV-V) with equal suitability, is intrinsically connected to neither unit. Unit I, however, does set a thematic context within which the quite independent concerns of IV-V may be explored. In order to clarify and refine these observations, we turn now to a formal and substantive analysis of LR/PRK's major units.

Unit I, of course, simply signals that a coherent unit of exegesis is to follow. Since it is unlikely that Tanhum bar Hanilai will begin an exegesis by citing himself (PRK IIb), or conclude it in his own name (LR IV), the attribution can hardly be accounted an "historical" tradition of Tanhum. Rather, it has simply been tacked on--probably because Tanhum plays a crucial role in LR IV. Thus, the superscription assumes the existence of LR II-V in its present form. PRK, which alters IV-V, nevertheless retains the attribution and imports Tanhum's name at the beginning of unit II.[11]

Unit II consists of three parts: a citation of David (IIa), an explanation of the citation (IIb), and a gloss of the latter (IIc). The center of the unit, IIb, cites IIa and provides a simple exegetical remark, to which is appended an amplifying parable. The point is that while God's promises are indeed trustworthy, those of men are not--hardly a controversial claim in rabbinic circles. IIc has been cited from its primary context in y., where it is one of a series of exegetical clauses introduced by the formulary, mhw ("what is . . ."). It is perfectly appropriate here as well, for it cites and explains the very verse with which IIb concludes.[12]

Unit III, certainly the most complex and engaging unit, is linked to IIa at IIIa. The bulk of the unit falls into two unequal sections, IIIb-c and IIId-h. Together, these sections carry forward IIb's contrast between the words of God and the words of men. Examples of God's concern to maintain purity of speech (b-c) parallel IIb's judgment about the constancy of God's word as promise, while the catalogue of catastrophic human misuses of language (d-h) is a thematic complement of IIb's estimation of the promises of kings.

It is important to stress that the thematic balance of IIIb-c +d-h is created by a redactor who knows his materials in an earlier context and wishes to employ them in amplification of IIb. IIIb-c, in a somewhat briefer version, finds its earliest documentary context in GR 32:4,[13] where it is appended to a citation of Gen. 7:2

("Take with you seven pairs . . . "). The materials of IIId-h, for their part, rearrange (with deletions and stylistic improvements) pericopae first redacted in y.Pe. and y.Sot. In the former, IIId-g offer autonomous discussion of the consequences of idle talk and gossip, a theme introduced by y.'s citation of Tos. Pe'ah 1:2, itself an explication of Pe'ah 1:1. IIIh, cited in y.Pe., is in fact original to y.Sot., where it serves a detailed inquiry into the traits of Abner. As a whole, then, III is an eclectic but cogent compilation of earlier literary sources, which have been gathered together to elucidate the theme established by IIb's exegesis of IIa. The entirety, II-III, stands on its own as a coherent exegetical unit, employing Ps. 12:6 as an occasion for contrasting God's speech with that of man.

Units IV-V ignore the foregoing, but are appended in order to bring the proem itself to its appropriate structural conclusion. It is striking that neither version of IV-V pretends to carry forward the work of IIb-III. Rather, in each version, IV is interested solely in the scriptural citation of IIa, providing the link between the latter and the concluding citation at V.

In LR, unit IV makes two assertions: 1) Num. 19:1ff. and Lev. 21:1ff.--both of which concern ritual defilement through contact with a corpse--are given to Israel by Moses, by virtue of his membership in the Levite tribe; 2) Ps. 12:6, as interpreted through the prophetic vision of Mal. 3:3, demonstrates that only the Levites, purified by God for their priestly vocation, are suitable to mediate God's commandments to Israel. These points prepare us for the concluding citation of the proem, V (Lev. 21:1). This citation, however, is simply a formal requirement of the proem; in substance it adds nothing to IV, which has already made its point quite independently. The sole task of IV, then, is to bring IIa (Ps. 12:6) into relation with V (Lev. 21:1). The point is that David's equation of the purity of God's word with refined silver is explicable in terms of God's revelation, through the priestly tribe of Levi, of the laws of cleanness. This point, of course, neither contributes to IIb-III nor acquires significance through it. Its sole purpose is to link the beginning of the proem, IIa, with its conclusion.

In sum, LR's version of this proem is an amalgam of materials that the redactor intends to coexist as independent and mutually uninforming units. That is, IIa is served equally well by IIb-III or by IV-V, yet neither unit serves the other. The formal unity of the proem alone, established by IIa and V, links these quite separate sets of pericopae into a literary and thematic whole.

The larger point of the entire proem, however, is difficult to ascertain.

These results apply with equal validity to the version of PRK. Here, too, units IV-V are substantively irrelevant to IIb-III. It is interesting, therefore, that PRK's version of IV-V thematically depends upon the corresponding units of LR. PRK clearly knows that Ps. 12:6 may be read in relationship to Mosaic legislation regarding the burning of the Red Heifer as a rite of purification from corpse-uncleanness. Thus Hanan b. Pazzi (IV) demonstrates the connection between Ps. 12:6 and Num. 19:1ff. in detail. PRK improves upon LR in a single respect. Unlike LR, PRK requires the citation of Scripture at V to make its point. That is, it is necessary to cite Scripture to demonstrate that there are indeed seven references to priests in Num. 19:1ff., as IV has claimed. The redactor of PRK, then, has more successfully linked form and substance in his exegetical task than has his counterpart in LR. It is all the more striking, therefore, that PRK's redactor still makes no effort to create a substantive link between IV-V and IIb-III. The substantive discontinuity, therefore, must be intentional --a requirement of the form--and not a careless error.

The results of this analysis of the versions of a single proem point to persistent traits of the form as a whole. In the bulk of extant examples,[14] unit III breaks the flow of discourse between IIa and IV-V. It does so by introducing a sequence of materials that illumine IIa to the exclusion of IV-V. Unit III, in turn, is ignored by IV-V, which proceeds as if III had never intervened. These substantive discontinuities among the basic components of the proem indicate that the form is an exegetical construct intended to create tension among its elements, even while it links them within a common thematic agendum--in the present case, the equation between God's pure word and his commandment of ritual purification. The form is hardly designed to offer unambiguous exegesis of any of the scriptural verses it cites, particularly of those central to its formal structure (IIb, V). If anything, the proem-form attempts the opposite task. The structurally central verses are given a wider range of meanings and referents than their surface language would suggest. By subverting the fixed sense of these Scriptures, the proem destroys their specificity to any one scriptural context. In our example, David's praise of God (IIb) points not only to the history of his own times, but can as well amplify the meaning of Mosaic legislation.

We have seen that the construction of new meanings for Scripture is the goal of the proem as an exegetical form. This task is performed by the redactor's selection from the materials of earlier exegetical literature to establish new contexts within which to locate discrete scriptural passages.[15] These materials, compiled into the structural units of the proem, establish a persistent tension among the scriptural selections of the proem, a tension that admits no explicit means of exegetical release. Scripture's numerous meanings--isolated and amplified by the proem's exegetical pericopae--remain distinct and unblurred. They are linked together, but never merged, in the medium of traditions cited in the names of rabbinic masters. These traditions play the senses of Scripture against each other, even while asserting a thematic relevance of all Scripture to the theme of the proem. The abiding exegetical tensions, however, remain unresolved, an intentional refusal to bring the established set of meanings to any final harmonious statement.

We are now in a position to restate the question with which this study began. What does the exegetical tension created by the proem tell us about the meaning this form--as form--is intended to convey? The most immediate point is that a document central to the lives of Jews--Scripture--does not mean what it says. The meaning of all Scripture is in a state of flux; each verse bears a range of potential meanings that is delimited in principle by any other random verse. Second, the only sure hermeneutical guide for plotting the multiplicity of Scripture's meaning is in the sole possession of the rabbinic masters, whose names and traditions serve as the literary context framing the proem's central scriptural citations. The key to the many meanings of Written Torah, that is, is in the hands of the masters of Oral Torah, who perceive the obscure links that bind both Torahs into a single continuum of revelation originating with the first rabbinic master, Moses. Finally, the proem itself, which intentionally leaves unresolved the conflict of senses imputed to Scripture, is not only an *act* of exegesis, but an *object* of exegesis as well. It is intended to raise problems, not to solve them; it is a riddle to which one may continually return without final solution. The act of solving the riddle--of resolving the tension created by the proem--is itself an act of Torah, a training of the mind in the ways of revelation. This final act, the response of the proem's audience to the riddle it poses, unfortunately has left few traces upon our literary sources--unless, of course, we understand the present redactional contexts of the proem in the extant documents to be our first clue.

If the proem is to be described as exegesis, therefore, it is exegesis of a peculiar sort. Meaning is not derived by explanation and argument, but rather is suggested through skillful contextualization of disparate items of information. Thus the exegesis does not appear to teach a content, i.e., Scripture or a particular theology, even though it does place before its audience a substantial body of Scripture and distinct theological themes. Rather, the proem seems more concerned to exercise its audience in the intricacies of a cognitive method. The formulator of the proem poses a riddle that must be solved within the conventional rules of intellect and belief specific to his audience. These rules, it seems certain, must be part of the audience's intellectual repertoire before it can begin to appreciate the proem.

If this be the case, it is time to revise the scholarly consensus regarding the original *Sitz im Leben* of the proem. The consensus is that the proem originates in homiletic sermons, the purpose of which was to inculcate in the masses the theological and ethical doctrines of rabbinic Judaism.[16] The evidence of the proem, however, reveals first of all that it is hardly suited for oral presentation. Its structure and method are purely literary. The form requires the discerning eye, which can ponder riddles and return to a text in order to find and resolve deeper ambiguities. Second, and in the same vein, the sophisticated exegetical rules assumed by the proem hardly suggest that its audience will be unlettered in rabbinic discipline. The proem appears not to be a homiletic form with which an intellectual or religious elite waters down its private knowledge for the consumption of a well-meaning but ignorant public. Quite to the contrary. A plausible (but unverifiable) *Sitz im Leben* for the proem would be that assumed by nearly all other rabbinic literature, the house of study or the circle of the master and disciple--any context, that is, in which masters of rabbinic tradition train disciples in the way of tradition.

The "midrashic" proem, it appears, provides its audience with an opportunity to exercise its special erudition. It confirms as well the central ideology that united the various rabbinic circles of Palestine and Babylonia during the culturally fertile centuries in which the way of Oral Torah became the way of the bulk of middle eastern Jewry. The proem expresses and verifies the fundamental conviction that truth flows only from Torah, as Torah is preserved in the special idiom of the rabbi. As an exegesis that itself requires exegesis, the proem extends the domain of Torah beyond the confines of Scripture and into the entire deposit of rabbinic tradition. The point is clear: a tradition that demands exegesis is no longer mere tradition, but has itself become Torah. Scripture and tradition, Written Torah and Oral Torah, are affirmed as one single revelation, a vast field within which to search out the meaning of God's word.[17]

FOOTNOTES

[1] Note that the present discussion of rabbinic exegesis avoids the difficult question of the definition of "midrash" in its rabbinic and non-rabbinic expressions. I am not inclined to view the term "midrash" as analytically useful. "Exegesis," however, is analytically valuable, for it permits a wide range of coloration appropriate to specific kinds of data, from the refined elucidation of mishnaic principles characteristic of the Talmuds, to the harmonization of scriptural and mishnaic law which occupies the bulk of the "halakhic" exegetical compositions, and ultimately, to the eclectic compilations of exposition particular to the "aggadic" collections.

The most recent--and useful--effort to provide the term "midrash" with some descriptive and analytic punch is the recent essay of G. Porton, "Midrash: Palestinian Jews and the Hebrew Bible in the Greco-Roman Period," in W. Haase, ed., *Aufstieg und Niedergang der römischen Welt*, II.19.2 (Berlin & New York, 1979), pp. 104-138. Porton writes: "Midrash is a type of literature, oral or written, which has its starting point in a fixed canonical text, considered the revealed word of God by the midrashist and his audience, and in which this original verse is explicitly cited or clearly alluded to" (p. 12). While I am indebted to Porton for my own rough-and-ready definition of what I mean by rabbinic exegesis, I draw my insights into the meaning of exegesis as a cultural form from students of non-Judaic exegesis. In particular, see the recent essay by Jonathan Z. Smith, "Sacred Persistence: Towards a Redescription of Canon," in W. Green, ed., *Approaches to Ancient Judaism*, I (Missoula, 1979), pp. 11-28.

Smith views the problem of canon and exegesis "as a way of exploring the proposition that sacrality persists insofar as there are communities which are persistent in applying their limited deposit of tradition; that sacred persistence is . . . primarily exegesis; that if there is anything distinctive about religion as a human activity it is . . . what might be described as the extremity of exegetical totalization" (p. 18). I view my own essay as an attempt to apply Smith's insight to a concrete case of rabbinic exegesis.

[2] This language is dependent upon that of C. Geertz, "Religion as a Cultural System," in C. Geertz, *The Interpretation of Cultures* (New York, 1973). See especially Geertz's discussion of the signifying capacity of symbols, pp. 93-94:

> Unlike genes and other non-symbolic information sources, which are models *for*, not models *of*, culture patterns have an intrinsic double aspect. They give meaning . . . to social and psychological reality both by shaping themselves to it and by shaping it to themselves. It is, in fact, this double aspect which sets true symbols off from other sorts of significative forms. Models *for* are found . . . through the whole order of nature; for wherever there is a communication of pattern, such programs are . . . required. . . . But models *of*--linguistic, graphic, mechanical, natural, etc., processes which function not to provide sources of information in terms of which other processes might be patterned, but to represent those patterned processes as such, to express their structure in an alternative medium-- are much rarer, and may perhaps be confined . . . to man. . . . The intertransposability of models

for and models *of* which symbolic formulation
makes possible is the distinctive characteristic
of our mentality.

[3] Smith, op. cit., p. 18. See note 1 above.

[4] In formulating this thesis I have learned much from J. Lightstone, "Structure as Ethos in the Halakhic Midrashim," in *Semeia* 27 (forthcoming). Prof. Lightstone generously made his Ms available to me at my request.

[5] I thus hope to contribute to exploring a new agendum for the study of midrashic literature. See the programmatic essay of R. S. Sarason, "Toward a New Agendum for the Study of Rabbinic Midrashic Literature," in J. Petuchowski, E. Fleischer, eds., *The Joseph Heinemann Memorial Volume* (to appear in 1981). There Sarason suggests that the proper focus of midrashic studies ought to be the character of the documents themselves, and the evidence they provide for determining the particular world view of each. My own essay, of course, falls far short of that ambitious undertaking. Concentration upon the details of specific exegetical forms, however, permits us to chart characteristic usages and patterns of meaning and to measure changes of meaning from document to document, as various redactors with their own biases and tastes manipulate the formulaic conventions at their disposal.

[6] The work begins with Leopold Zunz, *Die Gottesdienstliche Vorträge der Juden* (Berlin, 1832). See the Hebrew translation of A. Jaques, edited by H. Albeck, *HaDerashot BeYisrael* (Jerusalem, 1947), pp. 85ff. Zunz's work is of historical interest only, for later scholars vastly improved upon his hunches. The primary works I have consulted in the preparation of this paper are, in chronological order:
J. Theodor, "Der Komposition der Agadischen Homilien," *Monatschrift für Geschichte und Wissenschaft des Judentums*, 28 (1979), pp. 97-113, 164-175, 271-278.
P. Bloch, "Studien zur Aggadah," *MGWJ* 34 (1885), pp.166-184, 210-224.
H. Albeck, "Introduction" to J. Theodore, H. Albeck, eds., *Midrash Bereshit Rabba*, 3 vols. (2nd printing, Jerusalem, 1965), vol. III, pp. 1-138.
J. Heinemann, "The Proem in the Aggadic Midrashim: A Form-Critical Study," *Scripta Hierosolymitana* 22 (1971), pp. 100-122.
_____, "The Art of Composition in Midrash Vayiqra Rabba" (Hebrew), *Hasifrut* 2 (1971).

[7] The meaninglessness of the superscription, and thus its purely formal character, is first noticed by Bloch, op. cit., pp. 179-181.

[8] This literary characteristic is one of the primary sorts of evidence adduced in support of the theory that the proem--and even much of the midrashic literature as a whole--originally served as sermons of homiletic biblical exegesis. This theory, central to Zunz's pioneering work in midrashic literature, is represented most articulately among modern scholars by J. Heinemann. See his remarks in *Scripta Hierosolymitana*, p. 109ff. Sarason, op. cit., details the evidence for this view (his note 18) and, to my mind, successfully challenges it. My own viewpoint, stated in the conclusion of this essay, substantially agrees with Sarason's position.

[9] Bloch, op. cit., pp. 183-184, Heinemann, op. cit., pp. 104-107.

[10] For units I-III I have translated the text of M. Margoliot, ed., *Midrash Vayiqra Rabba* (Jerusalem, 1972), pp. 587-595. Where the parallel passage of PRK differs in formulation, I indicate the change in brackets, i.e., [PRK adds: . . .], translating the text of B. Mandelbaum, *Pesiqta d'Rab Kahana* (New York, 1962), pp. 54-59. Units IV and V, which differ entirely in each document, are translated consecutively for purposes of comparison, the text of PRK following that of LR. Marginal references indicate parallels in earlier documents (San.=Sanhedrin, Pe.=Peah, Sot.=Sotah). For translations of biblical passages I follow the Revised Standard Version (RSV), The Koren Jerusalem Bible (K) or the translations of William G. Braude (B), depending upon which best represents the sense imputed to the text in the proem. Braude's translations are found in his English translation of PRK, W. Braude and J. Kapstein, eds., *Pesikta de-Rab Kahana* (Philadelphia, 1975), pp. 59-65.

[11] The pseudepigraphic nature of the attributive superscription in the midrashic proem has been discussed at length by Albeck, op. cit., pp. 15ff.

[12] The very same lemma is cited in yet another context in LR 6:6, ed., Margoliot, p. 145, 1.2.

[13] Theodor-Albeck, pp. 291-292, 1s. 5ff.

[14] I have not made a statistical study of the proems in all the relevant documents, i.e., BR, LR, PRK, Lam. R. The results for the proems in LR 26 and PRK 4, however, are suggestive. Of the three proems in LR 26, the first two (26:1-3,4-5) exhibit disjunctive redactional technique I have described in detail. Of the five proems in PRK 4, four (4:2,3,4,5) conform to this model. In Lam. R., perhaps the richest source of proems, the percentage of proems fitting the model described is less massive, but nevertheless revealing. The first unit of Lam. R. consists of a series of thirty-six units identified as proems by appropriate superscriptions (I) and subscriptions (V). Of these, eighteen (1-2a,5,8-10, 12-17,20-22,30-31,33) clearly employ a wide range of techniques which establish disjunctive or complementary exegeses of a given verse within the body of the proem. The preponderance of proems conforming to our specifications is more striking, however, if we eliminate items 11 and 23-25 from the list of proems which do not conform. These are massive constructions which show significant signs of having been constructed with purposes other than the proem in mind. The redactor of Lam. R. has simply introduced and concluded them with appropriate superscriptions in order to render them suitable for use in his document. Thus, of the thirty units capable of serving as proems, eighteen (56%) exemplify traits I have described as characteristic of the proem-form.

[15] Since scriptural verses are routinely drawn from all biblical books, I cannot suggest any principle of selection which could explain why specific verses are juxtaposed in any given proems. The same holds for the thematic interests raised in midrashic proems. These seem no different than the well-attested themes appearing throughout rabbinic literature as a whole. As I have already indicated, the *content* of any given proem rarely issues in a novel theological statement. It is the *form* that yields the clearest statements of the distinctively rabbinic mind.

[16] Cf. Sarason, op. cit. and note 8 above.

[17] An earlier version of this paper, since completely revised, was presented in Prof. Richard S. Sarason's graduate seminar, The Modern Study of Midrash, at Brown University, Fall 1978. I am indebted to Prof. Sarason for introducing me to the field of midrashic studies, and for his criticisms of my earlier version. I bear full responsibility for the views of the present essay.

YERUSHALMI'S COMMENTARY TO MISHNAH TERUMOT:
FROM THEOLOGY TO LEGAL CODE
Alan J. Avery-Peck
Tulane University

The character of a work of exegesis is a product of the will of the interpreter, the fruit of the ideals and concerns the exegete brings to the text. Interpretation is not a reflex of some determinate nature of the document being explained.[1] A document presents a wide range of potential meanings and the interpreter determines which of these to underscore and elucidate. The others remain unnoticed either because the exegete elects to ignore them or because his or her own attitudes and purposes prevent the bringing of these to consciousness. The character of a work of exegesis thus offers an important key to the mind of the exegete; it can reveal as much about that individual as about the document subject to interpretation.

This paper uses this interpretive approach to analyze Tractate Terumot in the Talmud of the Land of Israel (hereafter, the Talmud, or the Yerushalmi). It asks what the nature of the Talmud's commentary to Mishnah Terumot reveals about the religious and social world view of those individuals who, in third through sixth century Palestine, read the Mishnah and attempted to make sense of it as a document that spoke in their own day and setting.[2] We thus examine the relationship between a work of interpretation, the Talmud, and the text it interprets, Mishnah Terumot, in order to probe the mind and purpose of the exegete.

This approach is particularly appropriate in the case of the Yerushalmi. Although Yerushalmi Terumot shows all the signs of a careful commentary, we shall see in some detail that it makes no attempt to locate the meanings that the Mishnah's own authors appear to have intended.[3] To be sure, the Talmud follows the order of the Mishnah's materials sentence by sentence; it purports to explain the Mishnah's rules and to develop the Mishnah's themes; and the vast majority of the facts the Talmud uses come from the Mishnah. Yet, while dependent upon Mishnah Terumot for structure, facts, and themes, the Talmud's authorities have an encompassing agendum of issues and concerns quite foreign to that proposed by Mishnaic rabbis whose work they claim to interpret. Whether consciously or unconsciously,[4] the talmudic masters subvert Mishnah Terumot and use their commentary as a context in which to express their own preoccupations, interests, and insights.

To limn the vision of Judaism promulgated by the Yerushalmi's authorities, this paper classifies each discussion in Yerushalmi Tractate Terumot according to the type of question it asks about Mishnah Terumot and the character of the information it uses. This typology of the Yerushalmi's materials suggests answers to basic questions about the intellectual program of the talmudic masters. This program, I argue, reveals their hopes--not the Mishnah's--for the Judaism of their own day.

Before turning to the classification of Yerushalmi Terumot's materials, however, we must review some of the essential theological claims and pedagogical traits of Mishnah Terumot itself. We then can be clear about the important differences between the Mishnaic and talmudic materials and can isolate the distinctive ways in which, through their work of exegesis, the Yerushalmi's authorities use the Mishnah to express their own ideals and concerns. Let us, then, briefly review the content and character of Mishnah Terumot.

Like the rest of the Mishnah, Tractate Terumot is composed of individual rules and legal statements attributed to authorities who lived over a period of roughly two hundred years. The Mishnah's final formulators and redactors conjoined these diverse laws to create a theological statement more powerful than any the tractate's individual components could devise or express. In full and eloquent detail Mishnah Terumot describes a system of sanctification. Speaking in the period after the destruction of the Temple in 70 C.E. and the Bar Kokhba revolt of 135 C.E.,[5] Mishnah Terumot's authorities claim that, despite these terrifying events of history, the people of Israel remain God's chosen nation, and the land of Israel remains His holy land. These claims are grounded and manifest in the tractate's assertion that, although the Temple is destroyed and the cult has ceased, an agricultural tithe, heave-offering, still is to be given to the priests. Although they have lost their original cultic function, these priests--God's designated representatives--retain their God-given station and must be given the portion God says is owed to them. This means that God still rules over the people of Israel. The deeper message of the tractate derives from the fact that heave-offering has a status of consecration comparable to that of the animals and grain once offered on the altar. According to Mishnah Terumot, the holiness that had filled the people and land of Israel before the destruction of the Temple still abides in the world. The God who once moved in response to the priestly invocation at the altar continues to sanctify Israelite life. Now he responds to the actions of ordinary

Israelites, who separate, and thereby consecrate, the holy offering that he had mandated.

Mishnah Terumot's statement of theology is produced through careful selection and arrangement of individual rules and diverse topics of discussion. The Mishnah's authorities do not speak in theological terms, nor do they explicitly state the deeper meaning their laws convey. But their message is clear and powerful in their system of law as a whole. The Mishnah's very strength comes in the fact that its point is made quietly, not through naked claims of theology, but through an expressive system of law and behavior to be understood and followed by all of the people of Israel.

Yet, the systemic character that gives the Mishnah its power also produces a statement that is flawed and fragile. When examined through its constituent parts, detached from the redactional context that lends coherence to the whole, Mishnah Terumot is enigmatic. Outside of their context within the Mishnah's system of sanctification, the tractate's discrete rules lose all vestige of meaning and importance. They are perplexing, for the Mishnah does not always provide the facts necessary for understanding them. Many are arcane, with no apparent concrete application. Perhaps the most severe problem is that, while claiming to speak of how things are and should be for the people of Israel as a whole, the Mishnah offers neither proof of nor basis for its authority. Those who do not already concede the Mishnah's ascendancy need not be persuaded by Tractate Terumot's specific directives.

In the centuries following the creation of the Mishnah, the authorities of the Yerushalmi attempted to correct what they regarded as the weaknesses of Mishnah Terumot. They did so by transforming the Mishnah's essay about the system of holiness into a collection of distinct, individually accessible, legal statements. Each rule was to have its own, independent, meaning, which could be interpreted outside of the Mishnah's complex system of laws. To accomplish this, the Yerushalmi's authorities provided the Mishnah with a secondary interpretive structure. The practical applications they ascribed to individual rules also needed to be shown for cases that in the Mishnah were purely theoretical. The talmudic rabbis therefore indicated the concrete cases in which the tractate's rules would apply. Finally, by linking Mishnaic laws to specific scriptural passages, the Yerushalmi's authorities provided for the Mishnah's rules a basis of authority that all Israelites would concede. In these ways, the Yerushalmi turned a closed and idiosyncratic network of interdependent rules into a compendium of discrete legal statements. Each was rendered accessible, intelligible, and manifestly significant.

The purpose of the Yerushalmi's masters is not far below the surface. For them Mishnah constituted Torah. Its stature, perhaps, was only slightly below that of Scripture itself. For the talmudic authorities, all of the people of Israel ultimately were to follow the Mishnah's law, under the guidance and rule of the rabbis themselves. The latter's work on Tractate Terumot, along with the rest of the Mishnah, was designed to facilitate their program. Mishnah was to serve as a code of law and basis for all legal decisions. The talmudic masters therefore needed to make explicit the source of the Mishnah's authority. More than that, they had to determine the exact details of its directives and to augment its corpus of laws. These tasks became the central focus of their work.

To prove these claims about the goal of the Yerushalmi's formulators, we must examine in detail the character of their work. After an overview of the Yerushalmi's approach to the Mishnah, we address specific questions about the sorts of issues raised by the Talmudic masters and the types of discussions they themselves provide.

The Yerushalmi is comprised of a line by line commentary to Mishnah Terumot. It takes up in sequence the Mishnah's individual rules and the statements of its various authorities. In this way it breaks the Mishnah down into a series of discrete sentences, analyzing each rule in its own right, without regard to the systemic context provided by Mishnah Terumot as a whole. What is striking, then, about the relationship between Yerushalmi Terumot and the Mishnah is what the Yerushalmi ignores. It ignores the most basic characteristic of the Mishnah, that it is a structured essay in which groups of legal statements make larger points and within which each topic follows logically from the preceding one.[6] Because the Talmud is a line by line, and often phrase by phrase, commentary, the student of the Yerushalmi is not permitted to perceive these facts. For the Talmud, for example, the authorities in a Mishnaic dispute do not necessarily argue a single proposition. Examined separately, each authority has his own perspective and concern, unrelated to that of the other. The views of each authority often are treated as equally valid, each to be applied in a specific case. For the Yerushalmi, moreover, groups of the Mishnah's parallel cases do not come together to establish a legal principle or ideal. Viewing each rule and statement separately, the talmudic masters find only a maze of details to be enumerated, explained, and applied in a variety of cases, often unknown to the Mishnah itself.

In its approach, accordingly, the Yerushalmi pays little or no attention to the overarching logic of the Mishnah's topic or to the structure of its presentation. The Yerushalmi's formulators thereby transform an anthological essay into a collection of distinct rules and legal statements. As I have said, the Yerushalmi is totally subservient to Mishnah's structure, consistently following the order of Tractate Terumot's rules. This passivity, however, masks the Yerushalmi's innovation. By ignoring the importance of the Mishnah's larger structure, the talmudic masters destroy the systemic power of the tractate. The Talmud reduces the Mishnah to a corpus of disjointed legal statements, each with its own meaning and practical application (albeit determined only by the Yerushalmi's own rabbis!), but with no contextual meaning.

Their atomistic approach points to the central concern of the Yerushalmi's framers. They focussed on the meaning of individual rules that could serve for the guidance of the Israelite community. Examination of the specific sorts of materials they created strengthens this impression. To accomplish this analysis, I have separated Yerushalmi Terumot's discussions into three basic types, dividing each type in turn into its constituent categories. This summary of the content of Yerushalmi Terumot shows that the greatest portion of the Talmud is comprised of explanatory comments attached to the Mishnah's individual rules. Within this exegetical material, the Yerushalmi's authorities desire to know what the Mishnah's rules mean and work to tie them to specific statements of Scripture, from which they claim the rules derive. The second most prominent material in Yerushalmi Terumot consists of supplementary rules and cases. These expand the Mishnah's laws so as to apply them in a wide variety of situations unforeseen within the Mishnah's own limited range of interests. They further contain a great number of rules that the Talmud's own authorities supplied to augment Mishnah's corpus of law. Only a small percentage of the tractate's content falls outside of these first two areas. These last materials are the synthetic discussions, which examine the relationship among discrete rules and statements within the Mishnah, the Tosefta, and talmudic literature as a whole. These few discussions differ from the ones just described in that their primary focus is not the specific meaning and applications of individual rules.

In what follows, each of the units within Yerushalmi Terumot is listed under the applicable category.[7] In the first section,

Exegetical Material, I list all units that explain a statement or rule of the Mishnah. This includes pericopae that cite neither Scripture nor any tannaitic text as the basis for their explanations (section 1), units in which there is an amoraic dispute over a rule's meaning (section 2), and materials which claim that the Mishnah's rule, or a specific authority's opinion, derives from Scripture (section 3), Tosefta (section 4) or from a different pericope within the Mishnah itself (section 5).

I. *Exegetical Material*
1. *Explanation based upon logic* [8]
    1. 1:6I   M. Ter. 1:6 explained (+ supplementary rules).
    2. 1:8III Conditions under which M. Ter. 1:8C-D applies.
    3. 2:1IV   Meaning of M. Ter. 2:1C.
    4. 2:1V   Logic of M. Ter. 2:1D-E.
    5. 2:1VI   Logic of M. Ter. 2:1D-E.
    6. 2:1VII Logic of M. Ter. 2:1.
    7. 2:1XIV At M. Ter. 2:1, which authority's opinion is law?
    8. 2:2I   Explanation of M. T.Y. 4:7.
    9. 2:2II   Clarification of dispute at M. Ter. 2:2K-M+R.
    10. 2:3I   M. Bes. 2:3 explained.
    11. 2:3III M. Ter. 2:3 explained.
    12. 2:4II Point of M. Ter. 2:4C made explicit.
    13. 2:5III Implications of M. Ter. 2:6V-W drawn out.
    14. 3:1I   Analysis of M. Ter. 3:1 (+ implications for other rules).
    15. 3:1VII General principle: Which tannaitic authority does the law follow?
    16. 3:3I   Dispute at M. Ter. 3:3 explained.
    17. 3:3II Opinion of Aqiba, M. Ter. 3:3, explained (+ secondary issue).
    18. 3:3III Opinion of Yose, M. Ter. 3:3, explained.
    19. 3:4II M. Ter. 3:4N-P explained.
    20. 3:8II Dispute at M. Ter. 3:9E-F explained.
    21. 4:1II M. Ter. 4:1A-B vs. C explained.
    22. 4:1IV Statement of circumstances under which M. Ter. 4:1B-C applies.
    23. 4:3VI Circumstances under which M. Ter. 4:3H applies.
    24. 4:4I   Circumstances under which M. Ter. 4:4 applies.
    25. 4:4II M. Ter. 4:4F explained.
    26. 4:8II M. Ter. 4:8A-B explained.
    27. 4:8III M. Hal. 1:4 explained.
    28. 4:8VII Circumstances under which M. Ter. 4:7 applies.
    29. 4:8VIII Circumstances under which M. Ter. 4:8 applies.
    30. 5:1V   Circumstances under which M. Ter. 5:1E applies.

31. 5:1VII Definition of term at M. Ter. 5:1I.
32. 5:2II   M. Ter. 5:2D-E explained.
33. 5:2III Definition of term at M. Ter. 5:2D
34. 5:3I   Clarification of M. Ter. 5:2 (+ expansion).
35. 5:4I   Clarification of M. Ter. 5:4N.
36. 5:5II   M. Ter. 5:5D explained.
37. 5:7II   M. Ter. 5:7E explained.
38. 5:8I   M. Ter. 5:8F-G+H explained.
39. 5:9I   Circumstances under which M. Ter. 5:9 applies.
40. 6:1V   M. Ter. 6:1E explained.
41. 6:1VII Circumstances under which M. Ter. 6:1F applies.
42. 6:4I   M. Ter. 6:4E-F explained.
43. 6:6V   Implications of M. Ter. 6:6E drawn out.
44. 7:1VII Implications of M. Meg. 1:5 (+ extended discussion).
45. 7:1IX   Clarification of facts of M. Ket. 3:1.
46. 7:2I   M. Ter. 7:2B explained.
47. 7:6II   Circumstances under which M. Ter. 7:6N-O applies.
48. 7:7I   Circumstances under which M. Ter. 7:7Y applies.
49. 8:1I   Factual basis of M. Ter. 8:1.
50. 8:1II   Reasoning of Eliezer, M. Ter. 8:1H explained.
51. 8:3I   Nature of dispute at M. Ter. 8:1-2 explained.
52. 8:3III Point of M. Ter. 8:2U expressed.
53. 8:5XX   Circumstances under which M. Ter. 8:4G applies.
54. 8:6II   Circumstances under which M. Ter. 8:5 applies.
55. 8:8I   Assumption behind M. Ter. 8:8 expressed.
56. 8:9VIII Point of Eliezer, M. Ter. 8:9-11, indicated.
57. 8:10I   Circumstances under which M. Ter. 8:12 applies.
58. 9:1I   Point of M. Ter. 9:1 indicated.
59. 9:1IV   Implications of M. Ter. 9:1 expressed.
60. 9:1V   Reason for M. Ter. 9:1F-G given.
61. 9:2-3III Meaning of M. Ter. 9:3N indicated.
62. 9:4I   Meaning of M. Ter. 9:3O expressed.
63. 9:4III Meaning of M. Ter. 9:3S expressed.
64. 9:4V   Circumstances under which M. Ter. 10:1 applies.
65. 9:5II   M. Ter. 9:4C explained.
66. 9:5IV   M. Ter. 9:4D-E explained.
67. 9:7I   Point of M. Ter. 9:6C-D indicated.
68. 9:7II   Clarification of M. Ter. 9:6F-G.
69. 9:8IV   M. Ter. 9:7N explained.
70. 10:1I   Circumstances under which M. Ter. 10:1A-B applies.
71. 10:1II Circumstances under which M. Ter. 10:1A-B applies.
72. 10:1III Circumstances under which M. Ter. 10:1A-B applies.
73. 10:1IV M. Ter. 10:1C explained.

74. 10:1V   Circumstances under which M. Ter. 10:1A-B applies.
75. 10:1VI   Circumstances under which M. Ter. 10:1H applies.
76. 10:5bII Meaning of term at M. Ter. 10:6.
77. 10:6I   Implications of M. Ter. 10:7B, C and F indicated.
78. 10:7II   Exact quantities referred to at M. Ter. 10:8A-C indicated.
79. 10:7V   M. Ter. 10:9B explained.
80. 10:8I   M. Ter. 10:10A explained.
81. 10:8II   Analysis of Aqiba's view, M. Ter. 10:10.
82. 10:8III M. Ter. 10:11C-D explained.
83. 10:10I   M. Ter. 10:12B explained.
84. 11:2I   M. Ter. 11:2A-C explained.
85. 11:2III Dispute at M. Ter. 11:2D-F explained.
86. 11:2V   Point of M. Mak. 6:4 indicated.
87. 11:7I   M. Ter. 11:10A-B explained.
88. 11:7II   M. Ter. 11:10 clarified.
89. 11:11X   M. Ter. 11:10E-H explained.
90. 11:7X   Who does law follow, M. Ter. 11:10E?

2. *Amoraic disputes over meaning*
1. 1:4II   Zeira disputes Yohanan's explanation of M. Ter. 1:4C.
2. 1:5II   Hezeqiah and Yohanan dispute meaning of M. Ter. 1:5.
3. 3:1VI   Dispute over Yohanan's explanation of T. Ter. 4:7G-H.
4. 3:6III   Hiyya bar Ba and Samuel b. R. Isaac dispute meaning of M. Ter. 3:6.
5. 3:8III   Anonymous dispute over meaning of M. Ter. 3:9E-F.
6. 4:1I   Samuel and anonymous authority dispute meaning of M. Ter. 4:1.
7. 4:3VII   Kahana and Yohanan dispute meaning of M. Ter. 4:3I-K.
8. 4:5II   Yohanan and Hezeqiah dispute meaning of M. Ter. 4:5A.
9. 4:6I   Huna and Hinena dispute meaning of M. Ter. 4:6C2.
10. 4:8I   Yohanan and Kahana dispute meaning of M. Ter. 4:8C.
11. 4:8IV   Rabbis and Bar Padiah dispute meaning of M. Ter. 4:8A-B.
12. 5:1II   Hezeqiah and Yohanan dispute meaning of M. Ter. 7:5.
13. 5:1III   Hezeqiah and Yohanan--continuation of #12.
14. 5:6I   Yose b. Hanina and Yohanan dispute meaning of M. Ter. 5:6G.
15. 5:6II   Hilpa and anonymous authorities dispute theory underlying M. Ter. 5:5-6.
16. 5:3I   Yohanan, Simeon b. Laqish and Yose b. Hanina dispute M. Ter. 6:3.
17. 6:5I   Yohanan, Simeon b. Laqish and anonymous authorities clarify dispute at M. Ter. 6:5A-D+E.
18. 6:6IV   Abin and anonymous authorities dispute implications of M. Ter. 6:6E.
19. 7:3I   Hiyya the elder and Yannai dispute case parallel to M. Ter. 7:3.

20. 7:7II   Yannai and Zeira dispute meaning of M. Ter. 9:6.
21. 8:4II   Anonymous authorities dispute meaning of M. Ter. 8:3X.
22. 8:5XV   Jeremiah and others dispute reasoning of rule at M. A.Z. 2:6.
23. 10:7III Yose b. Hanina and Simeon bar Hiyya dispute meaning of M. Ter. 10:8F.
24. 11:1III Eleazar and Yohanan dispute meaning of M. Ter. 11:1F-G.
25. 11:4F   Eleazar and Yohanan dispute meaning of M. Ter. 11:4B-D.

3. Explanation from Scripture

1. 1:1I   M. Ter. 1:1 derived from Ex. 25:1-2.
2. 1:1VII   M. Ter. 1:1D derived from Num. 18:28.
3. 1:1VIII   M. Ter. 1:1F derived from Num. 18:28.
4. 1:1II   M. Hag. 1:1 derived from Deut. 31:12.
5. 1:1I   M. Ter. 1:5A-D derived from Deut. 14:28-29.
6. 1:10I   M. Ter. 10:10A-E derived from Num. 18:27.
7. 2:1I   M. Ter. 2:1A derived from Num. 18:27.
8. 2:1II   General principle: rules for heave-offering from Num. 18:27.
9. 2:4I   M. Ter. 2:4A derived from Num. 18:11.
10. 2:5II   M. Ter. 2:6T derived from Num. 18:32.
11. 3:5III   M. Ter. 3:5C derived from Num. 18:27-28.
12. 3:6II   M. Ter. 3:6B derived from Ex. 22:29.
13. 3:7QI   M. Ter. 3:8 derived from Lev. 5:4.
14. 4:3I   M. Ter. 4:3 derived from Ez. 45:13 (=T. Ter. 5:8).
15. 4:3II   M. Ter. 4:3D derived from Num. 31:30 (=T. Ter. 5:8).
16. 4:3III   M. Ter. 4:3E derived from Ez. 45:13 (=T. Ter. 5:8).
17. 4:3V   M. Ter. 4:3F-G derived from Ez. 45:11.
18. 4:5III   M. Ter. 4:5E derived from Num. 18:12.
19. 4:5IV   M. Ter. 4:5F derived from Num. 16:21.
20. 4:7I   M. Ter. 4:7 derived from Num. 18:29.
21. 6:1I   Quantity of "added fifth" derived from Lev. 22:14.
22. 6:1II   M. Ter. 6:1 derived from Lev. 22:14.
23. 6:4II   M. Ter. 6:4E-G derived from Lev. 22:14.
24. 6:4III   M. Ter. 6:4G derived from Lev. 22:9 (=T. Ter. 7:8).
25. 7:2II   M. Ter. 7:2A-E derived from Lev. 21:9.
26. 7:2III   M. Ter. 7:2F-G derived from Lev. 21:9.
27. 8:2I   M. Ter. 8:1I-K derived from Deut. 26:3 and 33:11.
28. 8:3II   Lev. 11:20-23 is source for several rules for forbidden foods.
29. 8:9VII   M. Bek. 5:2 derived from Deut. 12:16.
30. 9:4VI   Deut. 25:4 source for rules concerning muzzling animals used in threshing.
31. 11:2IV   M. Ter. 11:2D, E-F derived from Lev. 11:23.
32. 11:6I   M. Ter. 11:9G derived from Lev. 22:11.

33. 11:6II   M. Ter. 11:9H derived from Lev. 22:11.

4. *Explanation from the Tosefta*

1. 1:1V   T. Ter. 1:3 explains M. Ter. 1:1C2.
2. 1:2I   T. Ber. 3:5 explains M. Ber. 2:3, M. Meg. 2:4.
3. 1:8IV   T. Ter. 3:4 clarifies M. Ter. 1:8.
4. 2:3V   T. Shab. 3:11 explains M. Ter. 2:3.
5. 4:9I   T. Ter. 5:10 explains M. Ter. 4:7A-C, 4:8.
6. 6:6I   T. Ter. 7:9 explains M. Ter. 6:6B.
7. 9:4IV   T. Ter. 8:3 explains M. Ter. 9:3T-U (+ Amoraic discussion).
8. 11:4II   T. Ter. 10:4 explains M. Ter. 11:5I-J.

5. *Explanation from the Mishnah*

1. 1:9I   M. Ter. 1:10 clarifies M. Ter. 1:9.
2. 1:9II   M. Ma. 1:6 explains M. Ter. 1:9.
3. 3:6I   M. Ter. 3:6B explains M. Ter. 3:6C.
4. 9:5I   M. Ter. 9:5B explains M. Ter. 9:4B.
5. 11:4IV   M. Ed. 3:3 explains M. Ter. 11:4-5.

This material comprises 161 units out of a total of 349 found in Yerushalmi Terumot as a whole, that is, 46.13 percent of the total. 71.43 percent of this material, in turn, is the Yerushalmi's authorities' own line by line exegesis of the Mishnah (sections 1 and 2). They clarify Mishnah's often abstruse language, define terms and, in the majority of cases, explain exactly what the Mishnah's rules prohibit and permit. Notably, only a relatively small percentage of these explanations (15.53 percent of the exegetical material as a whole) are under dispute by amoraic authorities.

20.5 percent of this exegetical material uses Scripture to derive and explain the Mishnah's rules. The claim in these discussions is that the Mishnah's own authorities only made explicit what Scripture itself requires of all Israelites. The Yerushalmi thus gives weight to the central rabbinic claim that the Mishnah comprises divine revelation. The assertion is proven by demonstrating that the Mishnah's rules correspond to those found in the document accepted by all Israelites as revealed. The meager amount of material in sections 4 and 5 indicates that the Yerushalmi's authorities did not consider the Mishnah and the Tosefta themselves to be important sources for the interpretation of the Mishnah. Such interpretation was better based upon the authoritative Scripture or upon the Talmudic masters' own sense for the meaning the Mishnah's rules should have.

In their second major category of discussion, the *Supplementary Material*, the Yerushalmi's rabbis fill out the corpus of rules found in the Mishnah. They do this by citing the Tosefta's cognate material (section 1) as well as by reporting tannaitic statements unknown in the Mishnah or the Tosefta (section 2). Yet more than this, the Talmudic authorities are themselves active in legislating rules unknown to the Mishnah (sections 3 and 4) and in developing the implications of the Mishnah's rules to show how they apply to new cases and problems unforeseen by the Mishnah (section 5). Finally, through stories and legal precedents they indicate how the law functions in concrete, contemporary, cases (section 6).

II. *Supplementary Material*

1. *Rules cited from the Tosefta*

1. 2:1III   T. Ter. 3:19C-D supplements M. Ter. 2:1 (+ cognate rules).
2. 2:1X   T. Ter. 3:8C-H supplements M. Ter. 2:1 (+ anonymous explanation).
3. 2:1XI   T. Ter. 3:7A supplements M. Ter. 2:1 (+ tannaitic and amoraic discussion).
4. 2:1XII   T. Ter. 3:18 complements M. Ter. 2:1 (+ amoraic explanation).
5. 2:1XIII   T. Ter. 3:7 complements M. Ter. 2:1 (+ amoraic explanation).
6. 2:3IV   T. Shab. 3:5 complements M. Ter. 2:3 (+ amoraic discussion and rules).
7. 2:4III   T. Ter. 4:1-2 supplements M. Ter. 2:4 (+ amoraic discussion).
8. 3:1III   T. Ter. 4:5J-K supplements M. Ter. 3:1 (+ amoraic explanation).
9. 3:1IV   T. Ter. 4:6A-D supplements M. Ter. 3:1 (+ amoraic explanation).
10. 3:4IV   T. Ter. 3:12 supplements M. Ter. 3:4.
11. 3:4V   T. Ter. 3:13 supplements M. Ter. 3:4 (+ amoraic discussion).
12. 3:5V   T. Ter. 4:9 supplements M. Ter. 3:5.
13. 3:6V   T. Ter. 4:10 supplements M. Ter. 3:5 (+ amoraic discussion).
14. 3:8I   T. Ter. 4:13 complements M. Ter. 3:9.
15. 4:3IV   T. Ter. 5:3 supplements M. Ter. 4:3 (+ scriptural prooftext).
16. 4:10I   T. Ter. 5:11 supplements M. Ter. 4:10 (+ amoraic discussion).
17. 4:10II   T. Ter. 5:11 supplements M. Ter. 4:10 (+ explanation).
18. 4:12I   T. Ter. 6:12 supplements M. Ter. 4:12 (+ amoraic analysis).
19. 4:12III T. Ter. 6:13 supplements M. Ter. 4:12 (+ amoraic analysis).

20. 5:3II   T. Ter. 6:1 complements M. Ter. 5:6E (+ amoraic discussion).
21. 5:9III   T. Ter. 6:10 supplements M. Ter. 5:9.
22. 6:1VI   T. Ter. 8:2 supplements M. Ter. 6:1.
23. 7:6   T. Ter. 6:16 supplements M. Ter. 7:6 (+ anonymous rules).
24. 8:5IX   T. Ter. 7:13 supplements M. Ter. 8:4.
25. 8:5X   T. Ter. 7:13 supplements M. Ter. 8:4.
26. 8:5XI   T. Ter. 7:13 supplements M. Ter. 8:4.
27. 8:5XII   T. Ter. 7:16 supplements M. Ter. 8:4.
28. 8:5XIII   T. Ter. 7:16 supplements M. Ter. 8:4.
29. 8:5XVII   T. Ter. 7:12 supplements M. Ter. 8:4 (+ amoraic discussion).
30. 8:6I   T. Ter. 7:14-15 supplements M. Ter. 8:5.
31. 8:10II   T. Ter. 7:20 supplements M. Ter. 8:12.
32. 9:4II   T. Ter. 8:5-6 supplements M. Ter. 9:4C-E.
33. 10:2II   T. Ter. 8:9 supplements M. Ter. 10:2 (+ amoraic discussion).
34. 10:10II   T. Ter. 9:5 supplements M. Ter. 10:12 (+ amoraic rules).
35. 10:10III T. Ter. 9:5 supplements M. Ter. 10:12 (+ amoraic rules).
36. 11:1I   T. Ter. 9:7 supplements M. Ter. 11:1 (+ amoraic discussion).
37. 11:2II   T. Ter. 9:8 supplements M. Ter. 11:2.
38. 11:3II   T. Ter. 9:9 supplements M. Ter. 11:3.
39. 11:5IV   T. Ter. 10:12 supplements M. Ter. 11:6-8.
40. 11:7III   T. Ter. 10:9 supplements M. Ter. 11:10 (+amoraic discussion).
41. 11:7IV   T. Ter. 10:9 supplements M. Ter. 11:10.

2. *Tannaitic rules not found in the Mishnah or Tosefta*[9]

1. 1:3I   Meir supplements M. Ter. 1:3 (+ amoraic discussion).
2. 5:8II   Supplement to rules of neutralization.
3. 5:9II   Supplement to rules of neutralization.
4. 6:1VIII   Supplement to M. Ter. 6:10.
5. 7:1V   Supplement to M. Ter. 7:1.
6. 8:7II   Eliezer supplements M. Ter. 8:6.
7. 9:8II   Supplements M. Ter. 9:7H-J.

3. *Rules in names of amoraim*

1. 1:1IX   Rule for agency, supplements M. Ter. 1:1D-F.
2. 1:10II   Amoraic supplement to M. Ter. 1:1C.
3. 2:1IX   Hiyya the elder expands M. Ter. 2:1D-E.
4. 2:3II   Hiyya bar Ashi: rule cognate to M. Ter. 2:3.
5. 3:1II   Yohanan supplements M. Ter. 3:1.

6.	3:5IV	Yohanan supplements M. Ter. 3:5.
7.	3:5VI	Yohanan and Simeon b. Laqish dispute rule cognate to M. Ter. 3:5.
8.	3:5VII	Hoshaya b. R. Shammai M. Ter. 3:5.
9.	4:3IX	Simeon b. Laqish supplements M. Ter. 4:3 (+ discussion).
10.	4:3X	Yohanan supplements M. Ter. 4:3 (+ biblical prooftext).
11.	4:8VI	Simeon b. Laqish supplements M. Ter. 4:8 (+ T. Ter. 5:10M-T).
12.	4:12II	Simeon supplements M. Ter. 4:12.
13.	5:1I	Hiyya paraphrases T. Ter. 6:1F-G.
14.	5:9V	Yohanan supplements M. Ter. 5:9.
15.	5:9VI	Rules on obligations of judge: several amoraim.
16.	6:1III	Yohanan: rules cognate to M. Ter. 6:1C.
17.	6:1IX	Yohanan and Simeon b. Laqish dispute rule cognate to M. Ter. 6:1F.
18.	7:1II	Yohanan and Simeon b. Laqish: rules for punishments.
19.	8:5I	Jacob bar Aha, Simeon bar Ba and Yohanan supplement M. Ter. 8:4.
20.	8:5II	Several amoraim supplement M. Ter. 8:4.
21.	8:5III	Abbahu supplements M. Ter. 8:4.
22.	8:5IV	Jacob bar Aha and Imi supplement M. Ter. 8:4 (+ incident).
23.	8:5VII	Hiyya bar Ba: rules concerning venom (+ incident).
24.	8:5VIII	Imi: folk health hints.
25.	8:5XIX	Jacob bar Aha supplements M. Ter. 8:4.
26.	8:7III	Jonah, Hezeqiah and Tabbi supplement M. Ter. 8:6.
27.	8:7IV	Hiyya bar Ba supplements M. Ter. 8:6.
28.	9:5III	Yohanan supplements M. Ter. 9:4D-E.
29.	9:8III	Supplement to M. Ter. 9:7: Abahu in the name of Yohanan.
30.	10:4I	Supplement to M. Ter. 10:4: Rav and Levi dispute.
31.	10:4III	Rav: rule cognate to #30.
32.	10:7IV	Rule cognate to 10:8-9: Ba bar Zabdah and Isaac.
33.	10:9I	Ba and Zeira supplement M. Ter. 10:11.
34.	11:5III	Rules loosely connected to M. Ter. 11:8H: Hilaphta b. Saul and Ba.
35.	11:7VI	Supplement to M. Ter. 11:10: Imi.
36.	11:7VIII	Supplement to M. Ter. 11:10: Yosa.
37.	11:7XI	Supplement to M. Ter. 11:10: house of Yannai.

4. *Rules cited anonymously*

1.	4:2II	Supplement to M. Ter. 4:2.
2.	6:1X	Complements M. Ter. 6:1 (+ T. Ter. 7:5).
3.	6:2I	Complements M. Ter. 6:2.
4.	6:6II	Supplements M. Ter. 6:6A-B.

5. 6:6III   Supplements M. Ter. 6:6C.
6. 7:4-5I   Supplements M. Ter. 7:4 (+ expanded discussion).

5. The Mishnah's rules applied to new cases

1. 1:3II   M. Ter. 1:3/0 serves as basis for set of rules concerning minor.
2. 1:9III   M. Ter. 1:9 supplemented with new cases.
3. 3:2V   M. Ter. 3:2/0 is basis for ruling in different cases.
4. 3:5II   M. Ter. 3:5A-B applied to new situation (T. provides ruling).
5. 3:6IV   M. Ter. 3:6 applied to case suggested by M. Ter. 1:10.
6. 4:1III   M. Ter. 4:1C applied to new case.
7. 4:1V   M. Ter. 4:1A-C applied to new case.
8. 4:3VIII   M. Ter. 4:3I-K+M serves to answer new legal question.
9. 4:8V   M. Ter. 4:8 applied to new case.
10. 4:12IV   M. Ter. 4:12 applied to new case.
11. 4:12V   M. Ter. 4:12 applied to new case.
12. 8:2II   M. Ter. 8:2K applied to new case.
13. 8:2III   M. Ter. 8:1I applied to new case.
14. 9:1II   M. Ter. 9:1 applied to new case.
15. 9:1III   M. Ter. 9:1 applied to new case.
16. 9:2-3I   M. Ter. 9:2 applied to new case.
17. 9:2-3II   M. Ter. 9:2L-M applied in case of T. Toh 8:4.
18. 9:6I   M. Ter. 9:5A-B applied to new case.
19. 9:6II   M. Ter. 9:5 and 5:9 produce new situation.
20. 10:3I   M. Ter. 10:3A-C analyzed within new situations.
21. 10:3III   M. Ter. 10:3D-F applied to new cases.
22. 10:4II   M. Ter. 10:2D-F applied to new cases.
23. 10:5bII   M. Ter. 10:6 applied to new case.
24. 11:5II   M. Ter. 11:8G applied to new cases.
25. 11:5V   Refinements of M. Ter. 11:8I-J.

6. Instantiation of the Mishnah's rules

1. 8:5V   Incident concerning improperly slaughtered meat.
2. 8:5VI   Incident concerning uncovered wine.
3. 8:5XIV   Incident concerning snake venom.
4. 8:5XVI   Incident concerning snake venom.
5. 8:5XVIII   Incident concerning snakes.
6. 8:7V   Incident concerning snakes.
7. 8:7VI   Incident concerning snakes.
8. 8:10III   Supplement to M. Ter. 8:12.
9. 8:10IV   Supplement to M. Ter. 8:12.
10. 8:10V   Supplement to M. Ter. 8:12.
11. 10:3II   Supplement to M. Ter. 10:3C.

12. 11:7V   Supplement to M. Ter. 11:10.
13. 11:7VII Supplement to M. Ter. 11:10.

Comprising 36.96 percent of the Yerushalmi's units, the complementary material takes up slightly less of the total then does the exegetical material (129 units in contrast to 161). 37.21 percent of these units consist of statements assigned to tannaitic authorities (sections 1 and 2). These present rules that supplement those found in the Mishnah, and they usually include a short amoraic gloss on their meaning. A further 28.68 percent of this material consists of rules suggested by amoraim to round out the Mishnah's corpus of law (section 3). One central aspect of the Yerushalmi's work thus was to complete the task of legislation that its authorities see the Mishnah's masters as having begun.

Along these same lines the Yerushalmi's rabbis devote a great deal of effort to defining the implications of the Mishnah's rules and applying them to cases unknown to the Mishnah. These units, listed in section 5, comprise 19.38 percent of the present material. The discussions in section 6 show how the Mishnah's rules served as a basis for behavior and legal decisions in the Yerushalmi's authorities' own lives. Not surprisingly, these cases concern the most practically applicable rules in the tractate, those concerning foods which might have been contaminated by snake venom. This material constitutes 10.08 percent of this category.

The final and smallest component of talmudic material is designated *Synthetic*. This refers to the treatment of issues that transcend individual laws and legal statements. These discussions compare and contrast rules taken from diverse contexts within the Mishnah, the rest of the tannaitic literature and, in some cases, the Yerushalmi itself. They represent the attempt to find overarching principles informing discrete units of law, rather than entire tractates, which can guide legal decision-making. They also point out apparent contradictions which might plague the corpus of law.

Alongside the discussion of contradictory rules (section 1) and correlated ones (section 2), I include in this section the Yerushalmi's units that discern which Mishnaic authority stands behind a rule stated anonymously in Mishnah Terumot (section 3). These discussions belong here because, just as in the treatment of apparently correlated rules, they point out agreements in the ideas of two or more discrete statements within the Mishnah. We also find a few cases in which an amoraic exegesis of one pericope of the Mishnah is applied to some other one (section 4) or in which the Yerushalmi points out that an interpretation proposed for one

Mishnaic rule is proven unviable by a different rule (section 5). In these several cases we see how the approach characteristic of the *Synthetic Material's* analysis of Mishnah Terumot might have been developed into a tertiary analysis of the Talmud's own discrete discussions and their relationship to the Mishnaic materials they claim to explain.

III. *Synthetic Materials*

1. Discussion of apparently contradictory tannaitic statements

1. 1:1II   M. Ter. 1:1 contradicts M. Makh. 6:1.
2. 1:1III T. Ter. 1:1 contradicts M. Yeb. 14:1.
3. 1:2III M. Ter. 1:2L contradicts M. Ter. 1:2H-J and M. Yeb. 12:4A-D.
4. 1:4I   M. Ter. 1:10 contradicts M. Ter. 1:4.
5. 1:4III T. Ter. 3:19A contradicts M. Ter. 2:2K-N (expansion discusses M. 1:4).
6. 1:7I   M. Ter. 4:6 contradicts M. Ter. 1:7 (+ biblical prooftext).
7. 1:8I   M. Ter. 1:10 contradicts M. Ter. 1:8.
8. 3:4III M. Ter. 3:4/O-P contradicts M. Ter. 1:8.
9. 4:4III M. Ter. 4:4F contradicts M. Ter. 4:4G.
10. 4:4IV   M. Me. 6:1 contradicts M. Ter. 4:4G.
11. 4:11I   M. Ter. 4:10N contradicts M. Ter. 4:11R-S.
12. 4:13I   T. Ter. 5:13E-F contradicts M. Ter. 4:13.
13. 5:1IV   M. Ter. 5:1E contradicts M. Ar. 6:5.
14. 5:7I   M. Ter. 5:9I-K contradicts M. Miq. 7:2.
15. 6:1IV   Anonymous tannaitic statement contradicts T. Ter. 7:7C-D.
16. 7:1I   M. Mak. 3:1 contradicts M. Ket. 3:1.
17. 7:1III M. Mak. 3:1 contradicts M. Ket. 3:1.
18. 7:2IV   M. Ter. 7:1A contradicts M. Ter. 8:1.
19. 10:1VI M. M.S. 2:1 contradicts M. Ter. 10:1H.
20. 10:2I   M. Ter. 10:2A-C contradicts T. Ter. 8:9H.
21. 10:7I   T. Ter. 9:2C contradicts T. Ter. 9:2B.
22. 10:10IV M. Ter. 10:12D contradicts M. Miq. 7:2.
23. 11:3I   M. Ter. 11:3E-F contradicts a tannaitic teaching.
24. 11:4III M. Ter. 11:4L contradicts a tannaitic teaching.
25. 11:5I   M. B.B. 5:8 contradicts M. Ter. 11:8H.

2. Discussion of apparently correlated tannaitic statements

1. 2:5V M. Ter. 2:6W-X = M. Kil. 1:2.
2. 3:1V M. Ter. 3:1/M. Ter. 2:2 together point to over-reaching principle.
3. 3:5I Simeon, M. Ter. 3:5B = Shammaites, M. Ter. 1:4C.
4. 4:2I M. Ter. 4:2C = M. Dem. 7:3.

5.	4:5I	M. Ter. 4:5B = M. Ter. 1:4C.
6.	5:2I	M. Ter. 5:2C = M. Zeb. 8:5.
7.	8:4I	M. Ter. 8:3X = Tarfon, M. Ma. 3:9.
8.	8:9I	M. Ter. 8:8+9-11 = M. Pes. 1:7.
9.	8:9II	M. Ter. 8:8+9-11 = M. Pes. 1:7.
10.	8:9IV	M. Bek. 5:2 + M. Ter. 8:9-11.
11.	8:9V	M. Bek. 5:2 + M. Ter. 8:9-11.
12.	8:9VI	M. Bek. 5:2 + M. Ter. 8:8.
13.	8:9IX	M. Ter. 8:9 = M. Pes. 1:7.
14.	9:8I	Simeon, T. Dem. 5:9 = M. Ter. 9:7H-J.

3. *Which tannaitic authority?*

1.	1:1IV	M. Ter. 1:1C1 does not accord with Judah.
2.	1:1VI	M. Ter. 1:1C3 does not accord with Judah.
3.	2:5I	M. Ter. 2:6/O is the opinion of Judah.
4.	2:5IV	M. Ter. 2:6T is the opinion of Ishmael b. R. Yose (+ expansion).
5.	3:7I	M. Ter. 3:8: Hillelites or Shammaites?
6.	5:9IV	M. Ter. 5:9H is the opinion of Yose.
7.	7:5III	M. Ter. 7:6P is the opinion of Judah (+ expansion).
8.	8:7I	M. Ter. 8:6A-F is the opinion of Gamaliel.
9.	11:1II	M. Ter. 11:1C is the opinion of Rabbi (+ expansion).

4. *Exegesis of one rule applied to a different rule*

1.	1:8II	Y. Ter. 1:4I and Y. Ter. 1:8I correlated for ambiguous case.
2.	5:1VI	Positions at Y. Ter. 2:1II applied to M. Ter. 5:1G.
3.	7:1VI	Positions at Y. Ter. 7:1I H and S applied to new cases.
4.	7:1VIII	Positions at Y. Ter. 7:1I V-X and 7:1VII D-E and K-M in new cases.
5.	8:9III	Jeremiah misinterprets view of Meir, T. Pes. 3:10.
6.	10:5aI	Y. Ter. 10:2II applies to M. Ter. 10:5E-F.
7.	10:6II	Y. Ter. 10:2II applied to M. Ter. 10:7.

5. *Exegesis of one rule contradicted by a different rule*

1.	2:1VIII	Yohanan, Y. Ter. 2:1I B-D, contradicts M. Ter. 2:1G.
2.	3:4I	Simeon b. Laqish's view contradicts M. Ter. 3:4K.
3.	5:5I	Yohanan's view contradicts M. Ter. 5:5D.
4.	7:1IV	Simeon b. Laqish's view contradicts M. Ter. 6:1.

As in the previous material, emphasis is upon those exegetical issues that play a central role in the development of a corpus of law and the creation of a guide to legal decision making. 66.1 percent of this material concerns either the discover of larger principles on whose basis a wide variety of cases may be adjudicated,[10] or the suggestion that certain rules might be contradictory and thus a problem for the judging of specific cases (sections 1 and 2).[11]

The Yerushalmi's masters are rather uninterested in the question of which Mishnaic authority stands behind a specific rule. This emphasizes the fact that the Yerushalmi's exegetical agendum is pointed to understanding practical and conceptual aspects of the Mishnah's rules. Therefore, the role of individual tannaitic authorities, section 3, is hardly of interest. It represents only 15.26 of the present material, 2.58 percent of the Yerushalmi as a whole. The question of the cogency of the Yerushalmi's own materials is only slightly more developed, sections 4 and 5. It comprises 18.64 percent of this material, 3.16 percent of the Yerushalmi as a whole.

By viewing all of the Yerushalmi's materials in synoptic form, we may draw a clear picture of the character of the talmudic corpus and the overall goal of its formulators. The chart at the end of the chapter summarizes the results of our preceding discussions.

The synoptic table allows us to answer the questions, What is Yerushalmi Terumot? The preponderance of exegetical materials shows that it is primarily an explanatory commentary to Mishnah Terumot. It delineates the basic meaning and point of the Mishnah's rules and, in many cases, establishes their scriptural origins. The second principal interest of Yerushalmi Terumot is the development of the Mishnah's corpus of laws. The Yerushalmi cites, and often gives a short explanation of, supplementary rules found in the Tosefta. Viewed as a whole, however, the Yerushalmi's authorities' own expansions of the Mishnah's corpus (II:3-6) take up the greatest portion of the *Supplementary Material*. By far the least prominent aspect of the Yerushalmi is the correlation of diverse rules from the Mishnaic and talmudic corpus as a whole. This synthetic material, a main component of later rabbinic exegesis, is only a minor facet of the Yerushalmi's discussion of this tractate.

The Yerushalmi's atomistic commentary and the overall focus of its questions point to the purpose of those who created Yerushalmi Terumot. They sought to transform a systematic statement of theology into a compendium of legal rulings that could serve as a basis for legal decisions about a wide range of topics and issues. This accounts for the Yerushalmi's exegetical interests, as well as for its concern for augmenting the Mishnah's corpus of law. The *Synthetic Material*, with its concern for the innerworkings of the law code as a whole, is equally at home within such an enterprise. Accordingly, roughly 11 percent of the talmudic discussions concern the locating of overarching principles and the delineation of rules that, while superficially contradictory, have their own, distinct, ranges of application.

What the Yerushalmi's masters failed to do is as informative as what they did. Although the Yerushalmi is concerned with the Mishnah's individual rules, we have seen that it exhibits little interest in Mishnah Terumot as a whole. This is shown by its atomistic commentary, as well as by its disregard of the Mishnah (or the Tosefta) as a source of facts and principles to explain the Mishnah's own rules (I:4-5). Further, while the source of a rule in Scripture mattered to the talmudic authorities, the possibility that it was the view of a specific Mishnaic rabbi did not. Attributing rules to tannaim did not meet the Talmud's goal of explaining the meaning of the law or of grounding it in the authoritative Scripture. Finally, the single-mindedness of the Yerushalmi's formulators bears noting. Nearly all of their material is dedicated to explaining and augmenting Mishnah Terumot. They stopped neither to tell us about the lives and character of the Yerushalmi's own masters, nor to develop a history of the Mishnah's authorities and period. These issues were irrelevant in the creation of a compendium of rules intended to serve all ages. Such material therefore occurs only in modest amounts, in cases in which it is relevant to the understanding of a specific legal ruling or to that rule's application in a concrete case (II:6).

The Yerushalmi's attentiveness to the explanation and expansion of discrete Mishnaic rules reveals that its authorities viewed the Mishnah as the central law code of the people Israel. As the chief interpreters of that code, the former would be the rightful leaders of the Israelite community. This vision shaped their overall approach to Mishnah Terumot. The questions they asked and the materials they themselves developed supply the key to understanding their vision. They initiated the work of creating a legal code that could unite the Israelite people under divine law, set out in the Mishnah and explained by the Yerushalmi's own rabbis. The striking shift from the ideal expressed by the Mishnah's tannaitic authorities is that, in the Yerushalmi's vision, the people of Israel were *not* to *believe* in the Mishnah's sophisticated theological views; they were, rather, to perform its rules and carry out its precepts.

Analysis of the organization of Yerushalmi Terumot and creation of a typology of its materials allow us to answer basic questions about that document. We find, first, that this talmudic tractate is a carefully crafted and redacted whole. The Talmud's organizers have placed materials deriving from diverse authorities and time periods in careful sequence so as to explicate, line by line, the materials in Mishnah Terumot. Within this sequence, almost every one of the Mishnah's constituent rules and legal statements is addressed. Second, categorization of the Yerushalmi's materials highlights the close correlation between the outward organization of the document and its actual content. Its redaction as a line by line reference work suggests that the Yerushalmi's central concern is the explication and expansion of each of the Mishnah's individual laws. In the Talmud, form and function thus merge to create a document that turns a theoretical legal anthology, the Mishnah, into a compendious code of law and basis for legal decision making.

The characterization of Yerushalmi Terumot on the basis of form and content has important implications for our understanding of the Talmud itself and of the religious and social program of the rabbis who created it. The first implication is that, so far as its contents can tell us, Yerushalmi Terumot is neither a haphazard nor incomplete document. Surely, as others have noted, it differs significantly in style from the Bablonian Talmud.[12] This should not, however, lead us to the conclusion that it is imperfectly or incompletely redacted.[13] By contrast, so far as its content and organization can be trusted to reveal the intentions of its creators, those individuals succeeded in putting together a complete and focussed commentary to Mishnah Terumot. In this commentary they applied a narrow set of questions to a large percentage of the Mishnah's laws.

These facts of the exegetical program that guided the formation of Yerushalmi Terumot in turn reveal the hopes and desires of the Talmud's authorities for the Judaism of their day. Unlike the Mishnah's rabbis, they seem clearly to have recognized their potential for leading the Israelite community on the basis of God's holy law, revealed in Scripture and expressed in full in the Mishnah. For this reason they turned away from the highly theoretical character of the Mishnaic text. They attempted instead to make clear the nature of each of the Mishnah's legal demands and to explicate the circumstances under which the Mishnah's particular rules would apply. The Talmud's rabbis began with an enigmatic collection of legal statements and disputes, intended by its own redactors to set forth a theology of sanctification. This they shaped into a legal code that they hoped would serve, under their own guidance, to rule the Israelite nation as a whole.

SYNOPTIC TABLE

	Number of units	% of category	% of Yerushalmi Terumot
I. *Exegetical Material*			
1. Explanation based upon logic	90	55.90	25.79
2. Amoraic dispute over meaning	25	15.53	7.16
3. Explanation from Scripture	33	20.50	9.46
4. Explanation from Tosefta	8	4.97	2.29
5. Explanation from Mishnah	5	3.10	1.43
Totals:	161	100.00	46.13
II. *Supplementary Material*			
1. Rules cited from Tosefta	41	31.78	11.75
2. Tannaitic rules not found in Mishnah or Tosefta	7	5.43	2.01
3. Rules cited in names of Amoraim	37	28.68	10.60
4. Rules cited anonymously	6	4.65	1.72
5. Mishnah's rules applied to new cases	25	19.38	7.16
6. Instantiation of Mishnah's rules	13	10.08	3.72
Totals:	129	100.00	36.96
III. *Synthetic Material*			
1. Discussion of contradictory Tannaitic statements	25	42.37	7.16
2. Discussion of correlated Tannaitic statements	14	23.73	4.01
3. Which Tannaitic authority?	9	15.26	2.58
4. Exegesis of one rule applied to a different rule	7	11.86	2.01
5. Exegesis of one rule contradicted by a different rule	4	6.78	1.15
Totals:	59	100.00	16.91
Final Totals:	349		100.00

FOOTNOTES

[1] See the introductory chapter ("Meaning and Significance") in E.D. Hirsch, *The Aims of Interpretation* (University of Chicago Press, Chicago, 1976), pp. 1-16. As Hirsch makes clear, and as I indicate in the following, this is not to claim that the text does not have some specific meaning intended, either consciously or unconsciously, by its author. It is only to say that this authorial meaning stands alongside other meanings that plausibly could be ascribed to the author's work. An interpreter may attempt to locate authorial meaning or may not. In either case, and particularly in the latter, this choice of goals reveals much about the attitudes and purposes of the exegete.

[2] The analysis of Yerushalmi Terumot upon which the following is based is found in my translation of and commentary to that tractate, *The Talmud of the Land of Israel. A Preliminary Translation and Explanation. Volume VI. Tractate Terumot* (University of Chicago Press, Chicago, projected 1986).

[3] A study of the meaning that the Mishnah's rules had for those who formulated them is found in my *The Priestly Gift in Mishnah. A Study of Tractate Terumot* (Scholars Press, Chico, 1981). See in particular pp. 1-21, on the meaning of the tractate, and pp. 21-27, where I describe the methods used in locating authorial meaning.

[4] I do not mean to argue that the talmudic masters consciously "misread" Mishnah Terumot in order to use it for their own purposes. Rather, they simply saw in it the meanings that best matched their own conceptions of and hopes for the Judaism of their day. On the question of unconscious meaning and the problems it presents for understanding a text, see E. D. Hirsch, *Validity in Interpretation*, (Yale University Press, New Haven, 1967), pp. 51-57.

[5] Both the major work of legislation and the final formulation of the tractate occur after 135 C.E. While three of the tractate's rules are attributed to the Houses of Hillel and Shammai, which were active before 70 C.E., only one of these appears to be authentic (see my argument in Jacob Neusner, *Judaism: The Evidence of the Mishnah* (University of Chicago Press, Chicago, 1981), pp. 292-293. Preliminary results of a study of the development of Tractate Terumot's law indicate that the vast majority of materials in the tractate, including those that are transmitted anonymously, derive from the period after the Bar Kokhba revolt.

[6] On the way in which the Mishnah's own formulators used literary constructions such as disputes or strings of linguistically parallel cases in order to highlight the points they wished to make, see my *The Priestly Gift in Mishnah*, pp. 23-24, and Jacob Neusner, *A History of the Mishnaic Law of Purities*. Vol. 21 (E. J. Brill, Leiden, 1977), pp. 165-196. For the way in which the organization of the tractate's topics directs the reader to the central point of the essay as a whole see *The Priestly Gift in Mishnah*, pp. 9-21.

[7] Y.'s materials are designated by the enumeration of pericope found in the Leiden manuscript and *editio princeps*, which parallels for the most part the division of pericope found in Mishnah Terumot itself. This same enumeration is found in Penei Moshe's commentary in standard printed editions. To the designation of the pericope I append a Roman numeral, which indicates my division of the pericope into its constituent units or *sugyot*. These are the shortest units of Talmudic discourse which 1) address and resolve a single issue and which 2) are substantively independent of the materials

which precede and follow. This designation of units, along with
my complete listing and brief description of each *sugya* under the
applicable category, should allow the reader both to see the basis
for my categorization of this material and to formulate independent
judgments about alternative classifications.

[8] I have included under this heading, as well as in the following ones, units in which the Yerushalmi explains a pericope
other than the one which is under discussion from Mishnah Terumot.
These normally are cases in which the cited pericope contains a
rule cognate to that of Mishnah Terumot. The Talmud's explanation
of it accordingly serves the same purpose as its explanation of
material from within Tractate Terumot itself.

[9] Under this heading I include rules and statements that,
while unknown in tannaitic documents, are cited by the talmud in
the names of tannaitic authorities and/or are introduced with the
formulaic *tny*. I intend no judgment as to the true antiquity of
these materials.

[10] Note that the principle the Yerushalmi's authorities derive
from several purportedly correlated rules is not normally the one
suggested by Mishnah Terumot concerning the processes of sanctification. See e.g., Y. Ter. 7:1 ff., in which the talmudic masters
determine which punishments and how many of them are applicable in
the cases of various offenses. While a central issue for those
who hope to implement the Mishnah's law in an actual community,
this issue was not on the minds of those who formulated the diverse
Mishnaic materials on the basis of which the Yerushalmi's Rabbis
draw their conclusions.

[11] The majority of units that begin by suggesting that two
rules or statements are contradictory ultimately prove that they
are not. This is accomplished by showing that the situations referred to in the rules are not comparable. The result of these
exercises thus is to indicate the correct circumstances in which
each of the cited rules or opinions properly is applied.

[12] See, e.g., J. N. Epstein, *Introduction to the Amoraic
Literature*, (Magnes Press, Jerusalem, 1962) (Hebrew), pp. 273-74,
who comments on the relative simplicity and undeveloped character
of the Yerushalmi's materials *vis a vis* the Babylonian Talmud's
sugyot.

[13] On the question of the extent to which Yerushalmi has been
"edited," see Saul Lieberman, "The Talmud of Caesarea," Supplement
to *Tarbiz* II, 4, 1931 (Hebrew), p. 21. Lieberman disagrees with
I.Y. Halevy, whom he cites, who claims that Yerushalmi was not
"edited" at all, but that its passages were copied as taught in
the academies without being reworked or ordered. Lieberman, by
contrast, claims that Yerushalmi did have an editor, who arranged
its passages according to the order of the *mishnayot* before him,
an order that often differs from our own. Halevy's theory clearly
is contrary to the evidence of Yerushalmi Terumot; Lieberman's
views, while not disproven, are not supported by the material
before us. For an analysis of Lieberman's "The Talmud of Caesarea,"
see Herman J. Blumberg, "Saul Lieberman on the Talmud of Caesarea
and Louis Ginzberg on Mishnah Tamid," in Jacob Neusner, ed.,
The Formation of the Babylonian Talmud (E.J. Brill, Leiden, 1970),
pp. 107-124.

THE MISHNAH IN TALMUDIC EXEGESIS:
OBSERVATIONS ON
TRACTATE MAASEROT OF THE TALMUD YERUSHALMI

Martin S. Jaffee
University of Virginia

A. *The Pretext of Interpretation*

The classical rabbinic literature of Late Antiquity is, with few exceptions,[1] self-consciously exegetical. Despite significant diversity in style and agenda, the great midrashic compilations, as well as the Tosefta and both Talmuds, are all extended commentaries on the twin canon of Rabbinism--the Hebrew Scriptures and the Mishnah. While bitter disputes may rage among modern scholarly circles about the way these sources are to be studied, why they are worthy of study and--needless to say--who is qualified by background and training to study them, all will agree that the texts at hand represent the efforts of their creators to explicate what they believed to be the word of God, revealed to Moses on Sinai and deposited as Written and Oral Torah in the hands of Israel.

To announce that rabbinic works are exegetical, therefore, can hardly be to inform anyone of an unrecognized state of affairs. To the contrary, I wish to direct attention to the significance of a fact that, precisely because it is so obvious, has ceased to be visible. My purpose is to transform the exegetical character of rabbinic literature from a fact of no special consequence into a question capable of bringing to light the remarkable work of interpretation pursued in these texts. Early rabbinic exegetical texts owe their existence to a "pre-text", the book of Scripture or the Mishnaic tractate that they are created to serve. This Scriptural or Mishnaic "pre-text" serves in striking ways also to promote a pretext. Not only does the Scriptural or Mishnaic text precede the commentary in time and stand above it in authority, it also serves as the ubiquitous filter through which the commentary's editors speak their own minds about fundamental matters. Thus the discourse of rabbinic exegesis constitutes itself in reference to the discourse of a primary text--Scripture or the Mishnah--the authority of which is grounded in the constitutive event of Sinai.

Before us, therefore, is a genuinely dialogical literature, a corpus of texts that quite literally "speak through" other texts more prestigious in origins. Midrash, tosefta, gemara--the classic genres of rabbinic literary discourse--all stake their claim to a hearing not on the special merits of those whose discussions are preserved therein, but rather on the merits of the texts in reference to which their words are intended to be understood. The pretext in this lies in the fact that in speaking through the "pre-text," rabbinic exegetes necessarily speak for it. They rewrite the authoritative "pre-text" through the pretext of interpretation. In rabbinism's vast project of rewriting Torah, therefore, we may discern not only an effort distinctively Judaic, but also a program most universally human. We trace in the rabbinic exegesis of Torah the human hunger for constructing a world upon immutable foundations of authority, and for forgetting most willfully that the world--of experience or of the text--is at bottom a human construction.[2]

This essay is an experiment in thinking through these observations and refining them in conversation with a small sample of rabbinic sources. It is in principle possible to use any and all early rabinic sources as the foundations of such a project. Nevertheless, certain considerations have governed my decision to begin with, and limit discussion to, a single text. I shall discuss in detail Tractate Maaserot ("Tithes") of the Talmud Yerushalmi ("The Palestinian Talmud"), a commentary on the Mishnah's tractate of the same name. Both works, as their titles announce, are substantially concerned to explain details of the Scriptural commandment, binding upon all Jews living in the Land of Israel, to remove tithes and other sanctified offerings from their seasonal harvests. Where necessary, I will explain some of the content of the Mishnah's discussion and the Talmud's commentary. For the most part, however, I discuss the content of the law only in order to highlight a more pressing question: How do the editors of Yerushalmi Maaserot create and sustain the reader's perception of communication between the text of Mishnah Maaserot and their own commentary? How, furthermore, do text and exegesis create a seamless conversation in which the firm distinction between text and commentary--between Torah and explication--looses all significance?

B. *The Generic Decision: The Mishnah as Law*

It is difficult, after eighteen centuries, to imagine the novelty of the Mishnah in its third-century Palestinian environment. Here is a text with little precedent in the Jewish world of Late Antiquity, conforming neither in form nor rhetoric to any of Israel's earlier legal or narrative traditions,[3] and exploiting as well few literary models available in the non-Israelite environment.[4] Those who might have chanced to see a copy of the Mishnah

or, as is more likely, would have heard portions of it recited by
disciples of rabbinic masters, would confront a text offering few
conventionally-recognizable signals that might guide the audience
in its efforts at interpretation.[5] While understanding the
Mishnah's language, the audience would nevertheless have been at
a loss to appropriate this text as a meaningful address to its own
situation and interests.

The fundamental task of the Mishnah's first proponents, therefore, would first of all have been to teach their audience how to
read the Mishnah as something else, as a work similar in genre and
meaning to others familiar to that audience. Only after appreciating the kind of meaning the Mishnah could be expected to convey
would the audience begin, with the help of qualified instruction,
to hear the text intelligently. E.D. Hirsch, the literary critic,
has discussed in some detail the crucial role of generic expectations in our capacity to interpret written and oral communications,
and it is useful to cite him at length in this context:

> Such expectations are always necessary to understanding,
> because only by virtue of them can the interpreter make
> sense of the words he experience[s] along the way. He
> entertains the notion that "this is a certain type of
> meaning", and his notion of the meaning as a whole
> grounds and helps determine his understanding of details...[6]
> It is essential to note that in most cases our expectations are not baffled and defeated. We [find] the
> types of meanings we expect to find, because what we
> [find] is in fact powerfully influenced by what we
> expect. All along the way we construe *this* meaning
> instead of *that* because *this* meaning belongs to the
> type of meaning we are interpreting while *that* does
> not. If we happen to encounter something which can
> only be interpreted as *that*, then we have to start all
> over and postulate another type of meaning altogether
> in which *that* will be at home. . . . Thus, while it is
> not accurate to say that an interpretation is helplessly
> dependent on the generic conception with which an interpreter happens to start, it is nonetheless true that his
> interpretation is dependent on the last, unrevised
> generic conception with which he starts. All understanding of verbal meaning is necessarily genre bound
> [author's italics].[7]

To return, then, to our point: if all understanding of verbal
meaning is genre-bound, then the Mishnah's early champions would
first have had to recommend that their audience interpret the text
within the framework of expectations appropriate to some familiar
genre. Now, the evidence of rabbinic literature,[8] which includes
among other things the description of the Mishnah as Revelation,[9]
suggests that the generic conception of the Mishnah promoted in
the early years of rabbinic proselytization was that of Torah, or
more specifically, law. Despite a substantial body of literary
evidence within the Mishnah itself suggesting that its editors

intended their work to be read as a series of discursive essays on the metaphysical foundations of law,[10] the Mishnah's early teachers choose to present the text as a kind of legal source-book. While not regarded as a normative code of law,[11] the Mishnah is nevertheless read as analogous to the legal portions of Scripture. Like these portions, it is construed as providing a series of prescriptions defining the content of personal and social behavior in areas deemed crucial to the public welfare of Israel.

This generic decision, the first traces of which are difficult to reconstruct, is nevertheless manifest in all strata and types of rabbinic literature, from the earliest halakhic midrashim to the Babylonian Talmud. I should like to focus, however, on how this conception of the Mishnah as a legal source informs the construction of the Talmud Yerushalmi in particular. The most important fact, of course, is the content of the Yerushalmi itself, which is devoted in great measure to exploring how the various statements of the Mishnah can be used to ground concrete social institutions of either the present-day or eschatological Israel. But even if we ignore for the moment the content of the Yerushalmi, its decision to interpret the Mishnah as a genre of legal literature is apparent in the very way that the Mishnah is presented to the reader by the Talmud. The Mishnah's paragraphs, sentences, and clauses are never presented to the reader as an essay, composed of complete units of thought leading to some overall conclusion in which each part contributes to the whole. Rather, any clause of the Mishnah can be interpreted as a distinct unit of thought in total isolation from its surrounding context in the Mishnah.[12] Insofar as the Talmud prevents the reader from construing the Mishnah's sentences as contributing to a cogent sequence of ideas out of which some larger unit of discourse is built, the Mishnah must be construed as a series of oracular utterances. Each such utterance gains whatever meaning it may have largely from the reader's expectation that here is some rule of action or statement of principle from which consequences of practical weight are to be deduced. Before the reader are not philosophical theorems, but concrete behavioral prescriptions.

The wholly typical case of Yerushalmi Maaserot can serve now as a means of making these general assertions more concrete. This commentary on the Mishnah's theory of tithing is, at least on superficial reading, a chaotic work. Composed of diverse sources, employing a wide variety of rhetorical conventions, and pursuing no single argument or set of problems, the commentary is rich in discordant literary voices competing with each other for the reader's attention. This immediate impression of literary chaos, however, conceals a most systematic conception of how the text of the Mishnah is to be presented for purposes of interpretation. Nowhere spelled out by the tractate's editors, this conception emerges from the concrete procedures by which every line of Mishnah Maaserot is mediated to the reader.

The tractate's method of presentation is to mount a sustained assault upon the literary coherence of the Mishnah, dismembering its text into discrete propositions that reach the reader only through the surrounding filter of the commentary's supplementary discourse. In this way Yerushalmi Maaserot deprives the Mishnah of the capacity to address the reader as an independent work. Such meaning as Mishnah Maaserot can have appears only when its textual shards are merged with the quite independent text of the commentary. Thus the commentary supplants the original text of Mishnah Maaserot by incorporating it into a new text, Yerushalmi Maaserot. In this new text, Mishnah Maaserot now participates only as one voice among many in the project of defining its own meaning. Its carefully-crafted units of thought, often extending to many paragraphs of sustained theoretical exploration,[13] must now be read as a series of isolated dicta, organized, to be sure, under the topical rubric of tithing regulations, but linked necessarily to the exemplary models of interpretation supplied by the Talmud's framing discussion. These bits and pieces of the Mishnah enjoy a relationship to each other only insofar as the Talmud itself chooses to bring them into conceptual correlation for purposes of its own. The result is a sustained line-by-line analysis of Mishnah Maaserot of a highly paradoxical character; for the more closely the Mishnah is inspected, the least likely is its own meaning to become clear.

Yerushalmi Maaserot, then, requires its reader to interpret each ruling of the Mishnah as if it were a single "word", having no necessary connection to the context (the paragraph, chapter or, indeed, tractate) in which it is uttered. As in a dictionary, in which lexical items are assigned conventional meanings in isolation from concrete speech-acts, each sentence of the Mishnah receives explanation in virtual independence of the documentary context of its original expression. Once Mishnah Maaserot is treated as a series of legal oracles, the Talmud's commentary--which contributes to these oracles a suggestive array of exegetical contexts--appears inevitable. In rabinic circles it becomes inconceivable to study Maaserot, or any other Mishnaic tractate, on its own terms. The Mishnah becomes inseparable from the exegesis appended to it, so that text and commentary become a literary and conceptual unity, a new text in which the independent outlines of the Mishnah are, for all practical purposes, obliterated.

C. *Strategies of Interpretation: Primary Exegetical Units and Their Functions*

The observations above, which focus on the significance of Yerushalmi's mode of presenting the Mishnah for analysis, may now be supplemented by a more detailed discussion of how such analysis proceeds. We turn, then, to a description of the Talmud's concrete acts of exegesis and explication. Here we may observe most clearly the Yerushalmi's creation of its dialogue with the text of Mishnah Maaserot, a dialogue that enables the "pre-text" of Mishnah Maaserot to be restated through the pretext of interpretation.

The Talmud's commentary on Mishnah Maaserot appears to have been constructed by means of three basic sorts of literary or editorial procedures. In various combinations these account for all pericopae in the tractate. They are: 1) the production of brief glosses on the Mishnah, which generally pursue a limited program of linguistic or logical clarification; 2) the construction of extended units of discourse (*sugyot*, sing.: *sugya*), which explore in detail issues deemed relevant to a given Mishnaic ruling or principle; 3) the sequential arrangement of a series of such glosses and extended *sugyot* for study with given pericopae of Mishnah Maaserot.[14] This final work of selection and arrangement naturally presupposes the others, and must be regarded as the act of tractate-construction itself, the final redaction of earlier pericopae deposited by means as yet unclear in the hands of the Yerushalmi's editors. In this context the Mishnah acquired whatever meaning it had to those for whom the Yerushalmi became the definitive context for the study of Oral Torah.

We focus initially on the relatively small number of simple glosses, which appear to have been formulated as aids to the study of Mishnah Maaserot at some point after the promulgation of the Mishnah but prior to the decision to produce a commentary on the order of Yerushalmi Maaserot. These are all freestanding pericopae that, unlike others of similar literary traits, have not been incorporated by later editors into fullscale *sugyot*. These glosses, only sixteen in number,[15] may be divided into two basic types on the basis of their literary characteristics.

A small proportion consist almost entirely of brief citations of other texts regarded as stemming from the Tannaim, the Sages of the Mishnah. Thus, in juxtaposition with a ruling of Mishnah Maaserot we may find a citation either of a text attested elsewhere in the extant Tannaitic collections or of a text attributed to the

Tannatic period but unknown in extant sources (i.e., *baraita*).
Such glosses serve two related purposes. First, the cited passage
explains, supplements, or even challenges the Mishnaic passage to
which it is joined. Second, these citations place the Mishnah's
ruling into a new continuum of tradition, making the point that
all Tannaitic statements--regardless of documentary context--are
in mutual converstation, discrete parts of a multi-documentary
super-text. Such glosses, in other words, initiate the procedure
of interpretating the Mishnah in terms of information that comes
from beyond the boundaries of a given tractate and its distinctive
concerns.

A representative example of such a gloss appears in Yerushalmi
Maaserot 2:6 (50a)[16], appended to Mishnah Maaserot 2:7. In the
Mishnah, first of all, we read:

- A. One who hires a worker to harvest figs for him--[if the worker] said to him, "On condition that I eat figs", he eats [during the harvest] and is exempt [from tithing].
- B. [If the worker] said to him, "On condition that I and my son eat", or ["On condition] that my son shall eat as [part of] my pay", he eats [during the harvest] and is exempt, while his son eats, but is required [to tithe].
- C. [If he said,] "On condition that I eat both during and after the harvest"--during the harvest he eats and is exempt, while after the harvest he eats, but is required [to tithe],
- D. for [if he eats after the harvest] he is granted no eating privileges by the Torah.
- E. This is the general principle: One who is granted eating privileges by the Torah is exempt [from tithing what he eats], while one who is granted no eating privileges by the Torah is required [to tithe what he eats].

Before we explain the Mishnaic pericopae, let us first turn to the
Yerushalmi's gloss of stich B above. The gloss is the fifth unit
in a series of six independent exegetical pericopae redacted for
circulation with M. 2:7. It states, quite simply:

- A. On the basis of this ruling [at M. 2:7B] they said [at M. Baba Meṣia 7:6]:
- B. 1. A man arbitrates [cash compensation for refraining from eating during his labor] on behalf of himself, on behalf of his son or daughter [if they are] of age, and on behalf of his manservant or maidservant [if they are] of age, and on behalf of his wife--for they have [mature] understanding [and will abide by his agreement to refrain from eating during their work in return for cash].
  2. But he does not arbitrate on behalf of his son or daughter [if they are] minors, or on behalf of his manservant or maidservant [if they are] minors, or on behalf of his beast--for they do not have [mature] understanding.

In order to appreciate the Yerushalmi's gloss, it is necessary
first of all to understand the role of M. 2:7B in articulating
its pericope's thesis that workers have, on the basis of Scriptural
law, the right to eat untithed produce which they are hired to

harvest. At issue for M. 2:7 as a whole is whether the worker's stipulation of a contract for the privilege of eating permits us to regard what he eats as a purchase, received in exchange for his labor. If so, he should tithe whatever he eats, for all purchases are liable to the removal of tithes (M. 2:5). M. 2:7A, for its part, argues that the contractual relationship is voided in the case of the worker because he has a prior right to eat, (M. 2:7E and M. Baba Meṣia 7:2) which supercedes the terms of his present contract. M. 2:7B now introduces an important qualification. While the worker's stipulation is voided with regard to his own eating, it remains in force regarding his son, who does no work and therefore does not enjoy the benefits explained at M. 2:7E.

The Yerushalmi's response to M. 2:7B is a complex one, despite its literary simplicity. The citation of M. Baba Meṣia 7:6 at Y. 2:6B makes two points. First, the argument that M. Baba Mesia 7:6 is consequence of M. 2:7B, requires us to interpret the latter solely in reference to a son who is a minor. As such, he is not bound by his father's contracts, for he is incapable of understanding its terms. For this reason alone, and not because of his failure to work, he must tithe what he eats of all produce received in exchange for his father's labor. Had the son been of age, naturally, he would have eaten untithed produce on the strength of his father's prior privilege. Contrary to the sense of M. 2:7B in its documentary context, but in accord with the view of M. Baba Meṣia 7:6, we are now given to understand that a worker's adult dependents do in fact share his privileges with regard to tithe-free eating. This simple gloss, by forcing us to read entirely independent Mishnaic pericopae in mutual conversation, has transformed the point of Mishnah Maaserot's ruling. A statement about the consequences of purchasing produce with the labor of another has now become a ruling about the distinction between the legal status of minors and adults.

The capacity of relatively simple glosses to restructure our reading of a given Mishnaic ruling is also apparent in the second type of gloss common in Yerushalmi Maaserot. Differing from the above primarily in literary style and source of authority, it exhibits as well a somewhat different relationship to the Mishnaic pericopae it serves. I refer to such glosses simply as "amoraic", for they make no effort to copy tannaitic literary forms and frequently cite a third or fourth-century master as their source. Such amoraic glosses offer brief textual elucidations of the Mishnah, focusing upon the identification of obscure realia, the meaning of difficult terms and ambiguous clauses, or the explication of logical principles.[17] As in the case of the tannaitic glosses, these contributions also bring to the Mishnah a range of extra-documentary facts and information.

By way of example, we point to the final unit of Y. 2:6, which immediately follows the gloss we have just examined. Addressed now is the general principle of the worker's privilege cited above in the Mishnah at M. 2:7E. The text reads:

> A. [At M. 2:7E] should it not rather say that one who is granted eating privileges by the Torah should be required to tithe [insofar as the produce is now regarded as the worker's property, to dispose of as he wishes]?[18]
> B. Said R. Yonah: "[In addition to the privilege of eating his employer's produce while at work] the Torah exempted him [as well from the requirement to remove tithes]."
> C. As it is written in Scripture: "When thou comest into thy neighbor's vineyard, then thou mayest eat grapes, as thou will, at thine own pleasure" (Deut. 23:24).

A is perplexed by an apparent contradiction between the principle of M. 2:7E, which exempts the worker from tithing produce eaten on the job, and the general thesis of Mishnah Maaserot that produce becomes liable to tithing as soon as a person appropriates it as his own (M. 1:5-8, M. 2:1-2, M. 2:5, M. 3:5, M. 4:1, M. 5:1-2). Why, then, should the worker at M. 2:7, who in effect becomes the owner of whatever he eats while at work, be exempt from tithing that produce? Yonah's response, B, asserts that the Torah's extension to the worker of eating privileges--precisely because this is a privilege--does not transform the worker into the owner of the produce. Accordingly, he need not tithe what he eats since, strictly speaking, it is not his. As a gift, in other words, it need not be tithed (see M. Bekhorot 8:10). C, which appears only in MS. Sirillo of the Yerushalmi, supplies the Scriptural proof-text presumed to ground Yonah's view. The point, however, is fully made by Yonah, whether or not we accept C as a genuine textual variant.

The gloss, like our tannaitic example, seems designed to reveal the complexity of an apparently straightforward passage of the Mishnah. Where before, however, the result of the gloss was to redefine the issue addressed by the Mishnah, here the result is rather to reinforce what is at any rate perfectly obvious on the basis of the Mishnah itself. Can there, indeed, be reasonable doubt that M. 2:7E is precisely intended to stress that whatever is eaten by M. 2:7A-C's laborer is exempt from tithing on the grounds that it is a gift, a privileged item? I think not. The attempt to raise such doubt, therefore, requires explanation. In my view, this gloss reflects and reinforces a frame of mind characteristic of Yerushalmi Maaserot as a whole. That is, the

Mishnah within its own limits is impenetrable. It requires the interpolation of the Talmud's exegetical contribution. It requires, in this particular case, a Yonah to tell us what is perfectly obvious from the start. The resolution of any *crux interpretum* in the Mishnah, that is, lies beyond the boundaries of the immediate text, in a continuum of theory that only the Talmud can provide.

We have seen that both tannaitic and amoraic glosses function in a manner analagous in some respects to explanatory notes on a literary classic. That is, they supply facts necessary for grasping the sense of the work, point out problems of interpretation (at times gratuitously), and reconcile these in light of extra-textual information. If Yerushalmi Maaserot were composed entirely of such glosses it could justifiably be regarded as a kind of annotative commentary on the Mishnah, constructed primarily for clarifying the text and suggesting the types of questions and problems that might be addressed to it. In fact, the percentage of Yerushalmi Maaserot consisting of such unadorned materials is quite small, only sixteen of the tractate's 124 units of discourse. This suggests that annotation as such, while perhaps important at some point in the history of rabbinic exegesis of the Mishnah, is peripheral to the goals of the present commentary. For the most part, as I have said, the simple glosses preserved in Yerushalmi Maaserot have lost whatever literary independence they may once have enjoyed, and have instead been incorporated into ambitious *sugyot* of impressive literary complexity and conceptual sophistication. As I shall point out in detail momentarily, the character of this tractate's *sugyot* is most impressive evidence that the goal of producing the commentary before us can hardly be described as *explication de texte*. Rather, the primary result of the Yerushalmi's commentary is to draw attention from the Mishnah and to focus instead upon the complex internal dialogue generated by the commentary's own materials. This commentary on the Mishnah, then, is in great measure no explanation of the Mishnah at all, but rather an extended exploration of a method by which the Mishnah's text may be manipulated to yield a potentially endless set of logical permutations.

Again, some examples will help explain. One of the unusual characteristics of Yerushalmi Maaserot is that a full 40.7% of this commentary is composed of *sugyot* that are either entirely intelligible without reference to a given pericope of Mishnah Maaserot, address issues of little relevance to those of the Mishnah, or make no allusion to the Mishnah in the course of their own discussions.[19] The radical autonomy of these *sugyot* from the Mishnaic pericopae with which they are redacted indicates that they originate in some context and for some purpose other than the creation of a commentary on Mishnah Maaserot. Thus, within this commentary on the Mishnah, we find much material that was not at first intended to function as Mishnah-exegesis. In order to appreciate how the redactors of our tractate have enlisted such materials for their own purposes--and in order to clarify those purposes--we may refer to a typical example from Y. 2:7 (50a), the fifth in a series of six *sugyot* redacted with Mishnah Maaserot 2:8.

Continuing in its own fashion M. 2:7's interest in the produce eaten by laborers, the first section of M. 2:8 states:

    A. [If the worker] was engaged with cooking-figs, he shall not eat fine figs, [and if he was engaged] with fine figs, he shall not eat cooking-figs.
    B. Yet, he [may] restrain himself [from eating altogether] until he reaches the area [in which] the high-quality [figs grow], and [then he may] eat.

The point, of course, is that the privilege of the laborer to eat his employer's produce extends only to the precise type of produce with which he is at the moment engaged. In the context of M. 2:7-8, the ruling offers an important qualification of M. 2:7E, which on its own might suggest that the worker is entitled to any produce owned by the employer.

The Mishnah's concern to prevent the worker from overstepping his rights is reflected as well in the Yerushalmi, but the *sugya* itself is clearly formulated with no interest either in M. 2:8A-B or in the contextual relationship of the latter to M. 2:7E. Rather, the Talmud observes:

    A. It is taught: A man may arrange with his workers that they may eat one fig and lay nine out to dry [in order to protect his profit].[20]
    B. There are teachers who teach it as follows: They lay nine out to dry and eat one.
    C. [With regard to A] it is quite appropriate [to rule that] they eat one and lay nine out to dry [for in this way the workers are clearly in the employ of the householder when they eat].
    D. [If so, what is added at B, which holds that] they lay nine out to dry and [afterwards] eat one?
    E. Said R. Abin: "The point is that you shall not[21] say, 'It is as though [he ate the fig] after the completion of his work'[22] such that he is culpable [for taking what is not rightfully his]."

Despite the general thematic congruence of M. 2:8A-B and this *sugya*, both of which deal with the possibility of the worker exploiting his employer, there is little intrinsic connection between text and commentary. Rather, the Yerushalmi supplies at *A-B* a pair of conflicting rulings of tannaitic vintage, and at *C-D+E* spells out the implications--all in total isolation from M. 2:8. Sbin's point at *E* is that our primary criterion for choosing between *A* and *B* must be the protection of the worker from the possibility of being accused by his employer of theft. In this view, *B* is the preferable ruling, for it permits the worker to eat only after he has actually begun his labor, at which point he can not be accused of eating what is not yet his due.

How, then, does this *sugya* constitute an exegesis of M. 2:8? The answer lies in Abin's explanation of Y. 2:7*B*, which stresses that at issue in legislation involving apparent restrictions upon the worker's eating privileges is, in fact, the protection of the worker from the employer, rather than the protection of the employer's profits. This point is quite relevant to M. 2:8A-B which, like Y. 2:7*B*, appears to restrict the worker's privilege (M. 2:8A), but actually has his interests in mind (M. 2:8B). This Mishnah's gloss, then, is designed to display the harmony of principle and perspective linking discussions unrelated by any literary criterion; to reveal a new horizon within which to interpret a superficially simple statement of law.

This example of how materials formed apart from explicit interest in Mishnah Maaserot are made to address its rulings yields an important functional principle of the autonomous *sugyot* in Yerushalmi Maaserot. The redactional strategy is a challenge to the Talmud's reader to construct the conceptual bridge by which the Mishnah's text and its talmudic context can be linked into a single literary and conceptual continuum. The frequency with which the reader of Yerushalmi Maaserot is required to perform this operation--in fourty of the tractate's 108 extended *sugyot*--testifies that the Mishnah itself can hardly be the primary focus of the tractate's editor. Rather, the *sugya*, superimposed as it is upon the Mishnaic text, and defining the parameters of the latter's meaning, presents itself as the primary problem of interpretation--the riddle that must be solved before Mishnah and *sugya* together resolve themselves into a single text pursuing a single line of thought. The Mishnaic text--the "pre-text" of the *sugya*--legitimates by its background presence the quite independent inquiry in which the Mishnah is submerged as an independent work.

This last point, generated by materials framed independently of Mishnah-exegesis, is strengthened by the evidence of the *sugyot* of Yerushalmi Maaserot--sixty-four in number--that are clearly dependent upon the Mishnaic passages to which they are appended.[23] Insofar as these spell out some clear issue arising from Mishnah

Maaserot itself, one would expect them to serve as evidence of the Talmud's interest in textual explication. The problem, however, is that even here the evidence for a sustained interest in the Mishnah as such is ambiguous at best. Discussions of any length that begin in some issue directly relevant to the Mishnah's language and topic are routinely expanded by a series of fresh discussions generated not by the Mishnah itself, but rather by issues located within the elements of the *sugya's* own discourse. Indeed, insofar as there are few *sugyot* of any length that fail to move beyond the task of Mishnaic analysis *per ce*, it appears that the *sugya* in its most complex and articulate form is designed as an exegesis of itself rather than of the Mishnaic text it is created to serve.

By way of example, we may turn to a relatively succinct discussion generated by Mishnah Maaserot 1:4. The Mishnaic pericope concludes a list, begun at M. 1:2, of criteria by which we determine that various kinds of produce have become ripe enough to be edible. In Mishnah Maaserot's view, such produce is now subject to the law of tithes. That is, it has formally entered the tithing system, and may be consumed in an untithed condition *only* as a random snack, but not as a formal meal.[24] The portion of M. 1:4 of interest to the Yerushalmi's *sugya* states:

    A. Apples and citrons are subject [to the law of tithes whether they are] large or small.
    B. R. Simeon exempts citrons which are immature.

Simeon disputes A's claim that citrons at an early stage of their development share with apples the capacity to serve as food. In Simeon's view, immature citrons are inedible, and thus are exempt from the law of tites, which holds that produce becomes subject to the law only when it has reached the point of edibility (M. 1:2). Anyone desiring to make a meal of immature citrons--for whatever peculiar reason--is therefore free to do so without removing tithes.

Let us see now to what extent Y. 1:4 (49a)--the third of four *sugyot* responding to M. 1:4 in its entirety--exploits Simeon's principle in ways certainly unimagined by the formulator of M. 1:4's dispute:

    A. 1. A citron which has begun to ripen [prior to maturity]--
        2. R. Aqiba says, "It is not [yet regarded as a fully viable] fruit [and so may not be waved with the *lulab* during the Feast of Sukkoth]."
        3. And Sages say, "It is [already regarded as a fully viable] fruit [and may indeed be waved with the *lulab*]."
    B. R. Ila, R. Yose in the name of R. Leazar: "The ruling of Simeon [who at M. 1:4B, exempts immature citrons from the law of tithes,] accords with the principle of R. Aqiba, his Master. Just as R. Aqiba held that the early-ripening citron is not yet regarded as a fully viable fruit [and

as such is ineligible for ritual use], so R. Simeon holds
that the immature citron is not regarded as a fully viable
fruit [and as such is exempt from the law of tithes]."
C. Said R. Yose: "All citrons suitable for ritual use with
the *lulab* are subject to the law of tithes [for in order
to qualify for the former, a citron must be ripe, a condition which qualifies it as well for use in tithing].
And all citrons which are not suitable for ritual use with
the *lulab* are not subject to the law of tithes [for unripe
citrons are exempt from the law]."
D. They retorted: "What about speckled citrons, or those
shaped unnaturally in a mold, or those artificially
rounded? Surely any of these is ineligible for ritual use
with the *lulab* [for it is not a perfect natural specimin,]
yet all are subject to the law of tithes [insofar as they
are edible]."
E. It follows from the foregoing that R. Simeon would concur
with R. Aqiba [who at A.2 seems to suggest that a citron
which is exempt from the law of tithes is also ineligible
for ritual use, but] R. Aqiba will not concur with R.
Simeon [who at M. 1:4B seems to hold that a citron which
is ineligible for ritual use need also be exempt from
tithing].
F. R. Simeon would concur with R. Aqiba, for it is written
in Scripture: "And ye shall take you on the first day
the fruit of goodly trees . . ." (Lev.23:40)--yet an early-
ripening citron is not fruit [in the full sense of the
term, and so cannot be regarded as subject to the law of
tithes either].
G. R. Aqiba would not concur with R. Simeon [on the basis of
the following]: "What about speckled citrons, or those
shaped unnaturally in a mold, or those artificially
rounded? Surely, any of these is ineligible for ritual
use with the *lulab*, yet all are subject to the law of
tithes."[25]

We may best appreciate this *sugya's* richness by attending to
the way in which its various elements are related to each other.
The primary unit is at *A-B*, with *B* establishing the relevance of
the independent dispute at *A* to Simeon's ruling at M. 1:4B. The
overall point, apparently, is that the principles of tithing coin-
cide with those regulating the ritual of Sukkot in that, in both
areas, the maturity of the citron determines whether it may be used
in the fulfillment of a commandment, i.e., to tithe or to wave.
Secondarily, we learn that this common principle is linked histor-
ically to Aqiba, whose ruling regarding the ritual disqualification
of early-ripening citrons (*A*.2) is interpreted by his disciple,
Simeon, as being applicable to the law of tithes. At this point,
then, the Yerushalmi provides us with a fine amplification of
M. 1:4B, demonstrating the relevance of Simeon's view to other
questions of law and linking the authority of that view to the
great Aqiba himself. The agendum, overall, is only slightly more
ambitiousthan those typical of tannaitic or amoraic glosses.

Matters take a sudden turn, however, at *C-D*. While it is
unclear whether Yose, *C*, responds directly to *A-B* or whether his

statement is entirely autonomous in formulation, he clearly states in his terms the inevitable conclusion to be drawn from B. D, however, changes our whole picture. Responding to C alone, in points out decisively that there need be no necessary correlation between the eligibility of a citron for ritual purposes and its suitability for use as tithes. Thus, C-D as a unit must be read as a rejection of B. At a stroke, then, we have moved from B's correlation of tannaitic texts--M. 1:4B and A--to an exploration of a philosophical issue hardly explicit in either--namely, do we regard edibility as necessary to the citron's inclusion in the class of "fruit", or is edibility an accidental quality, which may or may not be present? Only on the basis of the former view can there be any correlation between Aqiba and Simeon, for then the immature citron's lack of edibility would disqualify it as a member of its class (A.2). If we take the latter view, however, Aqiba's disqualification of the citron must be interpreted as being grounded in the insufficient size or imperfect shape of the fruit at its early period of growth, but not in any considerations of flavor. That is, the citron is unacceptable for ritual use on Sukkot because it does not look like a perfect member of its species. In this case, of course, there can be no correlation between Aqiba's ruling and that of Simeon, for each has different criteria in mind for excluding the immature or early-ripening citron from the scope of the relevant law.

This brings us to the decisive point of the *sugya*, stich E, which certainly knows A-B + C-D as a completed pericope. E employs the insight of D to redraw the lines of intellectual filiation suggested at B. While Simeon might wish to claim Aqiban warrant for his view, on the grounds that immature citrons are both inedible and poorly formed, Aqiba would deny that Simeon's view is in any way a genuine development of his own, for as D points out, Aqiba has no real concern for the edibility of the citron in the first place. Thus E, carrying forward the argument of D, challenges the original thesis of B, that Simeon and Aqiba share a common principle applicable to quite separate domains of law. In light of E, then, the conclusions of B are overturned. F-G, a useful afterthought, links E to relevant proof-texts--Lev. 23:40, on the one hand, and stich D itself, on the other. Scripture and an internal element of the *sugya* thus function here as equal authorities for E's revision of A-B's original point.

This *sugya* displays most explicity the fundamentally self-referential character of Yerushalmi Maaserot's exegetical discourse. Generated, to be sure, by A-B's genuine explication of M. 1:4B,

the discussion rapidly develops into an exercise in the analysis
of its own propositions--*C-D* challenging *A-B*, *E* drawing out the
implications of *C-D*, and *F-G* summing up the results of *E*. By the
conclusion of the exegesis, the reader is drawn entirely out of the
context of Simeon's original ruling. But, as I have tried to show,
the reader addressed by the Yerushalmi is hardly expected to display such a narrow frame of exegetical reference in the first place.
Rather, he is expected to want to know precisely what Y. 1:4
provides--a demonstration of the unsuspected richness of a given
Mishnaic utterance, and an example of how it may be woven into a
tapestry of other legal ideas. The *sugya*, perfecting methods
implicit in the simplest of the tractate's glosses, is itself the
thought-experiment in which the student learns to master the art of
interpretation, to weave, out of the Mishnah's threads, his own
cloth.

D. *Yerushalmi Maaserot as a Work of Interpretation*

It will be useful, in conclusion, to recall the questions that
have generated this discussion, and to restate the ways in which
the above analyses provide a set of preliminary answers. At issue
throughout is the problem of describing rabbinic exegesis so that
its all-too-familiar characteristics can be seen in a new way. I
have tried, therefore, to estrange the reader from what is familiar
in rabbinic exegesis by questioning whether, in fact, it is at all
exegetical and by asking how, indeed, it explains the texts it
serves. The problem, quite simply, has been to describe the kinds
of comments that, in the view of rabbinic editors, count as
explanation.

In order to discipline our inquiry into the problem, I have
suggested a kind of experiment. Might we imagine that the extensive literature of rabbinic exegesis is a vast project of subversion--
a way of reverently ascribing great authority to a text while, at
the same time, putting that authority to work in the interest of
those who, through the act of interpretation, appear to submit?
Out of this experimental question has emerged the notion that
rabbinic exegesis may be understood as a pretext that, in light of
the sacred purpose it serves, can hardly have been visible even
to its perpetrators. In this pretext of interpretation, the editors
of rabbinic commentaries to Scripture or the Mishnah acquire for
their own work the authority conceded in their world to the "pre-
text" against which their exegesis is mounted in the first place.
By means of explanation the aura of Scripture or the Mishnah comes
to rest as well upon the vehicle of explanation, the commentary.

To test this imagined state of affairs against the data of rabbinic texts I have chosen the specific case of the Talmud Yerushalmi's halakhic commentary on the Mishnah's tractate about tithing. Tractate Maaserot, as I have argued, is rich in evidence that is illumined by the model of "exegetical pretext." Section B of this essay shows how, in the first place, Yerushalmi Maaserot dismembers the text of Mishnah Maaserot so that the latter may convey meaning only within the framework established by the commentary itself. Thus the student, dependent entirely upon the commentary for access to the Mishnah, grants to the Talmud's exegetical pericopae (rather than his own powers of analysis) the sole authority to speak on behalf of the interpreted text. Second, as section C demonstrates in detail, the literary form and exegetical strategies of the commentary overwhelm by their complexity the Mishnaic text to which the Talmud's 124 distinct glosses and *sugyot* are keyed. The bulk of the reader's energy, therefore, must be devoted to explicating the commentary itself rather than the Mishnaic text it ostensibly serves. These two procedures, in combination, obscure the Mishnah as a text in its own right, and permit it to merge in the reader's understanding with the commentary. Thus Mishnah Maaserot and its commentary become a new text, studied as a primary source of the Torah of tithing. In this Torah, the Mishnah--largely ignored as a coherent theory of its own topic--nevertheless legitimates by its very presence the now-definitive Torah of interpretation.

In this exegetical pretext, by which the authority of Revelation is extended beyond the literary confines of the Mishnah to its talmudic context, I claim to locate processes both seminal to rabbinic Judaism and illuminating of the function of the "sacred" text in religious communities. Within the interpretive framework of the history of rabbinic Judaism, the Yerushalmi's appropriation of the Mishnah is a model of the process of Oral Torah, defining the primary means by which rabbinic Judaism sustains its unshakeable conviction of continuity with the ancient convenant-history of Israel. The canon of Oral Torah, opened by the Mishnah's complement to the Written Torah of Moses, is never again closed. As the evidence of Yerushalmi Maaserot suggests, each new interpretation of Oral Torah itself can enter the Torah canon, serving in time as yet a new "pre-text" through which the entire meaning of the Torah is restated and Israel's response redefined. The Yerushalmi's appropriation of the Mishnah, then, prefigures its own fate at the hands of later exegetes, who will mine its *sugyot* as sources for their own project of legal amplification and codification.

The fate of the Mishnah is the Yerushalmi's exegesis speaks not only about the history of rabbinic Judaism. It illumines as well the nature and destiny of all texts that enjoy the authority of Revelation and to which the epithet "sacred" is applied. In the community of faith, where the text serves as the model and source of redeemed existence, the "sacred" text suffers the high price of reverence and devotion. Its fate--as the word of God or of the gods--is to be mis-read and subverted, torn apart and reconstructed, so that the power it represents can remain a force for the shaping of life in the world.[26]

FOOTNOTES

[1] The most important of these is the diverse literature of heavenly ascent referred to collectively as the "merkabah" literature, however, despite its general claim to stem from reflections on the first chapter of Ezekiel, rarely employs exegetical formats. It belongs generically to the rich visionary and apocalyptic traditions, familiar from Late Antiquity, in which Scriptural sources play an important role in the description of the Heavenly World. Use of such sources, however, is not properly exegetical. Useful attempts at classifying this literature from a generic perspective may be found in Anthony J. Saldarini, "Apocalypses and 'Apocalyptic' in Rabbinic Literature and Mysticism", in John J. Collins, ed., *Semeia 14: Apocalypse--The Morphology of a Genre* (Chico, 1979), pp. 187-205, and Ithamar Gruenewald, *Apocalyptic and Merkabah Mysticism* (Leiden, 1980), pp. 127-234.

[2] This postulate of the discipline of Religious Studies, classically argued in sociological terms by Peter Berger, *The Sacred Canopy* (Garden City, NY, 1967), has for some time now made its mark among literary critics as well in their efforts to define the nature of the literary text and the modes of its interpretation. See, for example, the overview provided by Frank Lentricchia, *After the New Criticism* (Chicago, 1980).

[3] Perhaps the closest analogies to the Mishnah may be found in the esoteric library at Qumran, in which collections of sectarian rules are preserved. Unlike the Mishnah, however, these lists of rules are self-consciously "antiquarian", employing Scriptural style in an effort to legitimate their authority. See Lawrence H. Schiffman, *The Halakhah at Qumran* (Leiden, 1975) for discussion of the main texts, and--more recently--Ze'ev W. Falk, "The Temple Scroll and the Codification of Jewish Law", in *The Jewish Law Annual* II (Leiden, 1979), pp. 33-44.

[4] In light of the extensive research of such figures as Boaz Cohen, David Daube, Menahem Elon, Asher Gulak, Bernard Jackson and Saul Lieberman, there can be no doubt that the themes, principles and thought-forms of the Mishnah owe much to Roman legal traditions. It is equally clear, however--despite the fragmentary form in which the Roman texts have been preserved--that the Mishnah's literary forms and distinctive wedding of literary style and content have few analogues in contemporary Roman legal literature. See, for example, the extensive discussion of the forms and transmission of late-Classical Roman Codes and Digests in Fritz Schulz, *Roman Legal Science* (Oxford, 1946), pp. 141-261. Compare this with the literary description of the Mishnah in Jacob Neusner, "Redaction, Formulation and Form: The Case of the Mishnah", in *Idem., Method and Meaning in Ancient Judaism*, Second Series (Chico, 1981), pp. 35-44.

[5] The past ten or fifteen years have witnessed a proliferation of studies, from a variety of perspectives, on the role of textual conventions in enabling the reader to construe meaning. Useful collections of essays by important contributors are those of Susan R. Suleiman and Inge Crossman, eds., *The Reader in the Text: Essays on Audience and Interpretation* (Princeton, 1980) and Jane P. Tompkins, ed., *Reader-Response Criticism: From Formalism to Post-Structuralism* (Baltimore/London, 1980).

[6] E.D. Hirsch, Jr., *Validity in Interpretation* (New Haven/London, 1967), p. 72.

[7] *Ibid.*, p. 76.

[8] See Baruch M. Bokser, *Post Mishnaic Judaism in Transition: Samuel on Berachot and the Beginnings of Gemara* (Chico, 1980), for discussion of the earliest layers of Talmudic exegesis of the Mishnah. Bokser shows that the mid-third century leaders such as Samuel had defined the basic parameters within which the Mishnah would henceforth be interpreted.

[9] See, for example, Yerushalmi Pe'ah 2:6 (17a): "Said R. Zeira in the name of R. Yohanan: '. . . Lo, many legal directives (*hlkwt*) were stated to Moses on Sinai, and all of them are embedded in the Mishnah'".

[10] This view of the Mishnah is, of course, the discovery of Jacob Neusner. For the classic statement, see "Form and Meaning: The Mishnah's System and The Mishnah's Language", in *Idem., Method and Meaning in Ancient Judaism* (Missoula, 1979), pp. 155-181.

[11] See David Weiss Halivni, "The Reception Accorded to Rabbi Judah's Mishnah", in E.P. Sanders, ed. (with A.I. Baumgarten and Alan Mendelson), *Jewish and Christian Self-Definition: Volume Two, Aspects of Judaism in the Greco-Roman Period* (Philadelphia, 1981), pp. 204-213. Cf. M. Chigier, "Codification of Jewish Law", in *The Jewish Law Annual* II (Leiden, 1979), p. 7.

[12] The extent to which the Mishnah itself may encourage such a reading has been explored most convincingly by William S. Green, "Story Telling and Holy Man: The Case of Ancient Judaism", in Jacob Neusner, *Take Judaism, For Example: Studies Toward the Comparison of Religions* (Chicago, 1983), pp. 29-43. Indeed, parataxis eventually becomes the dominant literary trait of all the exegetical literature of Rabbinism, legal or otherwise.

[13] See Martin S. Jaffee, *Mishnah's Theology of Tithing: A Study of Tractate Maaserot* (Chico, 1981), pp. 6-22.

[14] In this particular trait, the Yerushalmi is strikingly similar to the lemmatic commentaries popularly among contemporary Roman jurists. Schulz, *op. cit.*, p. 183, describes these as follows:
> The text commented on and the commentary are separate works, written on separate rolls, and the reader of the commentary is informed of what particular passage of the text is being commented on by means of lemmata, that is to say by words of the text being used as headings or captions. The lemma may be the passage in question or its initial words, and it is made easy to find by being written outside the text . . . or by symbols or special spacing and the like. Then follows the commentary.

Certainly all extant MSS. of the Yerushalmi employ the lemmatic method described by Schulz, although MS. Leiden does indeed transcribe a text of the Mishnah at the head of each chapter.

[15] I have listed these in ns. 14-15 of the introduction to Martin S. Jaffee, *The Talmud of the Land of Israel, VII: Maaserot* (Chicago, forthcoming).

[16] All passages of Yerushalmi Maaserot translated here follow MS. Leiden unless otherwise specified. The citational system follows the pagination of ed. Venice.

[17] This program is nearly identical with that identified by Bokser as informing the work of Samuel. See Bokser, *op. cit.*, pp. 283-293.

[18] My interpretation follows that of *Penei Moshe* (M. Margoliot).

[19] These *sugyot* are listed in n. 18 of the introduction to the work cited in n. 15 above.

[20] At stichs *A* and *C* I follow the emendations of Z.W. Rabinowitz, *Sha^{c}arei Torat Eretz Yisrael* (Jerusalem, 1940), p. 107. See also Solomon Sirillio, "Commentary" and Elijah Gaon, "Emendations" in J. Dinklas, *Massekhet Ma^{c}aserot min Talmud Yerushalmi* (Jerusalem, 1953).

[21] *sl' twmr:* so MSS. Vatican and British Museum. MS. Leiden has been emended to conform to this reading.

[22] ^{c}*y^{c}sh kl'ḥr gmr ml'kh:* so MS. Leiden. Cf. MS. Vatican: *y^{c}sh kl 'ḥt gmr ml'kh*, and the comments of Sirillo.

[23] These *sugyot* are listed in n. 17 of the introduction to the work cited in n. 15.

[24] See Martin S. Jaffee, *Mishnah's Theology of Tithing*, pp. 3ff.

[25] This unit in its entirety is the sole contribution of Yerushalmi Sukkot 3:7 (53d) to M. Suk. 3:7. In light of its assumption that M. Maaserot 1:4 lies before the reader, I view the whole as having been constructed for use with M. 1:4 and thereafter used as well in conjunction with M. Suk. 3:7.

[26] My understanding of the nature of "sacred" texts is shaped in large measure by the essay of Jonathan Z. Smith, "Sacred Persistence: Towards a Redescription of Canon", in William S. Green, ed., *Approaches to Ancient Judaism: Theory and Practice* (Missoula, 1978), pp. 11-28, and recently anthologized in Jonathan Z. Smith, *Imagining Religion: From Babylon to Jonestown* (Chicago, 1982), pp. 36-52.

HISTORY AND IDEOLOGY IN TALMUDIC NARRATIVE

Robert Goldenberg

State University of New York, Stony Brook

I

A number of stories in Talmudic literature suggest that the "Hillelite" dynasty[1] experienced considerable difficulty in the decades after the year 70 before its hold on the Patriarchate was secure. Both Talmuds report that Gamaliel II, the first post-70 representative of the line, was temporarily removed from his position, and the Babylonian Talmud[2] relates that his son and eventual successor Simeon[3] barely escaped a conspiracy aimed at unseating him as well. Only Simeon's son Judah seems to have established his own position and that of his family beyond all challenge;[4] at least no such stories are told about him or any of his successors.

Narratives of this sort have usually been studied in connection with the events they purport to describe, normally with a view to determining how accurately they report those happenings.[5] Such typical adjectives as "reliable" or "authentic," and the contrary refusal to use them in certain cases, all reflect such an aim. The same can be said of fancier descriptive phrases such as "narrative improvement," which suggests that parts of a story were just made up, or "historical kernel," which insists that other parts were not.

Such an aim is understandable, and indeed the effort to make such distinctions is an indispensable part of the historian's task. Still, the approach just described does not always take account of the fact that even fabrication is an activity that occurs within history. Even a story that was "just made up" reflects historical reality, but the reality is that of the teller, not the subject of the tale. In what follows, therefore, I wish to re-examine the Talmudic narratives already mentioned, concentrating this time precisely on those aspects of the stories that were "just made up"; I wish to uncover the evidence that they were invented, and to figure out what the inventors had in mind. To be sure, I think these narratives do indeed have a "historical kernel," but for now that kernel does not interest me. I wish instead to examine these stories as ideological propaganda.

II

I have elsewhere analyzed the Gamaliel-story in some detail,[6] and it will suffice here to review certain salient points. The Jerusalem Talmud[7] tells the story as follows:[8] One day Gamaliel finds out that Joshua b. Hananiah and he have answered a certain student's question in contradiction to one another. He seizes the next opportunity to humiliate Joshua before the entire rabbinic conclave, but the others, having witnessed Gamaliel's wrath once too often, remove him and appoint Eleazar b. Azariah in his place.[9] The rabbis are described as quoting Nahum 3:19 (*For upon whom has not come your unceasing evil?*), and the rest of the story confirms that they feel they are all Gamaliel's victims; he has at one time or another offended each of them. Gamaliel, naturally anxious to recover his office, adopts a two-step strategy: he goes and apologizes to each member of the conclave, but he also circulates a message ("A sprinkler, son of a sprinkler--should sprinkle. . . .") the meaning of which is clear--he and only he has a hereditary right to his office; those who cannot match his claim have no right to question his manner of filling it. The strategy works; Gamaliel is restored to his office, and Eleazar b. Azariah is demoted to the post of Av Bet Din.

The Babylonian Talmud[10] begins its version of the story similarly; indeed, its description of Gamaliel's original provocation is almost word for word the same. After that, however, the versions differ in important respects. BT's rabbis do not quote Nahum. In fact, they express no personal grievances against Gamaliel at all. Instead, they recite a list of previous occasions on which Gamaliel has insulted Joshua, and continue throughout the story to act not on their own behalf but on his. Only Joshua now will need to be mollified in the end. Furthermore, Eleazar b. Azariah is not demoted in this version. The members of the conclave cite the ancient principle that "one may increase the sanctity of an object, but not decrease it" and arrange instead for Gamaliel to offer the chief Sabbath discourse twice (or three times) as often as Eleazar.

In one important detail, however, the two stories continue to match; both preserve the metaphor of the sprinkler by which Gamaliel asserts his claim of hereditary legitimacy. BT even adds a second one, more personal in meaning: Gamaliel simply claims the office is his, as a garment might be. No one else can simply come along and take it.

The major finding to emerge from detailed examination of these two stories can be cited from my earlier study: "The men who created the Talmud forgot as much of their own past as they remembered. . . . [T]heir stories may not be relied on as historical records."[11] In view of the significantly different relationships among the parties that the two versions depict, and the random appearance and disappearance of specific details as one passes from one to the other, no other conclusion seems possible. To that negative finding, however, a positive one can now be added: the ideological presuppositions of the two versions are precisely the same. Both see Gamaliel's opponents as acting purely out of resentment, indeed out of impulsive anger. They never give expression to a principled basis for their removal of their leader, while he, in opposition to them, expresses exactly such a principle--heredity. The stories leave it uncertain whether Gamaliel's priciple or his fence-mending got him his job back, but for the tellers of these stories one thing was certain. Tactical considerations aside, only one criterion of legitimacy was worthy of explicit recognition. Leadership in the rabbinic community belonged to those who had inherited it from their forebears. Outsiders had no right to judge them or their claim.

III

Because the Simeon-story has not yet been studied in comparable detail, it will be better to begin more slowly.

Rabbinic tradition records the titles of three officers in the Patriarchal court. These were the Nasi (Patriarch), the Av Bet Din, who was second in rank, and the Ḥakam, who was third. Although tradition traced the titles Nasi and Av Bet Din back to very early times,[12] there is no mention of a Ḥakam prior to the time of Simeon b. Gamaliel II himself.

A *baraita*, connected by both Talmuds to that same period, defines the honor due each of these officers:

> When the Nasi enters, the whole assembly rise, and they shall not be seated until he has said to them, "Sit." When the Av Bet Din enters, whey make him two rows, [one] on each side, until he has entered and sat in his place. [When] the Ḥakam enters, one rises and one sits down until he has entered and sat in his place.[13]

The rule in Tos. is unattributed. Its context provides a series of rulings as to which of the two questions has priority when both simultaneously come before the court. Questions of precedence also constitute the Talmudic contexts in which the *baraita* appears.

M. Bikkurim 3:3 reports that when groups of provincial farmers brought their first-fruits into Jerusalem, "all the artisans of Jerusalem used to rise before them." JT[14] *ad loc.* quotes Leviticus 19:32 (*you shall rise before a gray head, and honor the face of an elder*); the *baraita* then appears, followed by this story:

> [When] R. Meir used to come into the meetinghouse, everyone would see him and rise before him. When they heard this *baraita*, they wanted to treat him accordingly. He got angry and left, saying to them, "I have heard that 'one raises the sanctity [of an object] but does not lower [it].'"

This narrative reports a single incident in a few short sentences. It is told anonymously. The surrounding *gemara* contains a large number of names, mostly of third-generation Palestinian Amoriam, but the passage as a whole is simply a collection of short, diverse comments dealing with the honor due various kinds of people. It could have been compiled under a wide variety of circumstances.

The story does not explain the background of the *baraita*, nor does it explicitly claim to be describing its origin. It does, however, depict Meir as astonished by the effort to put this law into practice, and the verb "heard" suggests that the rule was new to Meir's colleagues as well. The story implies, but does not state, that Meir held one of the two subordinate offices named in the rule. It gives no basis for guessing which.

It should be noted that Meir expresses his annoyance here by citing a maxim used in BT to explain why an honor once extended to Eleazar b. Azariah could not then be taken from him. In the JT version of that incident, despite the Talmud's own claim, Eleazar is demoted, and here too Meir may resent what has happened but must accept his loss of prestige. In telling these stories, then, the two Talmuds reflect conflicting views on the legitimacy of demoting rabbinic officials. Neither Talmud acknowledges the view of the other.

BT connects the law in T. Sanhedrin with M. Horayot 3:6-8. That text deals with the question of precedence in a variety of contexts, such as sacrifice, support of dependents, redemption of prisoners, and general honor. The *gemara* wanders off on a series of tangents, and T. Sanh. is finally quoted without any connection to the preceding materials. The Talmud discusses other portions of the citation from Tos., and then the following story is told:[15]

> R. Yoḥanan said: This Mishnah was formulated in the days of R. Simeon b. Gamaliel. R. Simeon b. Gamaliel [was] Nasi; R. Meir, Ḥakam; and R. Nathan,

Av Bet Din. When Simeon b. Gamaliel was there,
all the people rose before him. When R. Meir
and R. Nathan entered, all the people rose before them. Said R. Simeon b. Gamaliel, "Should
there not be a distinction between my [office]
and theirs?" He enacted that Mishnah.
   That day, R. Meir and R. Nathan were not
there. When they came the next day, they saw
that the people did not rise before them as
usual. They said, "What is this?" [The others]
said, "Thus has R. Simeon b. Gamaliel enacted."
   R. Meir said to R. Nathan, "I am Ḥakam[16]
and you are Av Bet Din; let us respond in kind.
What shall[17] we do to him? Let us say to him,[18]
'Expound ʿUqṣin'--which he has not mastered.
Since he has not learned it, we shall say to him,
'"Who can express the mighty acts of the Lord,
make all his praise to be heard?"[19]--For whom
is it becoming to express the mighty acts of the
Lord? For him who can make all his praise to be
heard.' We shall depose him, and I shall become
Av Bet Din, and you, Nasi."
   R. Jacob b. Qorshai heard them, [and] said,
"The matter might, God forbid, lead to disgrace."
So he went and sat down behind R. Simeon b.
Gamaliel's upper chamber; he explained [the trac-
tate and] repeated it again and again. [R. Simeon
b. Gamaliel] said, "What is before me? Perhaps,
God forbid, something is [amiss] at the study-
house." He concentrated his attention and repeated it.
   The next day, they said to him, "Let the
Master teach ʿUqṣin." He began and recited it.
After he had finished, he said to them, "Had I
not learned it, you would have disgraced me!"
He gave the order, and they were removed from
the study-house. They wrote down scholastic dif-
ficulties on slips of paper and threw them there
[i.e., into the study-house]. Whatever he solved
was solved; when he did not solve [any] they wrote
down the answers and threw them in. R. Yose said
to them, "Torah is outside and we are inside."
R. Simeon b. Gamaliel said to them, "We shall let
them in, but we shall penalize them; no traditions
are to be reported in their names." R. Meir was
designated "others," and R. Nathan "some say."
   In their dreams they were shown [a message]:
"Go and pacify R. Simeon b. Gamaliel." R. Nathan
went, R. Meir did not; he said, "Dreams are of no
consequence." When R. Nathan came, R. Simeon b.
Gamaliel said to him, "Your father's badge of
office[20] may have helped you become Av Bet Din;
shall we also make you Nasi?"

The story as it now stands reveals a clear shift of interest at the end of the first paragraph.[21] Yoḥanan's apparent interest is in the background of Simeon's enactment,[22] while the rest of the story presupposes the enactment and goes on to tell how other people reacted to it. The translation refrains from indicating with quotation-marks the extent of Yoḥanan's words, but they probably end with the summary statement, "He enacted that Mishnah."

What follows is a separate story, told by an unidentified narrator at an unidentified time. As will presently emerge, this narrator had purposes of his own.

The Simeon-story, like the Gamaliel-story, is told in personal terms. Meir and Nathan resented Simeon's enactment, and decided to get even with him. Simeon, however, is reported as wanting to distinguish his <u>office</u> from theirs, so this story, again like the other, may be taken as reflecting broader issues. Simeon seeks to institutionalize the primacy of the Patriarchate, and his opponents respond by suggesting that he has no right to any office at all.

In the course of this story, Simeon's inadequacy as a student of Torah is never explained away. He avoids initial disaster only through the timely warning of a loyal supporter. Later, when directly challenged by his rivals, his inferiority becomes clear to all; "Torah" is elsewhere, not with him. Simeon preserves his position, but only because he has the power to do so. He appeals at no time to any ideological basis for his acts; his side of the dispute is never expressed in terms of legitimacy. This means either or both of two things: *a*) the ideological basis of his position was clear, and known to all concerned, and *b*) his opponents did not recognize it at all, and viewed his exercise of leadership as based exclusively on power. Of these, however, *a* is not credible. Even if an ideology of heredity was "known to all," it was not accepted by all. This story offers a wonderful chance to reiterate it, a chance no one who accepted that ideology would have thrown away.

The Talmud preserves here, then, another ideological narrative, only the ideology of this one contradicts entirely that of the Gamaliel-story. The only sound claim for leadership here is one derived from Torah-learning; all other claims (e.g., one based on ancestry) have no legitimacy whatever.

The ideological aim of this story has led to some striking results. For one thing, Simeon's original enactment is explicitly described as reflecting a programmatic purpose of its own--the enhancement of the Patriarch's position at the expense of his colleagues'--yet this aim is forgotten as soon as it has been mentioned. No one ever hears of it again; the later narrator was glad to have it forgotten.

The present narrator's bias also explains Simeon's astonishing remark to Nathan. Here the hereditary Patriarch tells his own second-in-command that people whose only claim to high office is that they have the right fathers are on very shaky ground and ought to watch their step. This is not the sort of argument one would have expected from a Nasi, and its implausibility is matched only by the unlikely silence in which Nathan receives it. The narrator would have his hearers believe Nathan had nothing to say in return, when in fact such a comment from his rival all but invited a crushing rejoinder.

Finally, the story's ideological character explains its focus on Meir. Except at the very end, the narrator always names Meir before Nathan. The plot is launched at Meir's initiative, and indeed aside from joining Meir in the chorus "What is this?" Nathan never utters a word. The *baraita* itself, on the other hand, preserves the order Nasi/Av Bet Din/Ḥakam, and the report of Meir's proposal demonstrates that the narrator knew of Nathan's higher rank. The author of this story evidently was more interested in Meir than in Nathan, and shaped his narrative to highlight its connection with him.

I have suggested elsewhere[23] that the Gamaliel-story reflects a contest for power among the three most significant parties of the Yavnean period, with Gamaliel representing the "Hillelite" faction, Eleazar b. Azariah the priests, and Joshua the circle of Yoḥanan b. Zakkai. A similar political balance, now reflecting the period following Bar Kokhba, can be detected here. The text itself suggests that Nathan's position resulted from his high connections in Babylonia. Meir in turn was known as an important disciple of R. ᶜAqiva, and ᶜAqiva's fame and influence rested largely on his contributions to the ideology and techniques of Torah-study. That Meir should stand for resistance, in the name of that same ideology, to a hereditary Patriarchate was entirely appropriate. The Patriarchal party may have been more concerned with the rival Exilarchic house in Babylonia,[24] but the Torah-party would have aimed its most serious attacks at targets closer to home.

IV

These stories, or sets of stories, share the common element of resentment as the motivating factor in their plots. Gamaliel's opponents resent his manner and unseat him. Meir and Nathan resent Simeon's new enactment, and plot against him; he in turn resents their plot and tries to expel them from the conclave. None of this need have much to do with ideology, or with a principled basis for behavior. People become irritated, and try to harm those who have irritated them.

One could, of course, try to derive ideological implications from these resentful actions. Gamaliel's opponents could be taken to hold an implied philosophy of leadership--"a proper leader never shames his subordinates," or something like that--but they never express such thoughts, and there is no evidence that the narrator was interested in suggesting them. Indeed, Joshua in one passage in BT both expresses resentment along these very lines ("Woe to the generation of which you are the leader!"),[25] and concedes the legitimacy of Gamaliel's hereditary claim. In JT Meir does express a principle ("One may raise the sanctity of an object . . .") but takes no action; in BT Meir plots against Simeon but does not cite this reason. The factor of resentment, then, plays its own role in these stories, and ideologies are kept quite distinct from it.

Yet each story does reflect an ideology. These are always clearly expressed, and in the end each ideology always prevails over whatever resentment had led people to consider rejecting it. Gamaliel gets his position back after circulating the message about the sprinkler. Simeon, having been reminded that Torah is outside and he inside, has no choice but to re-admit Meir and Nathan, his feelings notwithstanding, and despite the immense threat they pose. The two sets of stories, as already noted, thus stand in mutual opposition. One endorses the Patriarchs' claim that their hereditary occupancy of their office was exempt from challenge. The other honors Torah, and only Torah; everything else is power politics and personal spite.

Neither ideology, to be sure, triumphs unambiguously. Gamaliel asserts his hereditary claim, but he also mends his fences. The expulsion of Meir and Nathan is only partially overcome; Simeon agrees to let them back for now, but he sets out to make later generations forget their names.[26] The Simeon-story is in any case more complicated in that each side bears resentment toward the other. Meir and Nathan use Torah in their effort to unseat Simeon, but their real motive is something else.

Thus, while the narrator of each story seems wholly to support a particular ideology of leadership, the stories themselves do not entirely serve their authors' points of view. Earlier versions of these tales eveidently were reshaped by later narrators for the purpose of supporting the ideologies they now reflect. Older non-ideological elements (resentment, the basic story-lines, etc.) were not entirely eliminated,[27] and probably in some dim way reflect real events, while the added ideological cast of each story was grafted on as best the narrator could manage.[28]

V

The clearest sign that these stories were indeed created as propaganda can be found through what they omit. If, for example, the Gamaliel-story really is at all "reliable," then Gamaliel provided a tactical precedent for his son which it is astonishing that Simeon failed to employ. Why does Simeon, faced as he is with the loss of his office, make no reference at all to his inherited right to hold it? It is hard to believe that he in fact would have refrained from doing so. It is easier to believe either that the Gamaliel-story is a fabrication invented only later, or that Simeon's reference to his ancestry is something that a later narrator preferred to pass over in silence. Indeed, the narrator in B. Hor. has Simeon of all people make a nasty remark about people who expect high office merely because of who their fathers were, and then has Nathan say nothing at all in response! Gamaliel's opponents, who are depicted as rightly offended by him, eventually restore him to office without any guarantee that Gamaliel will behave differently in the future. In short, all sorts of actions that the situations would seem to require go unreported in these stories, and the most likely explanation for this is that to report them would have forced the narrators to recognize a point of view which was uncongenial to their own.

For the same reason, none of these narratives ever refers to any of the others. Each seeks to defeat the other's purpose by establishing a certain belief; this belief, once accepted, nullifies the basis of the other stories. No narrator who shared the inclination of either of these tales would have seen anything to gain by helping to spread the other as well. On the contrary: anyone who considered one of these stories edifying would have considered the other wicked and dangerous. The narrators' apparent ignorance of one another, in other words, is studied and intentional; neither side wished to further the other's interests. The obvious strategy was to ignore the other's very existence.

My earlier study of the Gamaliel-story was led to its sceptical conclusion because of the variations between that one story's versions. Now it has emerged that these stories reflect ulterior purposes which motivated narrators to fabricate or to suppress elements in the stories they transmitted. They sought not merely to "improve" the materials they had received, but to bend them to purposes that older narrators had not introduced and might well have opposed. These stories are treacherous historical sources not because their tradents were careless; on the contrary, they knew quite well what they were doing. What the Talmuds now contain are later efforts to use incidents from the past--in this case by recounting them in such a way that the prestige of the Patriarchal house would either be discredited (the Simeon-story) or enhanced (the Gamaliel-story). "The Sages," even if they ceased trying to unseat the "Hillelite" dynasty altogether, never relented in their efforts to limit its role in the life of the nation and to strengthen their own. These stories are not pious memories of the great men of old, but rather skillfully crafted weapons used by both sides in that ongoing rivalry.[29]

NOTES

HISTORY AND IDEOLOGY

[1] The quotation marks are designed to accommodate the customary term without accepting as fact the dynasty's claim to have descended from Hillel. See J. Neusner, *The Rabbinic Traditions about the Pharisees before 70* (Leiden: E. J. Brill, 1971), 1:375.

[2] Henceforth BT or B.

[3] "Eventual" because Gamaliel seems to have disappeared well before the Bar Kokhba uprising, but there is no sign of his son until after the rebellion had been crushed. The status of the Patriarchate during the interval between father and son remains unclear. See G. Alon, *History of the Jews in the Land of Israel during the Period of the Mishnah and the Talmud* [Hebrew] (Tel Aviv: Ha-Kibbutz ha-Meuchad, 1967), 1:293-4.

[4] See A. I. Baumgarten, "Rabbi Judah I and His Opponents," *Journal for the Study of Judaism in the Persian, Hellenistic, and Roman Periods* (forthcoming). I thank Professor Baumgarten for sharing his work with me.

[5] A classical and typical study of the Simeon-story is Büchler's "The Conspiracy of R. Nathan and R. Meir against the Patriarch Simeon ben Gamaliel," reprinted in *Studies in Jewish History* (London: Oxford University Press, 1956), 160-178. J. Neusner, *History of the Jews in Babylonia*, I^2 (Leiden: Brill, 1969), 79-85, while far more critical of the sources, is no less concerned with extracting from them substantive historical conclusions. With regard to the Gamaliel-story, my own study (see below, note 6) reached mostly negative conclusions because at the time I wrote it, I, too, was chiefly interested in achieving results of this kind.

[6] R. Goldenberg, "The Deposition of Rabban Gamaliel II: An Examination of the Sources," *Journal of Jewish Studies* 23 (1972) 167-190. Henceforth cited as "Deposition."

[7] Henceforth J or JT.

[8] J. Berakhot 4:1 7c-d, J. Ta^{c}anit 4:1 67d.

[9] Here and elsewhere I have taken for granted interpretations of the story which go beyond the actual text. See "Deposition" for details.

[10] B. Berakhot 27b-28a.

[11] "Deposition," p. 190.

[12] See Mishnah (henceforth M.) Ḥagigah 2:2.

[13] Tosefta (henceforth Tos. or T.) Sanhedrin 7:8. The *baraita* appears with minor variants at B. Horayot 13b. A more substantially different version appears at J. Bikkurim 3:3 65c, but none of these differences is relevant to the question now at hand.

[14] J. Bikkurim 3:3 65c.

[15] B. Horayot 13b.

[16] Lit., let us innovate something like ours.

[17] Lit., reveal.

[18] Lit., which he does not have.

[19] Psalm 106:2.

[20] On QMR', see Neusner, *History*, I^2, pp. 81ff.

[21] The division into paragraphs is of course my own.

[22] Yoḥanan displays a similar interest elsewhere; see B. Bava Qama 94b, B. Bekhorot 30b.

[23] "Deposition," p. 190.

[24] See Neusner, *History*, I^2, pp. 107-118.

[25] The rebuke, but not the concession of legitimacy, appears in JT as well.

[26] Simeon's plan is less outrageous than may at first appear. Despite the sentiment expressed in Avot 6:6, tradents do seem to have tolerated relative laxity in the attribution of rabbinic dicta. See Goldenberg, *The Sabbath-Law of Rabbi Meir* (Missoula: Scholars Press, 1978), pp. 206-207 and p. 211, note 18.

[27] It can be objected that a fabricator would not likely have inserted the name of so obscure a personage as Jacob b. Qorshai, but it should be kept in mind that I have not called these stories simple fabrications. I have suggested only that ideological concerns not drawn from the original events have shaped the stories as we now have them. It is possible that Jacob's name appears because Jacob was there. It is also possible that Jacob was less obscure than we think: certain traditions (J. Shab. 10:5 12c, J. Pes. 10:1 37b) identify him as the chief, or the only, teacher of Simeon's successor Judah the Patriarch.

[28] Speculation as to how these narratives actually developed is best kept to a footnote. I would propose the following: Yoḥanan's brief report came first; as already noted, it is one of several such attributed to him. It was then taken and turned into a longer story designed to show that Torah and only Torah ought to propel a person into positions of leadership in the community of Israel. I would guess, but cannot demonstrate, that Yoḥanan was not the author of this longer narrative.

The Gamaliel-story, its earlier setting notwithstanding, arose as a response to this one. In its present form, it is demonstrably the result of a complex development; it is full of interpolations, and names authorities who lived well into the fourth century. The Talmuds supply a version of this story which was acceptable in the rabbinic academies, but still it defends the hereditary Patriarchate against its opponents, and provides a story which the Patriarchs' defenders could recount whenever the other tale seemed to be gaining undesirable currency.

After my earlier story of the Gamaliel-story appeared, Professor Morton Smith of Columbia University sent me a personal letter dated July 27, 1973, containing his further thoughts on the subject. On other grounds, he, too, concluded that the Gamaliel-narrative was "originally rabbinic propaganda vs. the patriarchate." I have awaited the proper occasion to thank Professor Smith for his kindness.

See also M. Avi-Yonah, *The Jews of Palestine* (New York: Schocken: 1976), pp. 116-121, and G. Alon, *Jews, Judaism, and the Classical World* (Jerusalem: Magnes Press, 1977), pp. 374-457. Alon notes, pp. 436ff., the growing tendency in the third century to turn the very status of "Sage" into something hereditary.

Finally, see now A. I. Baumgarten, "The Akiban Opposition," *Hebrew Union College Annual* 50 (1979), 179-197.

[29] An earlier version of this apper was read before the Early Rabbinic Studies section of the 1979 Annual Meeting of the Society for Biblical Literature. I thank my audience on that occasion for their helpful and stimulating questions and responses, though of course no one but myself should be held responsible for this paper in its present form.

I. INDEX OF LITURGICAL TERMS,
RUBRICS, AND CONCEPTS

"Acceptance of the Yoke
of the Commandments"
       18, 22

"Acceptance of the Yoke
of the Kingdom of Heaven"
       18, 22

'amen   4

^{c}Amidah   3, 38, 39

Ashkenazi Rite   4, 6, 13,
    15, 23, 29, 38,
    43, 47, 51

Babylonian Rite 5, 6, 41

Balkanese Rite   4

barukh   9, 10

barukh 'attah   11, 12

barukh 'attah 'adonai 9

"Benediction of
Redemption"   23

berakhah   8-12, 15-18,
    20-27, 30-31,
    34

birkhoth hashaḥar   25

"Call to Worship" 1, 26-27

Day of Atonement 3, 12-13,
    17, 26, 30,
    32, 38, 45

debharim   25, 27

'edah   1

Egyptian Rite   6

Eighteen Benedictions 3
  4, 6-13, 15-
  16, 18, 20,
  23-26, 31, 37,
  39, 41, 43-45

'emeth weyaṣibh   20, 25

'Emeq Berakhah   9

Evening Service ($Ma^c aribh$)
         18

Fast of the Ninth of Abh
       30, 45

Grace after Meals 10, 15,
      25, 43

"Great Sabbath"   30

Hanukkah   27

Haphtarah   27, 30-31, 82

hashkibhenu   23

ḥathimah   11, 17, 24, 37

"Hear, O Israel"   6

hithpallel   18, 20

Hodayoth   11

hodu le   11

"Holiness of the Day"   17

"Holiness of God"   17

Italian Rite   4, 6, 24, 30

kawwanah   3, 40, 41, 43,
     47, 48, 50

Kingship   17

Kol Nidrey   44-46

"Laws of Prayer"   5

Lekhah Dodi   43

lulab   45

maḥzor   47

Maḥzor Vitry   5, 36

methurgeman   31, 32

"Morning Benedictions" 25

Morning Service (Saḥar th) 18,
      27, 37-8, 41

"Mourner's Qaddish"   36

Musaph   13, 16-18, 34,
     38-40, 45

$Ne^c ilah$ 13, 18, 38

nephilath 'apayim   25

New Moon   13, 27, 30, 33

New Year   13, 16-17

Nine Benedictions 16-17, 37,
        45

Nosaḥ 'Ereṣ Yisrael   4

Nosaḥ Sepharad   4

'odekha   12

"Order of Benedictions" 31

"Order of Prayers"   5

Palestinian Rite 4-6, 15, 22-
     23, 27, 41,
     51

Passover	6, 28, 30, 32	Tabernacles	45
Pentecost	45	*tahanunim*	25
pesuqey de-zimra'	25	*tebhah*	30
petitionary prayer	10	*tehillah*	9
piyyutim	5, 45-46, 48	Ten Days of Repentance	45
"Praise"	15	"Thanksgiving"	15
Praised be the Lord	26	Thanksgiving Hymns	11
Praise the Lord	26	*Trisagion*	20, 37
"Prayers of House of Study origin"	33	"Verses of Song"	25, 37
		Yemenite Rite	4, 24, 51
Purim	27	*Yoser*	39

Qaddish 1, 33-37, 41
Qaddish de-Rabbanan 35
qebha^c 3, 40-44, 47-48, 50
Qedushah 37-41, 51-53
Qedushah De-Sidra' 38
qeri'ath Shema^c 18
Rites of Poland 4
Sabbath Afternoon Service 38
Sabbath Morning Service 40
Sanctus 37
seder 6, 8
seder berakhoth 8-9, 16, 31
Seder Ḥibbur Berakhoth 6
Seder Rabh 'Amram Ga'on 26, 40
seder tephilloth 47
Sephardi Rite 4, 6, 24, 30, 38
Seven Benedictions 12-13, 15-18, 31, 37, 40, 45
sheliaḥ ṣibbur 4
Shema^c 18-27, 37-41, 43, 45-6
siddur 47
Siddur Rashi 5
Siddur Sephath 'Emeth 47
Siyyon 42
"Standards and Variations" 40
synagogé 1

II. INDEX OF BIBLICAL SOURCES

OLD TESTAMENT

Chronicles, I
29:10	10

Chronicles, II
20:26	9

Daniel
2:20	34

Deuteronomy
6:4-9ff	18, 19, 38
6:7	19, 20
11:13-21ff	18
12:16	121
14:28-29	121
23:24	145
25:4	121
26:1-10	55
26:3	121
31:12	121
33:11	121

Ecclesiastes
10:11	100

Exodus
12:12	68
15:18	38, 53
22:29	121
25:1-2	121

Ezekiel
3:12ff	37, 38, 40, 52, 53
45:11	121
45:13	121

Genesis
7:2	98, 103
12:1	81
15	72. 73
15:1	87
15:10	73
26:1	82
28:7	82

Isaiah
6:3ff	37, 38, 40, 51, 52, 53
10:30	81, 86
41:5	87
45:7	21
55:1	42
55:7ff	72, 73

Jeremiah
1:1	82, 83
1:1-2:3	82, 86
1:5	91
4:6	89
4:7	82, 89
10:10	98

Job
1:21	36

Joel
2:17	77

Joshua | 27

Judges | 27

Kings, I
18:13	100
18:22	100

Lamentations | 27

Leviticus
1:10	75
1:13	74
1:14	75
1:16	74
1:17ff	74, 76
2:1-2ff	67, 70, 71, 72, 73, 74, 75, 76, 77, 78, 80
2:2-3	77, 78, 80
2:8	72
5:4	121
5:5	55
6:11	78

11:4	99	22:4	38
11:5	99	22:23-24ff	71
11:6	99	54:1	99
11:20-23	121	57:5	99
16:12	70	57:6	100
21:1	97, 101, 102, 104	68:18	52
		74:8	2
21:9	121	78:16	42
22:9	121	80:9	42
22:11	121, 122	87:2	41, 42
22:14	121	95	43
23:40	150, 151	99	43
		106:2	170
		113:2	34
Malachi		119:12ff	10
2:5-7	78	133:1-3	79, 80
2:6	79	146:10ff	37, 38
2:7	79	Qoheleth	
3:3	101, 104	4:6	67, 69. 70
Nahum		Ruth	27
3:19	160	Samuel, I	
Nehemiah		22:17	101
9:5	9	23:12	99
Numbers		24:11	101
15:37-41ff	18, 38, 56	26:14	101
16:21	121	Samuel, II	
18:11	121	2:14	101
18:12	121	3:12	101
18:27	121	Song of Songs	
18:28	121	1:4	79
18:29	121	Zechariah	
18:32	121	1:5	88
19:1ff	97, 102, 103, 106	NEW TESTAMENT	
28 & 29	12, 13, 16	Luke	
31:30	121	4:16-27	55, 61
Proverbs			
14:28	77		
17:2	88		
Psalms			
12:6	98, 101, 102, 104, 105		
12:7	99		
17:14	77		

III. INDEX OF RABBINIC AND OTHER ANCIENT SOURCES

MISHNAH

^cAbodah Zarah
2:6 — 121

Arakhin
6:5 — 128

Baba Batra
5:8 — 128

Baba Mesia
7:2 — 144
7:6 — 143, 144

Bekhorot
5:2 — 121, 129
8:10 — 145

Berakhot
1:1-2 — 58
1:3 — 58
1:4 — 58
1:5 — 58
2:2 — 58
2:3 — 122
4:3 — 55
4:7 — 57
7:3 — 59
6 — 59
7 — 59

Besah
2:3 — 118

Bikkurim
3:3 — 162

Demai
7:3 — 128

^cEduyyot
3:3 — 122

Hagigah
2:2 — 169

Hallah
1:4 — 118

Horayot
3:6-8 — 162

Ketubot
3:1 — 119, 128

Kila'im
1:2 — 128

Ma^caserot
1:2 — 149
1:4 — 149, 151, 157
1:5-8 — 145
1:6 — 122
2:1-2 — 145
2:5 — 144, 145
2:8 — 147
2:7 — 143, 144, 145, 148
3:5 — 145
3:9 — 129
4:1 — 145
5:1-2 — 145

Ma^caser Sheni
2:1 — 128

Makhshirin
3:1 — 128
6:1 — 128
6:4 — 120

Megillah
1:5 — 119
2:4 — 122
3:4-6 — 60
4:1-2 — 61
4:4 — 60, 61

Me^cilah
6:1 — 128

Miqva'ot
7:2 — 128

Pesahim
1:7 — 129

Rosh Ha Shanah
4:6 — 57

Sotah			Terumot		
7:1		63	3:19		128
7:7-8		57	4:1		118, 120, 126
Sukkah			4:2		125, 128
3:7		157	4:3		118, 120, 121, 123, 125, 126
Ta^canit			4:4		118, 128
4:1		57	4:5		120, 121, 129
Tamid			4:6		120, 128
4:3-5:1		55, 56	4:7		118, 121, 122
5:1		58	4:8		118, 120, 125, 126
Tebul Yom					
4:7		118	4:10		123, 128
Terumot			4:11		128
1:1		121, 124, 128, 129	4:12		123, 125, 126
1:2		128	4:13		128
1:3		124, 126	5:1		118, 128, 129
1:4		120, 128, 129	5:2		119, 129
1:5		120, 121	5:4		119
1:6		118	5:5		119, 120, 129
1:7		128	5:6		120, 124
1:8		122, 126	5:7		119
1:9		122, 126	5:8		119
1:10		122, 126, 128	5:9		119, 124, 125, 128, 129
2:1		118, 121, 123, 124, 129	5:11		119
2:2		118, 128	6:1		119, 121, 124, 125, 129
2:3		118, 122, 123, 124	6:2		125
2:4		118, 121, 123	6:3		120
2:6		118, 121, 128, 129	6:4		119, 121
3:1		118, 123, 124, 128	6:4		121
			6:5		120
3:2		126	6:6		119, 120, 122, 125, 126
3:3		118	6:10		124
3:4		118, 123, 128, 129	7:1		124, 128
3:5		121, 123, 125, 126, 128	7:2		119, 121
			7:3		120
3:6		120, 121, 122, 126	7:4		126
			7:5		120
3:8		121, 129	7:6		119, 124, 129
3:9		120, 123	7:7		119
3:19		128	8:1		119, 121, 126, 128

Terumot	
8:2	119, 126
8:3	121, 129
8:4	119, 124, 125
8:5	119, 124
8:6	124, 125, 129
8:8	119, 129
8:9-11	119, 129
8:12	119, 124, 126
9:1	119, 126
9:2	126
9:3	119, 122
9:4	119, 122, 124, 125
9:5	122, 126
9:6	119, 121
9:7	119, 124, 125, 129
10:1	119, 120, 128
10:2	124, 128
10:3	126
10:4	125
10:5	129
10:6	120
10:7	120, 129
10:8	121, 125
10:9	120, 125
10:10	120, 121
10:11	120, 125
10:12	120, 124, 128
11:1	121, 124, 129
11:2	121, 124
11:3	128
11:4	121, 122, 128
11:5	122
11:6-8	124
11:8	125, 126, 128
11:9	121, 122
11:10	120, 124, 125, 127

Yebamot	
12:4	128
14:1	128

Yoma	
3:8	55
4:2	55
7:1	57

Zebahim	
8:5	129

TOSEFTA

Berakhot	
3:5	122
3:25	56
3:6	60

Demai	
5:9	129

Megillah	
3(4):10	60

Pesahim	
3:10	129

Sanhedrin	
7:8	161, 170

Shabbat	
3:5	

Terumot	
1:3	122
3:4	122
3:7	123
3:8	123
3:12	123
3:13	123
3:18	123
3:19	123
4:1-2	123
4:5	123
4:6	123
4:7	119
4:9	123
4:10	123
4:13	123
5:3	123
5:10	125
5:11	123
6:12	123
6:1	124, 125

Terumot			Horayot	
6:10		124	12b	78
6:13		123	13b	162-3, 170
6:16		124	Keritot	
7:5		125	5a	78
7:7		128	Menahot	
7:9		122	43b	56
7:12		124	Sanhedrin	
7:13		124	6b	79
7:14-15		124	Shabbat	
7:16		124	115b	55
7:20		124	118b	59
8:2		124	Sotah	
8:3		122	49a	61
8:5-6		124	Yoma	
8:9		124, 128	36b	55
9:2		128	*PALESTINIAN TALMUD*	
9:5		124	Berakhot	
9:7		124	1:8(3c)	58
9:8		124	4:1(7c-d)	169
9:9		124	4:3	57
10:4		122	4:5(8c)	59
10:9		124	Bikkurim	
10:12		124	3:3	162
BABYLONIAN TALMUD			Ma^{c}aserot	
Berakhot			1:4(49a)	149
2A		58	2:6(50a)	143, 144, 145
4b		58, 59	2:7(50a)	147, 148
8a		63	Megillah	
11a		58	1:10	71
11b		58, 59, 63	4:1(75a)	60
12a		58	Pe'ah	
14b		58	1:1(16a)(16b)	99, 100, 101
16b-17a		60	2:6(17a)	156
26b		56, 57	Pesahim	
27b-28a		57, 169	10:1(376)	170
28b		55, 56	Sanhedrin	
29a		57	1:1(18a)	98
29b		55	Shabbat	
30b		57	10:5(12c)	170
33a		56	Sotah	
Baba Mesia			1:8(176)	101
59a		60		

Sukkot
3:7(53d)   157
Ta^{c}anit
4:1(67d)   169
4:1   57
Terumot
1:4   129
1:8   129
2:1   129
7:1   129
10:2   129
Yoma
8:7   72, 73

MIDRASHIM AND OTHER SOURCES
Genesis Rabbah
32:4   98
Lamentations Rabbah
1-33   111
Leviticus Rabbah
3   67-79
26:1-3   98-102
Pesiqta de Rav Kahanah
4   111
4:2   98-102
Pesiqta Rabbati
13:1   81-82
Sifra
Nedabah, 1:10   76
Shemini Mekhilta de Miluim
37   78
Sifre Deuteronomy
Qeut, pisqa, 306   60, 61
Masseket Soferim
13:10-14   61
14:8   60
19:12   61
21:6   61
Shulhan ^{c}Arukh
Orah Hayyim, #131   60
Josephus
Antiquities IV, viii, 13,
                         58

Apocrypha
Ecclesiasticus   11, 56
Dead Sea Scrolls
IQHV, 20   11-12, 57
Apostolic Constitutions
Book VII, Chapter 35   52

IV. GENERAL INDEX

Aaron 68, 76, 77, 79, 102
Abba bar Kahana 81, 82, 86
Abbahu, R. 71, 125
Abimelech 82, 101
Abin (Abyn), R. 98, 147, 148
Abner 101
Abraham 7, 79, 81, 87
Adler, H. M. 64
Agrippas 75
Ahab 100
Ahitophel 99
Al-Bargeloni, Judah ben Barzillai 64
Albert, H. 110, 111
Aleppo 4
Alon, G. 169
Altaner, B. 62
Amram 5, 13, 26
Anathoth 82, 90
Antonius 71
Apostolic Constitution 40
Aptowitzer, V. 63
Aqiba 4, 15, 120, 149, 150, 151
Ark 30
Assaf, S. 55, 58, 63
Av Bet Din 161, 163, 165
Ba bar Zabdah 125
Bachner, W. 55
Baer, S. 58
Baghdad 4
Bar Padia 120
Bath-gallim 81, 87, 88
Baumgarten, A. I. 169
Benjamin b. R. Levi 71
Berakhah, pattern and function 9-12

Berekhiah, R. 68, 98
Berger, P. 155
beth hammidrash 33, 38, 84
Biba b. R. Abina 72
Bloch, P. 97, 110, 111
Blumberg, H. J. 136
Bohemia 4, 36
Bokser, B. 156, 157
Braude, W. 83, 111
Brocke, M. 56
Buber, M. 59
Buber, S. 55
Buchler, Adolph 28, 29, 60, 169
Burkitt, F. C. 58
Buttrick, G. A. 55
Byzantuim 39, 45-6
Chigier, M. 156
Cohen, B. 155
Collins, J. J. 155
Creation 6, 18, 21-22
Crossman, I. 155
darshanim 84
Daube, D. 155
David 99, 101, 103, 105
Davidson, I. 47, 55, 58, 63
Davis, A. 64
De Sola Pool, David 61
demiourgos 21
Dibrey Yirmiyahu 82
Dinklas, J. 157
Doeg 99, 101
Ebionites 19
Eighteen Benedictions 6-9, 12-18
Elbogen, I. 25, 32, 39, 59, 60, 61, 63, 64
Eleazar, R. 71, 98, 121, 149
Eleazar ben Azariah 19, 160, 162, 165
Eliezer, R. 89, 124
Elijah 100

Elijah Gaon	157	Heinemann, Joseph	7, 29, 31, 33, 42, 56, 57, 60, 61, 63, 83, 110, 111
Elon, M.	155		
England	6, 16, 36		
Epstein, J. N	135	*Hekhaloth*	39
Essenes	18, 40	Hezekiah, R.	71, 120, 125
Exile	87, 88	Higger, Michael	56
Ezekiel	88, 91	High Priest	3, 12
Falk, F. W.	155	Hilpa	120
Finkelstein, Louis	7, 56	Hinena	120
Five Scrolls	27	Hirsch, E. D.	135, 139, 155
Fleischer, E.	64, 110	Hiyya	125
Flusser, David	62	Hiyya bar Abba	69, 76, 120, 125
Freimann, J.	55	Hiyya bar Ashi	124
Gad	69	Hiyya the Elder	120, 124
Gamaliel, Rabban	3, 6-9, 12, 41, 129, 159, 160, 161, 165, 166, 167, 171	Hoffman, L. A.	63
		Holy Spirit	79
Gaster, M.	60, 61	Horeb	42
Geertz, C.	109	Hoshaya b. R. Shammai	125
Genizah	4, 6, 8, 9, 13, 26, 28, 41	Huna	120
		Hungary	4
Gerar	82	Hurwitz, S.	55
Gnosticism	21	Idelsohn, A. Z.	64
Goldenberg, R.	169, 170	Ila, R.	149
Goldschmidt, E. D.	55, 56, 60, 62	Imi, R.	125
		Isaac	7, 82
Graetz, H.	55	Isaac Or Zaru'a	36
Grant, R. M.	59	Isaac, R.	67, 69, 72, 125
Green, W. S.	56, 109, 156, 157	Isaiah	21, 37, 38, 40, 42, 86, 89, 91
Gruenwald, I.	155	Ishmael, R.	26
Gulak, A.	155	Ishmael b. R. Nehemiah	71
Gutmann, J.	55	Israel	12, 22, 37, 41, 71, 86, 88, 104, 115
Guttmann, A.	64		
Haase, W.	109	Israelstam, J.	65
Hakam	161, 162, 163, 165	Italiener, B.	62
Halevi, Judah	43	Jackson, B.	155
Halivni, D. W.	156	Jacob	7, 71, 82, 87
Hanan bar Pazzi	102, 105	Jacob bar Aha	125
Hananiah bar R. Aha	77	Jacob bar Qorshai	69, 163, 170
Hannah	2	Jacob of Kefar Hanin	98
Hasidim	43	Jaffee, M. S.	156, 157
Heidenheim, Wolf	47	Jaques, A.	110

Jeremiah	2, 82, 88, 89, 90, 91, 98
Jeremiah, R.	121, 129
Jerusalem	8, 18, 31, 43, 86, 90
Joel, B. I.	55, 58
Jonah, R.	125, 145
Josephus	2, 18, 19
Joshua, R.	12, 15, 160
Joshua, b. Levi	91, 98, 101
Joshua of Sikhnin	99
Judaeo-Christians	9, 19
Judah the Patriarch	159, 170
Judah, R.	29, 39, 129
Judah b. R. Simon	73
Judah, R.	98
Justinian	32, 45, 46
Kahana, R.	120
Kallir, Eleazar	45
Kallir, Yannai	45
Kapstein, J.	111
Kaufmann, Y.	59
Kawwanah and *Qebha^c*, dialectics of	40-50
Kieval, H.	60, 63
Kimelman, R.	56
Kohler, Kaufmann	18, 21, 40, 58, 62
Laish	82, 89
Lentricchia, F.	155
Levi	78
Levi, I.	63
Levi, R.	99
Lewin, B. M.	64
Lieberman, Saul	39, 136
Lightstone, J.	110
Lohse, E.	57
Luzzatto, S. D.	60
maggidim	32
mahzor	47
Mahzor Vitry	5, 36, 55
Maier, J.	56, 58
Maimonides	5, 9, 12, 16, 38, 56, 57
Mandelbaum, B.	93, 111
Mann, J.	27, 39, 41, 59, 60, 62
Margulies (Margoliot), M.	65, 66, 80, 111, 157
Meir, R.	10, 124, 129, 162, 163, 165, 166
mesadrim	84
Mirsky, A.	57
Moravia	4
Morgenstern, Julian	2, 55
Moses	18, 19, 68, 78, 79, 90, 95, 101, 102, 104, 106, 137, 153
Munk, E.	57
Nash Papyrus	19
Nasi	161, 162, 163, 165
Nathan, R.	163, 164, 165, 166
Nehemiah	7, 9
Nebuchadnezzer	82, 89, 90
Neusner, J.	56, 135, 155, 156, 169, 170
New Moons	13, 27, 30, 33
Ninth of Av	27, 30, 45, 82, 89
Nob	101
Obadiah	100
Origen	84, 91
'orkhim	84
Otto, Rudolf	38
Paddan-aram	82
Palestine	2, 6, 18, 28, 29, 31, 32, 39, 42, 43, 45, 49
Persia	39, 45
Petiha (petihta)	83, 84, 85, 86, 88, 90, 92, 95-112
Petuchowski, J. J.	56, 57, 64, 110
Phineas	88
Plaut, W. G.	64
Porton, G.	109
Qaddish, pattern and function	33-37

Qedushah	37-40, 51-53	*Seder Rabh 'Amram Ga'on*	5, 40, 55, 60, 62
Rabbina	26	Segal, M. H.	56
Rabinowitz, F. W.	157	Septuagint	1, 9
Rashi	5, 10	Shem	87
Rav	17, 125	*Shema^c*, pattern and usage	18-24
Redemption	17, 18, 22	*Shulhan 'Arukh*	26
Reform Judaism	2, 4, 16, 28, 32, 36, 44, 48-50	*Siddur Rabh Saadja Gaon*	55, 58
		Siddur Rashi	55
Resurrection	35	Simeon, R.	125, 128, 149, 150, 151, 159, 166, 167, 170
Reuben	69		
Revelation	17, 18, 22, 42, 138, 139	Simeon bar Ba	125
Rhineland	6, 36	Simeon b. Gamaliel II	161, 162, 163, 164
Rosenfeld, A.	63	Simeon bar Yohai	72, 129
Rudolph, K	59	Simeon ben Laqish	101, 120, 125
Russia	4	Simeon ben Zoma	19
Sa'adya Gaon	5	Simeon Hap'qoli	6
Sabbath	12, 13, 15, 16, 23, 24, 27, 28, 29, 30, 31, 32, 33, 34, 37, 38, 39, 43, 44, 45, 47, 49, 77, 82, 86, 90	Simhah ben Samuel	5
		Sinai	19, 42
		Sirillio, S.	157
		Solomon	2
Sachs, M	64	Smith, J. Z.	109, 110, 157
Safed	43, 48	Smith, M.	171
Saldarini, A. J.	155	Spanier, Arthur	7
Samuel, R.	120	Suleiman, S. R.	155
Samuel bar Nahman	100	Synagogue service, structure of	24-27
Samuel b. R. Isaac	120	Tabbi	125
sanhedrin	7	Tanhum b. R. Hanilai	74, 98, 101, 103
Sanders, E. P.	56, 156		
Sarason, R.	56, 83, 84, 85, 93, 110, 111, 112	Targum	32, 38
		Teman	4
Saul	99, 101	Temple	2, 3, 6, 7, 12, 18-20, 33, 45, 49, 82, 90, 114
Schechter, A. I.	56	Theodor, T.	110, 111
Schechter, S.	57	Tompkins, J. P.	155
Schiffman, L. H.	155	Torah	12, 22, 27, 31, 41, 42, 45, 78, 79, 82, 88, 89, 95, 98, 99, 106, 108, 116, 137, 153, 164, 165, 170
Schoeps, H. J.	58		
Schorr, J.	64		
Schulz, F.	155, 156		
Schreiner, M.	64	Uriah	88, 89
Scripture, reading of	27-33, 84	Venice	47
		Volz, P.	61

Weinfeld, Moshe 39, 40
Werner, E. 62, 64
Wieder, N. 63
Wolff, A. A. 48, 64
Yavneh 3, 6, 8, 9, 12, 16
Yannai 120, 121
Yohanan, R. 74, 77, 89, 120, 121, 124, 125, 129, 156, 162
Yohanan b. Zakkai 165
Yoredeay merkabhah 39
Yose 34, 125, 149, 150, 163
Yose b. R. Hanina 72, 120, 121
Yose ben Yose 17, 45, 46
Yose of Mimlah 99
Zechariah 89
Zeirah, R. 73, 121
Zion 42, 43
Zoroastrianism 21
Zunz, Leopold 32, 33, 61, 64, 110